CONTENTS

FOREWORD

The explosion of interest in jujitsu around the world has been extremely gratifying to my family. Most martial artists are now familiar with some of the core precepts of my family's philosophy of combat—that the outcome of almost all fights is largely determined by grappling, especially on the ground. What is needed now is a deeper look at the theory and strategy of grappling-based approaches to jujitsu that can take students to a higher level of understanding. Rather than stopping at the level of glib generalizations such as "all fights go the ground," my nephew Renzo and his friend and student, John Danaher, make a concerted analysis of all aspects of combat. Their intention is to show how different combat skills can be used to take an opponent out of his area of expertise and thus render him more vulnerable to attack.

As one of Renzo's main teachers, I find it wonderful to have observed his development into one of the foremost members of our family. Still more interesting is observing the development of his own personal approach to combat, based upon his own experiences as a professional fighter. Now martial artists around the world can look into that thoroughly modern approach. It is my pleasure to commend this book—an expression of modern jujitsu—to the public and martial arts world.

—Carlos Gracie, Jr.

PREFACE

Almost every culture and society on earth has a martial tradition, a style and approach to fighting that emerged within that culture and came to be associated with it. The result is that a vast number of martial arts exist, each teaching a unique means of achieving victory over a potential adversary. A long-standing question among martial artists has always been—which of the many styles is best? In other words, which is the most efficient fighting style?

Regardless of the difficulties in furnishing an answer to this perennial question, a massive step forward was taken in the 1990s when mixed martial arts (MMA) events were staged across North America. In these events, different martial arts were matched up against one another with few rules. To the great surprise of many, the hallowed theories of many martial arts were repudiated by hard experience. The public expected the biggest, strongest, hardest-punching-and-kicking man to win. In fact, the consistent winners of these tournaments were almost always men who were simply well-versed in grappling styles of martial arts—particularly certain forms of jujitsu. Rather than smashing their way to victory with pugilistic skills and power, these grapplers, despite being outweighed in almost every fight, wrapped up their opponents in a tight clinch, then took the fight to the ground. Here, their opponents had little idea of how to conduct themselves, and their striking skill was strongly negated. Once on the ground, the grapplers had little difficulty in applying efficient submission holds—joint locks and chokes—that forced their hapless opponents into a bloodless surrender.

The tremendous and unexpected success of these jujitsu fighters in early MMA events invoked a massive surge of interest toward jujitsu. People quickly came to realize that the techniques and training philosophy of jujitsu were essential to success in real combat and that the grappling skill that lies at the heart of jujitsu's dominance in MMA events had been neglected by the martial arts community for decades. People from all fighting styles had to sit up and take notice of what quickly came to be known as "the grappling revolution." Although public demand for instruction in jujitsu rose to unprecedented levels, there was, strangely enough, almost no reflection of this in printed form. Dozens of jujitsu videos were produced, and jujitsu seminars were routinely sold out; however, books on the radical changes in jujitsu and the martial arts have yet not emerged.

This book is intended to satisfy the enormous demand for quality, written jujitsu instruction. Unlike previous books on jujitsu, this book analyzes the recent changes in jujitsu and proposes new directions for this ancient martial art.

Most martial artists have come to recognize the tremendous need for grappling skill in real combat. MMA events have consistently shown that grappling skill is probably the single most important indicator of success in fighting. The highly effective grappling techniques of jujitsu (combat-proven in MMA events) are presented clearly and fully outlined to the reader by one of the most important figures in modern jujitsu and MMA competition, Renzo Gracie, and his student John Danaher.

Every martial artist is affected by the current shift toward grappling skill. Even stylists who largely reject grappling for self-defense purposes must learn the grappling techniques to defend themselves against grapplers. Those who do accept the validity of grappling technique for self-defense stand in need of a modern jujitsu book that details the key skills that lead to grappling mastery—and those who do not accept it should nevertheless consider the book's content for the sake of defending themselves in the event of a grappling attack.

In any activity, mastery of the fundamentals is critical to success. At the same time, however, students stand in need of higher-level technical instruction that can give them a competitive edge in both tournaments and combat. *Mastering Jujitsu* is intended to break new ground in jujitsu instruction. As such, much of the material must be covered in detail from beginner level and up. Through the use of detailed explanations of the fundamental concepts that lie at the heart of the new approaches to jujitsu, the beginner can be brought quickly to the advanced level that is the focus of this book. We hope, then, that the scope of the book ranges successfully from the beginner to the advanced. The key to sound instruction lies in the depth in which technique is analyzed and outlined; therefore, we offer in this book what may seem to be an unusual amount of detail and explanation for all techniques, so that any reader can understand the concepts being taught.

Part of the problem in offering an instructional guide to jujitsu technique is the extraordinarily wide range of material that needs to be covered. Jujitsu is an art that encompasses all manner of strikes; in addition, what must also be covered are throws, takedowns, counters to takedowns, joint locks and chokes, positional pins and transitions, sweeps, and so on. Any one of these topics is worthy of a book in itself, and to cover them all in a single volume is unrealistic. But by organizing this book into two basic areas—standing position and ground fighting—we believe that we can successfully handle the complexity and breadth of the subject matter in two convenient categories that best represent the recent changes in jujitsu. These two broad categories are further subdivided into relevant subcategories so that we can successfully execute a cohesive coverage of this wide-ranging topic.

The hard-won experience and knowledge gained by martial arts athletes in MMA competition, particularly the outstanding jujitsu competitors, can now be offered to the reader. This knowledge is the best available and the closest approximation we have as to what are the most combat-effective techniques and tactics for martial artists, security professionals, law-enforcement personnel, and the general public. In addition, our book provides the cutting-edge developments for martial arts athletes who are interested in competitive success in the rapidly expanding sport of submission grappling, sport jujitsu, and other related arts, such as judo and sambo.

This book is unique in that it seeks to avoid the stagnation and repetition found in the current crop of jujitsu manuals. We seek to replace the preoccupation of historical tradition with the combat-proven information that has emerged in recent times. By conveying the clearest, most complete knowledge and insight of one of the leading figures in the contemporary jujitsu-grappling revolution, *Mastering Jujitsu* will change the way people approach and study this ancient but ever-changing art.

ACKNOWLEDGMENTS

To my family, my wife, my children.

"And as for proof—how can a man ever be certain?
Certainty, surely, is beyond human grasp.
But however that may be, it is usually the case
that glory comes to those who act,
not to the over cautious and hesitant.
Only by great risks can great results be achieved."
—Herodotus, *The Histories*, book seven.

—Renzo Gracie

To my dear brother, Tom, and all my wonderful family.

My light, my inspiration, my best friend, my blood.

If night were eternal
And winter the only season
Could I not still live, love and persevere
To turn the corner of your smile?

—John Danaher

Many thanks to Renzo Gracie's outstanding students who helped in the production of this book; Matt Serra, Renzo Gracie's first American black belt, world champion in Brazilian jiu jitsu and truly outstanding MMA fighter, along with his black belt brother Nick Serra; Shawn Williams, Renzo Gracie black belt, and Paul Creighton, Renzo Gracie student and distinguished MMA fighter.

INTRODUCTION

Most major styles of martial arts to enter the West from Asia since World War II have enjoyed a certain vogue status. In fact, judo was the most well-known Asian martial art in the 1950s, but with each succeeding decade came karate and kenpo, kung fu, taekwondo, and ninjitsu. Little attention, however, was paid to one of the oldest of the Asiatic martial arts—jujitsu. This changed dramatically when mixed martial arts (MMA) competition was introduced to North America in the 1990s.

The guiding idea behind this type of event was to pit the various styles, methods, and philosophies of combat against one another under few rules to see which prevailed. The unexpected and dramatic success of certain styles of jujitsu brought tremendous recognition and interest to this previously neglected style of combat. In a short time, the public's perception of jujitsu went from an obsolescent and ineffective art to a formidable fighting style indeed. Along with this change in perception came a massive interest in learning the techniques that enabled jujitsu fighters to do so well in MMA fights. Soon, almost every martial arts school in North America was offering "grappling and ground fighting" as part of their instruction and syllabus. This inclusion was in direct recognition of the success jujitsu had experienced as a result of its highly effective grappling technique, most of which was applied on the ground.

THE CURRENT SPLIT IN JUJITSU

Although the tremendous increase in interest toward jujitsu is gratifying, it has also given rise to a problem that has split jujitsu into different camps. The fighters who did so much to renew interest in jujitsu came almost exclusively from one particular style of jujitsu—*Brazilian jiu jitsu*. This unique offshoot of jujitsu has Japanese origins, but over time, it has evolved into an art whose techniques, philosophy of combat, strategy, and training methods are quite different from those of traditional jujitsu. There has been a tremendous imbalance between the fighters from the Brazilian schools—which have been massively (and successfully) represented at MMA events—and the traditional jujitsu schools, which have been underrepresented. Indeed, many traditional jujitsu people feel the whole concept of challenge matches and MMA tournaments (so much a part of Brazilian jiu jitsu) is contrary to the spirit of their martial art. Others feel that the emphasis placed on ground grappling in Brazilian jiu jitsu is good for MMA events but is disastrous for street combat and self-defense. The result has been a split in jujitsu between those following the lead of the Brazilian stylists and those more interested in a historically or classically motivated program. The split is unfortunate because both approaches to jujitsu have much to offer each other.

Traditional jujitsu was an art that aimed for what is called *combative completeness*. It encompassed all manner of striking techniques, takedowns, throws, locks, chokes, and pins. There were even techniques for weapon disarmament, body-guarding, and tying up and restraining an opponent, in addition to a host of other skills. Modern approaches to jujitsu, however, tend to be much more narrowly focused toward ground grappling. This emphasis led jujitsu into the foreground because ground grappling was a skill that enabled jujitsu fighters to easily dominate their opposition in early MMA tournaments. In time, opponents learned how to fight on the ground and how to counter many of the ground-grappling aspects of jujitsu. *The result is that contemporary mixed martial arts matches tend to involve much more than ground grappling.* Fighters must now be well-versed in all aspects of combat, striking, clinching, and groundwork.

Thus, the ideal of *completeness* that was so important in traditional jujitsu is now coming back in vogue, and both traditionalists and modernists of jujitsu can benefit from each other. Traditional jujitsu can offer its ideal of the *complete fighter* as a positive influence on the more modern grappling styles of jujitsu. Likewise, modern grappling styles of jujitsu can offer traditionalists the extremely effective ground-fighting techniques and modern training methodology that catapulted it to the top of the mixed martial arts world.

Classical Jujitsu: Theory and History

Two key components are involved in understanding the nature of jujitsu. The first is the theoretical element of jujitsu, which is concerned with the philosophical basis of the art, its overall goal, and the strategy by which it attempts to reach that goal. The second is the historical element, which is concerned with the actual history of the art and its development and changes. A clear understanding of jujitsu as a martial art requires analysis of both components.

THEORETICAL BASIS OF JUJITSU

A strict translation of the term *jujitsu* offers little insight into the art. Taken at face value, the character *ju* means *gentle, soft,* or *flexible. Jitsu* is variously translated as *technique* or *art. Gentle art* or *flexible art* does not help us much. In fact, there is a definite irony in the idea of jujitsu as a "gentle art" because many of its techniques are extremely brutal. Clearly, a deeper analysis of the term is required. The key to the theoretical core of jujitsu is an adequate understanding of *ju*. To comprehend the meaning of *gentleness* or *flexibility* as it is used in jujitsu, we need to consider their opposites. *Gentle* stands in sharp contrast to the quality we normally associate with fighting prowess—strength. Typically, we think of the stronger man as having a definite advantage in any combat situation. Thus, jujitsu identifies itself in contrast to raw strength.

Seen in this light, the theoretical basis of jujitsu becomes clearer. *The guiding principle behind* ju *is the idea of a weaker (gentler) force overcoming a stronger force through the application of technique, or* jitsu, *rather than strength and aggression.* Reduced to its core, jujitsu is the employment of intelligence and skill to overcome brute strength and aggression. In this context, we can make sense of a martial art that regularly makes use of a potentially life-threatening technique in violent confrontations as "gentle." This should not be misunderstood as a notion of gentleness or softness. Strength *is* used in jujitsu. It can definitely help to be strong, but strength is used in an intelligent, rational manner as part of a strategy guided by efficient technique. Rather than confront strength with strength, jujitsu confronts strength with efficient technique and strategy so that the weaker fighter can attain victory. In practice, this means applying a high percentage of your total strength to a low percentage of your opponent's strength.

A simple example can illustrate this principle. If a weaker fighter applies an efficient stranglehold on an opponent, he uses a large proportion of his overall strength to a small proportion of his opponent's strength (the neck and throat). Thus, if a weaker fighter can attack a vulnerable part of his opponent's body (such as the neck or joints) with greater strength than his opponent can defend it with, he is effectively stronger than his opponent, even if his overall strength is less. This is the theoretical basis of jujitsu conveyed by *ju*. Technically skilled fighters can then efficiently apply what strength they have in a way that can cause sufficient damage to end the fight.

A way to understand the meaning that lies behind *ju* comes from an analysis of the phrase *ju yoku sei go*, which translates as *softness controls hardness.* This phrase conveys the idea of a smaller force initially giving way or yielding to a stronger force to eventually overcome it. Thus, it amounts to the use of strategy, one that resists strength with technique, and not additional strength.

VALUE OF MARTIAL ARTS HISTORY

Traditional martial arts have always maintained a strong sense of history. Most can give at least a coherent account of the origins of their art, even if it is not backed by concrete evidence. It is often thought that observance of history reveals important truths about the nature of a given combat style and thus enables the student to grasp the fundamental goals and attributes of that style. In assessing the social, political, and practical elements that lie behind the history of an art, much can be learned about its core commitments and goals. Every martial art arises and develops as a response to a given problem or set of problems. By looking at the history of an art, we can see clearly how it arose and changed in the face of these problems.

THEORIES ON THE HISTORY OF MARTIAL ARTS

In attempting to offer a historical explanation of the martial arts in general or any martial art in particular, several key questions need to be addressed. An effective test of any historical explanation is its ability to furnish adequate answers to these questions. The first question involves fighting styles. If one were to take a broad survey of the martial systems of the world, one notices a number of striking features. First, there are many similarities in the techniques used by the different styles, even when they are separated by vast geographical distances and time periods. For example, almost every striking style has a variation of the basic kick, front kick, side kick, and roundhouse kick. Almost every grappling art has a variation of the double-leg takedown or the hip throw. This first problem, then, is explaining the many similarities that exist between fighting styles. In other words, how did the many different martial arts evolve in similar directions?

Second, and in opposition to the first question, one cannot help but be equally struck by the obvious differences that have evolved among the different fighting styles. One sees dramatic differences between the arts of one nation or region and those of another. For example, there are many shared techniques between Japanese karate and Korean taekwondo, yet the way those same techniques are used give rise to two different fighting styles. The result, despite much overlapping technique, is two different martial arts.

The third problem is that of explaining the changes that occur over time within a given martial art and across the martial arts in general. In the past century, one martial art would rise to prominence for a period, only to be eventually outshone by another, which would then be replaced by some newcomer. Even within a given martial art, massive changes can occur. For example, the judo currently seen in the Olympic Games is different from pre–World War II judo.

Our attempts to offer a theory of martial arts history, then, must be able to account for these three problems.

Centralized Origins Theory

In answering questions about the historical origins of a martial art, three major approaches are commonly used. The first may be termed *centralized origins theory*.

This is the idea that a single person or a small group of people were the originators of an art—or indeed, of *all* the martial arts—and that from their original work stem all the subsequent variations of fighting styles that we see in later time periods and locations. Often one hears reference to semilegendary figures such as the sixth-century *Bodhidharma*, who traveled from India to China and taught his combat exercises to the monks of the Shaolin Temple.

From this centralized origin, the various arts allegedly emerged and spread out over time. Undoubtedly, this theory of martial arts history has been widely used by many martial arts to explain their origins. This is somewhat surprising because there is little hard evidence or inherent credibility for the claim that one person or one group laid an original and unprecedented foundation for the fighting arts.

Such a theory has several serious problems. Too often, the date given for the central origin of an art conflicts with hard historical evidence that shows the prior existence of related fighting styles. For example, the purported influence of the Shaolin temple on Japanese fighting styles comes late in the sixth century. Yet, we have a well-known reference to an empty-hand duel in 23 B.C. between two local champions (Kuyehaya and Nomi no Sukune) before the emperor in the *Nihongi*, a work that chronicles early Japanese history. After an exchange of grappling, the match ended with one of the contestants being kicked to death. Clearly, this predates any possible influence from the alleged singular source of the martial arts. In fact, the ancient Greeks in the West had a highly developed martial art called *pankration* that bears a striking resemblance to modern grappling forms of jujitsu hundreds of years before the birth of Christ.

Clearly then, the development of a complete martial art long before the most commonly cited central origin is not without precedent. In the case of jujitsu, another character often identified as the central origin is Chin Genpin, a man who excelled in such diverse arts as literature, poetry, architecture, and combat. Often, he is cited as the originator of jujitsu. Although he certainly did exist and did travel from his native China to Japan some time in the 17th century (circa 1619), it seems unlikely that he could have done any more than exert an influence on jujitsu technique in those localized areas where he traversed.

A former student of the Shaolin temple, Chin Genpin met Fukuno Masakatsu, a man much interested in combat arts. It appears Genpin taught his kenpo to a small but interested audience. That jujitsu has Genpin as its source, however, is implausible. Many documents show the existence of established ryu (jujitsu schools) long before 1626, when Fukuno met Genpin. Fukuno was obviously a student of the martial arts himself before ever meeting Genpin, which shows the prior existence of martial arts schools in Japan. Once again, the idea of a solitary source of a martial art is fraught with problems.

Another problem for the centralized origins theory is its clash with common sense. It would seem quite extraordinary that one person or one small group should gain a unique insight into combat technique that had eluded the rest of the world. In addition, the conditions that create a need for martial skills—war and civil strife—are not unique to one region or time. The reality of conflict would naturally inspire people of every region to create a fighting system, and the development of such a system is not so difficult that it requires unique genius to construct it. Accordingly, it would seem unlikely that the people of the world had to wait for the arrival of a martial arts messiah to gain insight and mastery of the fighting arts.

A third weakness of the centralized origins theory is that it cannot account for the obvious differences between the martial arts of different regions and times. If the true foundations of the martial arts genuinely came from one birthplace and were so much superior to anything else, why do we see such variation among them? To say that people subsequently modified them at a later date is inadequate. If we can presume that autonomous development of fighting arts is that common and simple, then we can probably doubt that it took one central originator to develop them all in the first place. Fundamental weaknesses such as these severely undermine the credibility of the centralized origins theory and force us to look elsewhere for a satisfactory account of the history of the martial arts.

Shared Conditions Theory

Another theory of the history of the martial arts that has gained widespread acceptance is *shared conditions theory*. The idea behind this theory is that the central problems and conditions that create a need for a martial art—warfare, interpersonal conflict, crime—are present in virtually every culture and time. In addition, the raw material around which a martial art is designed—the human body—is roughly the same at all times and places. Accordingly, different people in different regions at different times have been faced with the same problems. Given the physical similarities between the peoples in these different times and places, it is unsurprising that similar answers were provided to those original problems. An excellent statement of shared conditions theory was made by Koizumi Sensei, seventh dan, kodokan judo.

> As to the origin and native land of jujitsu, there are several opinions, but these are found to be mere assumptions based on narratives relating to the founding of certain schools or some incidental records or illustrations found in ancient manuscripts, not only in Japan, but also in China, Persia, Germany and Egypt. There is no record by which the origins of jujitsu can be definitely established. It would however, be rational to assume that ever since the creation, with the instinct of self-preservation, man has had to fight for his existence and was inspired to develop an art or skill to implement the body mechanism for this purpose. In such efforts, the development may have taken various courses according to the conditions of life or tribal circumstance, but the objects of the body being common, the results could not have been so different from each other. No doubt this is the reason for finding records relating to the practice of arts similar to jujitsu in various parts of the world. . . . (Sterling Publishing 1960)

The historical evidence in support of this theory is strong. Several clear instructional manuals, illustrations, and art works that depict combat styles similar to jujitsu are from areas and times that cannot possibly be related to the development of jujitsu in Japan, or anywhere else in the Far East. The implication is clear: Combat styles evolved and developed in disparate regions out of necessity. The same conditions and problems were encountered in all places and times, and the human body is relatively the same in all times and places. It can only be locked, punched, kicked, thrown, off-balanced, tripped, and swept in so many ways. Therefore, and unsurprisingly, each group arrived at similar answers to the shared problems. No culture has a monopoly on inventiveness;

hence, it makes perfect sense to think of every culture independently developing an indigenous fighting style with some strong family resemblances to styles of other cultures.

The main problem with the shared conditions theory, however, is its difficulty in accounting for important differences between fighting styles and also for the changes and revolutions that periodically occur both within a specific martial art and across the martial arts in general. Although there are clear similarities between the arts of different times and places, it is equally clear some important differences exist as well. Some arts emphasize long-range kicking attacks (Korean taekwondo); some favor gymnastics and rhythmic skills (Afro-Brazilian capoiera); others favor linear striking (karate); others specialize in clinching and in-fighting (Thai and Burmese boxing). The list of styles is long, and each brings its own particular emphasis to the table. Shared condition theory has little to say about these deviations, other than the obvious point that local conditions may have influenced the unique direction of a particular martial art's growth. In addition, there is the problem of change and evolution within the arts. How and why did styles change over time? Why do some come into favor and then get replaced? To adequately answer these questions, we must turn to another theory of martial arts history.

Great Person Theory

The *great person theory* of martial arts history posits the following idea: The history of the arts is essentially the history of great individuals who rose to prominence in their place and time through a combination of skill, innovation, personal charisma, teaching ability, and achievement. These individuals gained attention through some extraordinary demonstration of skill, often through the use of challenge matches or combat. If they had the capacity to teach these skills to others and if they had the ability to recruit and retain enough students, they could then build a new tradition, school, or style of combat. Quite often, these people themselves began under an established style. As they gained knowledge and experience, their innovative insights began to emerge. They could go on to develop or emphasize some new element and thus change the way that people view martial arts training and theory.

The great person theory is a commendable approach to the history of the martial arts. A survey of the arts in general, and jujitsu in particular, reveals a cast of truly fascinating characters who have created radical new directions and movements in combat training. The chief advantage of the great person theory is the ease with which it can help explain the many changes in direction that have occurred within jujitsu. Talented leaders create some new body of technique or way of training and drilling technique into students that enables them to excel in combat or combative events. This success creates a following that results in the development of a new school or style.

In recent times, the Gracie family from Brazil is a good example of a talented group of people who gained a large following through success in combative events. These jujitsu exponents embraced a controversial and initially unpopular thesis—that grappling (in particular, ground grappling) was absolutely essential to success in real fights. They pushed this concept to an initially skeptical public through their unprecedented success in mixed martial arts (MMA) competition. People became won over by the sight of small and physically ungifted

Gracie-trained fighters defeating much larger and more aggressive opponents with relative ease.

It is important to note the difference between the great person theory of history and the centralized origins theory. The latter was described earlier as largely untenable. The centralized origins theory posits the existence of an original person or group who laid out the foundations of the martial arts. All subsequent developments are thus a watering down of the original art. This might appear similar to the great person theory, since the alleged original founding figure must surely qualify as a great person in the history of the martial arts. The difference, however, is that the centralized origins theory puts all the credit and significance on the founder of the arts, with everyone else playing a secondary role, sometimes even a detrimental role as the diluter of an original system. The great person theory, on the other hand, sees the alleged founder of a style as just one great figure in a long line of great figures that stretches into the future. There is thus no special veneration of age and tradition. When we come to look at the actual history of jujitsu in Japan, we shall see the pivotal role played by great figures, such as Takenouchi Hisamori and Jigoro Kano, among others.

Politico-Historical Conditions Theory

Another key strand in any serious attempt to explain the history of jujitsu is *politico-historical conditions theory*. Every given culture has a large and complex set of local political and cultural traditions within which a martial art is born. Often these political and cultural traditions change over time as the forces of history come into play. Likewise, changes in direction and development of the martial arts are often in response to the changing political, historical, and cultural conditions. For example, the political conditions of feudal Japan changed enormously with successive political regimes. There were long periods of warfare, long periods of relative peace—and these changes had significant effects on the subsequent development of jujitsu. Ultimately, they all led jujitsu away from its initial role as a supplemental, battlefield art and into an autonomous art of personal protection and self-defense in a civilian setting.

Sociological Class Theory

Finally, we come to *sociological class theory*. This is the idea that every culture has a class system in place that ranks citizens into various groups based on income, occupation, lineage, and so on. Feudal Japan used an extreme example of this hierarchy, as different sociological classes had different social roles and conditions. Accordingly, they also had quite different approaches to martial arts. There was, for example, a different set of standards and attributes for the peasant classes who engaged in jujitsu practice than for the elevated warrior classes. Such sociological factors played a significant role in the subsequent development of jujitsu technique.

To conclude, we can easily consider the number of different theories as to how the martial arts in general, and jujitsu in particular, came to develop as they did. Each theory has its strengths and weaknesses, and a satisfactory account of the history of jujitsu will have to include elements of all these theories (with the exception of centralized origins theory). Having introduced these differing accounts of martial arts history, we are now in a position to begin an overview of the development of jujitsu, in which we shall see the role played by each of these theories.

BASIC JAPANESE HISTORY

A useful aid in studying the history of jujitsu is the practice of breaking up Japanese history into distinct stages, each based on different political orders. The name of the period is normally linked to the geographical location of the prevailing governmental forces of the time. One great advantage of this approach is the degree to which it clearly demonstrates the strong influence of political and historical factors in the development of Japanese martial arts (the politico-historical theory). There is usually a direct link between the prevailing political climate of the time and the type of martial arts that were developed. These historical stages are often arranged as follows.

Ancient Period (A.D. pre-650)

Politically and historically, the central feature of the ancient period is the establishment of the Yamoto line of emperors. This succession began the establishment of the royal dynasty, which created the possibility of a central imperial government (along the same lines as the Chinese system), and this line has been unbroken to this day. In fact, much of Japanese history is bound up with the quest for centralized control of the nation; however, control of the entire nation was not always possible.

Quite often, powerful provincial warlords *(daimyo)* gathered up sufficient military muscle to seize local authority and go on to fight for effective political control of the nation. The pattern was one of establishing effective political control in the form of a military dictatorship *(shogunate)* while keeping the emperor in a submissive role. Sometimes these powerful clans and warlords had to fight each other to assert dominance. It was the civil and military strife created within these power struggles that created the military class *(bushi* or *samurai)* and the martial arts of classical Japan. At various times, the lack of control on the part of the emperor over rural areas meant that local warlords could take effective control of their domains, then overtake other domains until they became effective controllers of virtually the entire nation. Such was the entrenchment of the imperial right to govern in the popular consciousness of Japan that these military rulers *(shogun)* had to rule in the name of the emperor, even though they were the ones with effective political control.

The earliest stage of Japanese history gives rise to the beginnings of Japanese martial culture in the form of *sumai,* which was the ancient forerunner of modern sumo wrestling. It was a much rougher, more combative variety of all-in wrestling, and it appears to have been the method employed by Nomi no Sukune in the epic death match of 23 B.C. (which was mentioned earlier as the starting point of Japanese martial arts). The lack of any hard historical evidence and the prevalence of myth and legend prevent any sound discussion of the beginnings of sumai. It would seem that the most sensible explanation is in terms of the shared conditions theory. People engaged in combat seek techniques to attain easier victories. Similarities in body mechanics and local conditions inevitably result in different people coming up with similar answers to the problems they confront.

Nara Period (A.D. 650–793)

Relatively little is said about the development of martial arts systems in this era. We can, however, safely speculate that there was a general shift from combative sumai to a more sportive and religious sumo-wrestling style. There is a decree from the Emperor Nimmyo (834–850) in the early Heian period that demanded the return to a more combative, military style of wrestling from which we can only assume that sumai had evolved earlier into a spectator sport.

Heian Period (A.D. 794–1191)

The chief development of the Heian period was the widespread development of sumo and sumai into the military style of grappling known as *kumiuchi*, or *yori-kumiuchi*. By the close of the Heian period, this was more or less standardized training for the rising social class of warriors. One of the most important martial institutions in Japanese history, the Butokuden, "the hall of martial virtue," was constructed on imperial orders in what was then the capital of Japan, Kyoto. Emperor Kanmu sent an edict that called for anyone skilled in fighting technique to come to the Butokuden to demonstrate his prowess. The result was a center for technical development that enjoyed full imperial support, which predates the rise of the classical combat schools.

Kamakura Period (A.D. 1192–1336)

The next two periods of Japanese history, the Kamakura and Muromachi periods, were a time of constant political struggle within Japan. The political chaos gave rise to constant warfare and a solidification of the role of a professional warrior caste—the samurai. There was a resultant need for instruction and expertise in the art of war. In response to this need came the development of the classical military schools—the *bugei (kakuto bugei),* or *bujutsu ryu-ha*. The intent of these schools was to prepare the bushi (warrior) class for open warfare on the battlefield. As such, weapons craft was the primary focus because there was no independent, weaponless martial art in the modern sense. Empty-hand fighting was simply a small part of the program, and it was strictly seen as a means of last resort in the case of weapons failure or loss. Hand-to-hand skills were thus merely a part of a holistic approach to battlefield combat.

Muromachi Period (A.D. 1337–1563)

With the continuing political instability within Japan and the resulting protracted state of war, the bushi (warrior) caste became an ever more important social group. Over time, the bushi had evolved into the samurai caste with an emphasis on faithful service to a lord of a feudal domain. Zealous servitude was a strong feature of the samurai lifestyle, and this was best displayed on the battlefield. The result was an ever-stronger demand for military instruction. In the Muromachi period, the number of bugei/bujutsu ryu greatly increased. In addition, gains in weapons technology created new military arts, and the introduction of firearms in 1543 created *hojutsu* (gunnery art). A general trend in this time was for bugei ryu to become specialized in their teaching. Often, there was a focus on a few selected weapons or skills for which a particular ryu became famous.

The bugei arts were thus centered on an aristocratic military class and were quite removed from the lower strata of Japanese society. This was the result of both the high cost of weapons and armor and the ever-tightening social constraints that made weapons possession illegal for commoners. It is near the end of the Muromachi period that the first documented jujitsu school is established in Japan—the Takenouchi ryu, in 1532. This ryu had an unusually high number of empty-hand techniques and is almost always cited as the outstanding forerunner of the modern, self-defense style of jujitsu.

Azuchi Period (A.D. 1564–1602)

In societal terms, the Azuchi period saw the solidification of the class differences between commoners and samurai greatly strengthened with the sword harvest *(katana gari)* of 1588. Commoners were prevented from carrying or even owning swords, and ownership of bladed weapons was limited to the samurai. This created the need for a separate jujitsu for commoners *(shomin yawara)* that did not involve weapons training and that helped set the basis for the development of a civilian style of empty-hand combat. Political strife came to the fore in what is often known as the "warring states period" *(sengoku)*, which culminated in the great battle of Sekigahara in 1601 and set up the Tokugawa shogunate as the sole political power base in Japan.

Edo Period (A.D. 1603–1867)

Without doubt, the Edo period was the most important time span in the development of what we think of as classical jujitsu today, and there are a number of factors behind this thinking. First, the Tokugawa shogunate looked to solidify its hard-won power base through the imposition of a harsh set of societal controls that isolated Japan from the rest of the world. Japanese ships were prevented from leaving Japan in 1635, and all foreigners (except the Dutch, who were isolated in Nagasaki) were expelled by 1639. Travel within Japan was greatly curtailed; permits were needed to leave one's own domain. Religious oppression was the norm, and strict controls on education, public discourse, and social mobility were enforced. In this way, freedom from civil strife and warfare was achieved, though at the cost of complete isolation and social repression. For the first time in centuries, there was an enduring peace in Japan. The result, however, was a total shift in emphasis on the part of the warrior class (bushi).

With their traditional role as servants to local rulers during military struggle undercut by peace, the primary role of the warrior caste became bureaucratic rather than military. There was a decline in the bugei/bujutsu arts that had been their great feature, and education and culture came to replace military prowess as the chief concern of the samurai class. As the battlefield arts declined, the study of combat in a civilian setting became dominant. Many ryu came to abandon weapons training altogether, and new ryu emerged whose sole emphasis was on empty-hand fighting.

It was in the Edo period that the vast majority of classical jujitsu schools *(koryu jujitsu)* arose and separated from the earlier bujutsu tradition. Jujitsu in some areas of Japan was doubtlessly influenced by the arrival of the Chinese national Chin Genpin in 1619. He was well versed in the art of kenpo, and it appears that he taught this art to some jujitsu practitioners. His emphasis seems to have been more on striking techniques, unlike the more typical grappling technique of Japan. From this story, some people have inferred that Genpin brought jujitsu to Japan. Clearly, however, there was a long history of martial arts in Japan long before Chin Genpin was even born.

The Tokugawa shogunate ruled from Edo for over two and a half centuries. In that span of time, the koryu jujitsu schools expanded greatly, both in number (over 700 documented ryu) and technical depth. However, by the end of the Edo period, classical jujitsu began to decline. The long-standing peace of the Edo period created a fundamental change in the bushi class, and it greatly reduced interest in combative disciplines. Moreover, as time wore on, the Tokugawa leadership came to be seen more and more as misguided in its isolationist policies and thus became increasingly unpopular. Jujitsu came to be identified with the old order of Japan, as opposed to new foreign ideas. There were so many ryu competing for students that interschool rivalry flared. Often, the results were brutal challenge matches to demonstrate the superiority of one style over another. Jujitsu was thus often seen as the business of brawlers and thugs, and its social image suffered, triggering the decline of koryu jujitsu. Thus, the Edo period saw the rise, zenith, and ultimate decline of koryu jujitsu.

Meiji Period (1868–present)

Growing internal dissatisfaction with isolation, along with the embarrassment caused by Commodore Perry's gunboat diplomacy in 1854, created a strong movement to remove the oppressive Tokugawa regime. A popular movement that was centered on the intelligentsia put Emperor Meiji in control of the nation through a bloodless revolution, and it began an attempt to drag Japan into the modern age in the shortest possible time. In the rush to adopt Western ideas and technology, traditional Japanese concepts and activities (such as jujitsu) were often disparaged and regarded as backward. In the face of this concerted drive toward new ideas, there was a danger of jujitsu's dying out altogether. The social class that had been the backbone of participation in jujitsu, the samurai class, were completely discredited and removed during the Meiji period. The symbol of the samurai, the sword (katana), was rendered illegal in public in 1877.

Many of the masters of jujitsu ryu were forced to find other kinds of work. It was in this period that Jigoro Kano began his study of jujitsu. By his early 20s, he had risen to prominence in the two styles of koryu jujitsu that he studied. Dissatisfied with many crucial aspects of traditional jujitsu, Kano sought to reform the martial arts of Japan by developing *kodokan judo* and opening his ryu in 1882. Within a short period, he gathered a large and talented pool of students whose skills he sharpened with new training methods. The kodokan fought a number of challenge tournaments with traditional jujitsu schools, which culminated in the Tokyo police tournament of 1886. A resounding win in this event gave great credibility to the young Kano and his school at the expense of the older styles of jujitsu. From this period on, judo became the foremost combat style of Japan while koryu jujitsu slowly sank away.

The historical eras of Japanese history provide the necessary background for a full understanding of the context in which jujitsu came into being and flourished in Japan. We need to go on now and look more closely at the history of the rise and fall of traditional jujitsu.

ORIGINS OF JUJITSU

The ultimate origins of jujitsu are unclear. India, China, and even Ancient Greece are often cited as the original sources of jujitsu. All such claims are entirely lacking in hard evidence and can never rise above the level of mere speculation. Indeed, we saw earlier that the whole notion of an ultimate origin of jujitsu (or any other martial art for that matter) is inherently implausible. The need for combat prowess is in every culture, and the rough similarities in physique, inventiveness, and combat conditions exist across cultures, race, and time. It therefore makes much more sense to think of local fighting styles as emerging without the need for some ultimate or central origin. Indeed, this is exactly what we observe from the historical record in Japan.

The theory of history that best explains and accounts for the origins of jujitsu in Japan is the shared conditions theory. Early Japanese society shared the same conditions that created a demand for fighting prowess in other societies. Combat skill arose from a basic need for efficient fighting technique, which was created by social conflict. In the face of this need, different people in different areas constructed methods of combat that gave them some advantage over an opponent. Since the raw material of combat—the human body—is roughly the same in all regions, it is unsurprising that there is considerable overlap in technique between the arts of different regions and times.

The unsystematic nature of these initial attempts at a method of combat is reflected in the fact that the first combative art forms were given many different names and titles in these early years. Indeed, the term *jujitsu* was not coined until relatively late in Japanese history. Instead, we see reference to arts of *yori-kumiuchi, taijitsu, Ya-wara,* and *wajutsu.* What was lacking in these early efforts at creating a combat method, however, was a systematic approach to the problem. There were no formal places of study and no full-time research or ordering of a syllabus of instruction. What was needed was a professional approach to the development, collection, and dissemination of the knowledge gained.

Establishment of the Ryu System

In the ancient period before A.D. 650, there is no record of an ultimate originator of jujitsu; rather, we see references to people who clearly engaged in the study and practice of local fighting arts. We have seen already the most famous of these, the passage from the *Nihongi,* that depicted the fight between Kuyehaya and Nomi no Sukune in 23 B.C. Other than a few scattered references to fights and grappling matches, there is little historical documentation that shows any systematic approach to the development and study of a complete fighting style.

In this early period of Japanese history, the fighting arts therefore appear to have no systematic means of instruction, and it seems individuals and small groups tried to develop their combat skills as best they could. The development of a fighting style, however, cannot make much progress under these conditions. Even the most enthusiastic amateur cannot devote the time and gather the resources necessary to systematically develop a complete fighting style from scratch. Isolated practitioners can gain some expertise on their own, but whatever skills they develop are lost if such skills are not passed on to students. Under these conditions, the early fighting arts of Japan could not have hoped to make much progress. This phenomenon stands in contrast to other areas of the world.

In ancient Greece, a different set of social conditions allowed for tremendous development and refinement of the local martial arts. The Greek city-states sponsored the construction and maintenance of gymnasiums where wrestling, boxing, and pankration were practiced. Professional coaches taught at these gymnasiums to a significant numbers of athletes, many of whom competed in large-scale sporting events such as the Olympic Games.

Tremendous prestige was associated with success in these arts. Accordingly, large amounts of money and resources were allocated to their development. The result was a systematic approach to training, technical development, and coaching, similar to a modern sports program. This produced a surge in skill level and technique that was literally hundreds of years ahead of its time. The development of such a professional and systematic approach to combat training would not arise in Japan until much later, but when it did, it shared many of the features that helped make the Greek program so successful.

What is needed for the development of a systematic and complete fighting style is first a need for combat technique. This need is created by political or social instability, which creates conflict. Early Japanese history (all the way up through the feudal era) certainly had a good deal of social and political conflict; thus, there was a definite demand for fighting technique. Second, a venue must exist where a group of practitioners can gather to develop and refine technique through constant experimentation and practice. The more time and resources these people can bring into the project, the better. These developments and refinements of technique must be systematized and passed on so that over time they can be further improved and modified and made part of an ever-growing corpus of knowledge.

Essentially, what is required is a school system for combat. In time, this is exactly what emerged in Japan, with the advent of the ryu (school) system. Various jujitsu ryu were created where professional teachers (sensei) developed and refined combat technique that they had themselves learned from their teachers. As long as unstable social and political conditions created a need for fighting technique, such schools could flourish and gain a good deal of prestige. This need opened the way for large numbers of prospective students, and it provided the resources to maintain and develop the ryu and the fighting system it taught.

The financial backing for these ryu typically came from the local *daimyo*, a district overseer who provided local governmental control. In feudal Japan, these local warlords had total power over their domain. In times of strife, they were often called on to supply warriors to other warlords with whom they were allied. Accordingly, they had a need to keep a well-trained force on hand. The training of that force became the task of the local ryu. Initially, these ryu had a fairly general curriculum, but over time, tremendous specialization took place and some ryu gained great fame in one particular art. A ryu was begun by a *ryuso* who passed on his knowledge to students in the form of physical training, theory, and written notes or drawings. Continuity and a sense of progress over time was ensured by handing the instruction on to new teachers who then became the heir to that ryu *(denshoha)* and who in turn became responsible for the development and propagation of that school's knowledge.

Rise of Battlefield Grappling Arts

By the time of the Kamakura period (1192), a clear and distinct combative style had emerged in Japan that was intrinsically linked to clashes on the battlefield. This was the art known generally as *kumiuchi*, a somewhat generic phrase that denotes grappling skills. In the course of fighting, warriors often had a need for a range of hand-to-hand combat skills, or empty-hand versus weapons skills in case of weapons breakage or loss in the midst of battlefield combat.

During this period, military combat was done in heavy, protective armor. Since heavy armor made the use of strikes impractical (seeing that a punch or a kick will probably not hurt a man who is wearing armor), these arts tended to revolve around grappling skills. Most of the techniques were designed to be used in full battlefield armor. They had a specific application that centered on off-balancing the opponent to the ground, where he could be disposed of with a short-bladed weapon or he could be tied up for capture. As the armor worn by soldiers became much lighter and handier over time, so the techniques of kumiuchi changed, allowing for freer movement and a wider range of grappling technique.

As long as military confrontation (caused by political instability) remained a feature of Japanese history, the prevalence of these battlefield arts survived. Unarmed fighting technique simply became one of many areas of combat expertise (but not a particularly important one, since weapons training obviously takes precedence on the battlefield).

The prevalence of warfare in feudal Japan led directly to the establishment of a professional warrior caste. Their desire to succeed in their military endeavors was what created the need for expertise and instruction in the battlefield arts. The development of *bugei ryu*, schools for the military arts, represents the direct prelude to the development of classical jujitsu ryu. These military schools would teach expertise in some aspect of weapons craft, sometimes specializing in one weapon—*kenjutsu* (swordplay), *sojutsu* (skill with the spear), and so on.

It should be made clear that Japan appears to have had a strong tradition of martial prowess and technical development before the confirmed establishment of the bugei ryuha. For instance, the Butokuden was established by the Emperor Kanmu around the beginning of the Heian period to encourage the development of martial skills. The establishment of genuine bugei/bujutsu ryu, where military skills were promulgated in a more systematic fashion, did not occur until the Muromachi period.

The beginnings of jujitsu were in this atmosphere of battlefield technique. The warrior caste clearly had a need for some empty-hand techniques because there was always a chance of losing one's weapon or being caught without one. Thus, even though empty-hand combat was a distinctly secondary skill to an armed warrior, some development of unarmed combative skill occurred in these bujutsu ryu. This was the initial seed from which a complete approach to unarmed combat was born.

Rise of Koryu Jujitsu

With the gradual decline of battlefield combat in Japan after 1601, the emphasis in combat instruction changed from battlefield art to personal protection in a civilian setting. It became more and more a means for an individual to defend himself in the face of attack in daily life. Thus, the nature of jujitsu changed in response to changing social conditions. It was the last period of open feudal warfare in Japan that gave rise to what is generally considered the first jujitsu ryu, as opposed to bugei ryu, which was concerned only with military combat.

The Takenouchi ryu was founded in 1532. Although it certainly taught many military weapons skills, it also taught a large array of empty-hand combat skills that were derived from *yoroi-kumiuchi* grappling arts (grappling in armor). Takenouchi ryu began a shift in emphasis toward hand-to-hand skills that grew stronger in the peaceful Edo period. Succession was passed on only to family members, and within two generations, the emphasis was almost entirely on nonmilitary technique. This shift was due to the wish of the school's founder, Takenouchi Hisamori. He declared that his sons should divorce themselves from allegiance to any powerful warlords (daimyo). This decision was the result of his own bad experiences with the warlords, and this declaration meant the school taught people from all social castes, most of whom were not allowed weapons and were not of the military classes. Thus, the emphasis naturally had to fall on civilian self-defense.

The Takenouchi ryu had a tremendous influence on many ryu in Japan. As the long-term peace of the Edo period wound on and the military arts withered, it became the standard model for the koryu jujitsu schools. It was in this time that traditional jujitsu (as we think of it today) arose as an independent, predominantly weaponless system of self-defense in everyday situations. Whereas the roots of the earlier bugei/bujutsu arts are set in the aristocratic warrior caste, the roots of koryu jujitsu are much more plebeian. Most of the demand for a weaponless fighting art came from the commoners, who were forbidden from carrying weapons. This "common people's yawara" (or *shomin yawara*) became popular in the Edo period with manuals that demonstrated techniques written and released for the public. The idea was to give civilians the techniques to defend themselves from the kinds of situations that they might find themselves in during the course of daily living. Old documents show the existence of at least 170 koryu jujitsu schools by the mid-Edo period, demonstrating well the degree of popularity they enjoyed as they came to replace the classical military arts.

Sociological Change and the Decline of Traditional Jujitsu

Ironically, the same social stability and peace that allowed for the rise of koryu jujitsu also brought about its decline. The extreme isolationist policies of the Tokugawa shogunate meant that Japan stayed locked in a feudal age while the rest of the world went through the scientific and industrial revolutions, which caused a gap between the technological, economic, industrial, and military strength of Japan and the European nations. This came to a head when Commodore Perry sailed his modern gunboats into Japanese waters in 1854 and demanded access to Japanese ports.

Japanese political and military weakness was apparent, and it became increasingly obvious that the old order would have to go. Japan became divided between the forces of conservatism that demanded the preservation of the old feudal system and the growing intellectual classes who clamored for immediate change. In 1868, the old order crumbled, and Emperor Meiji was put in power. The result was a dizzying rush to adopt new, mostly European ideas and catch up with the almost 300 years of European progress. When the Meiji restoration took effect, the samurai class, their feudal overlords, and the domains *(han)* they governed were an immediate casualty. The phasing out of the professional warrior caste and the fighting methods that they employed undercut much of the need for traditional jujitsu schools. Demand for instruction fell away drastically, and the result was a decline in jujitsu ryu, both in quantity and quality. More significant, jujitsu was heavily associated with old Japan and with the old order that had been responsible for the decline of Japanese power relative to the rest of the world. As such, it was seen as obsolete and without value.

Interest in koryu jujitsu plummeted. In addition, the breakdown of the feudal system of domains and restrictions on travel, along with the rapid growth of industrialization, meant that many Japanese moved from the countryside to the city. Thus, many jujitsu instructors, no longer financially supported by a daimyo, also moved to the cities. This, along with falling numbers of students, created great competition for paying students. The result was a large number of bloody challenge matches that were designed to prove the superiority of one ryu over another in the quest to attract followers. Jujitsu came to gain an unsavory reputation as the activity of thugs and ruffians, which further dampened public interest. The overall result was a real crisis for koryu jujitsu. Most teachers sought out other occupations to make a living.

Jigoro Kano and the Rise of Judo

When Jigoro Kano began jujitsu instruction in the late 1870s, the state of jujitsu was so poor it was difficult for him to even find a school. He noted the unfavorable public perception of jujitsu as a violent and outmoded relic from a past era. Despite this, Kano saw jujitsu as an important and vital part of Japan's heritage. He sought to modify it and bring the combat arts back into favor as part of an overall education. Reacting to constant bullying as a child and teenager, Kano turned to jujitsu as a way to improve his physique and overall ruggedness. This he had to do against the express wishes of his father, who had the low opinion of jujitsu so prevalent at that time. While in Tokyo University, Kano began an intense study of Tenjin-shinyo ryu jujitsu under Fukuda-sensei for a two-year period. Fukuda died in 1879, which forced Kano to study under Mataemon Iso. He too died, in 1881. That loss forced Kano to switch to Kito ryu jujitsu under Tsunetoshi Ikubo, where the throwing technique so associated with judo was emphasized. In all, Kano studied jujitsu for four years, and in that time, he distinguished himself as an extremely dedicated and innovative student. For his reward, he was given the symbol of leadership of Tenshin Shinyo jujitsu ryu—the written scrolls that depicted that system's history and technique.

Kano's vision, however, is much greater than merely that of carrying on an old tradition. While studying jujitsu, he made note of what he thought were the fundamental weaknesses of koryu jujitsu and resolved to improve them. These weaknesses are interesting to consider. First, the social question lingered about jujitsu's dubious reputation as the choice of thugs and ruffians. Kano came from a respectable, intellectual family; the image of brawling street fights did not go well with a man of his upbringing. One of Kano's great achievements was to bring about legitimate, sanctioned competitions (shiai) that allowed for socially acceptable matches and competition. Kano's concern was to make martial arts training part of the road to self-perfection rather than merely practice for fighting. It was as much about character building as it was combat training.

In addition, Kano implemented a strict code of ethics that forbade fighting for money (among other things). In this way, he was able to greatly repair the public's view of martial arts as mere roughhousing. It was for this reason that Kano adopted the term *judo* rather than *jujitsu* to describe his art. Instead of being a mere art or skill (jitsu), judo implied the theme of striving after something greater. *Do* means *the way* (tao in Chinese), and it carries with it the notion of self-mastery and perfection, as opposed to the simple accumulation of skills.

Second, koryu jujitsu had no set curriculum of instruction or ranking. This open format meant that novices often trained with experts, since there were no belt levels to divide students by experience and expertise. This policy, however, increased the likelihood of serious injury in training. For instance, there was no systematic training of beginners in the methods of safe falling *(ukemi)* to allow them to be thrown without harm. Instruction was random and idiosyncratic.

Third, the most important problem that Kano saw in koryu jujitsu was its lack of overall strategy. In essence, it was a collection of tricks to defeat an opponent in certain situations. Some of these were in accordance with the idea of an individual's using efficient technique to overcome brute strength, but not all. Kano took seriously the notion of *seiryoku zenyo* (maximum efficiency, minimum effort) as a guiding principle of his new martial art. All technique was to be put in line with this principle. The single most important development made by Kano in the implementation of this principle was his emphasis on *kuzushi* (off-balancing). Kano noted in the course of his study that if an opponent was kept off-balance, he could not attack nor could he defend throws and takedowns effectively. The amount of strength required to throw a man whose balance is disturbed is dramatically less than that of a man in good balance.

Accordingly, Kano put great emphasis on the skill of off-balancing an opponent as a prelude to throwing him. In this way, a smaller man had an excellent chance of controlling and throwing a larger man. Kano thus had an overall principle to guide the combatant's technique, to use minimal effort to gain maximum effect, and to achieve a physical means of acting out that principle, kuzushi, or off-balancing.

A fourth crucial problem with koryu jujitsu was the lack of adequate training methods. Traditional jujitsu was taught almost entirely by *kata*. The idea was for two partners to have a prearranged sequence of moves that they performed on each other without resistance. The main reason for this arrangement was the fact that koryu jujitsu relied heavily on techniques that could not be used in any situation other than an all-out fight for survival. This was a legacy from its battlefield roots when hair pulling, eye gouging, groin attacking, fish hooking, clawing, and so on were commonly used. Obviously, techniques such as these cannot be used with full power on a training partner. In time, the heavily idealized movement of the kata forms became an end in itself. Mastery of the kata movements was taken to imply mastery of combat. Although kata was a safe means of teaching moves to students, it was totally inadequate in preparing them for actual combat. There is a world of difference between applying a move on an unresisting, cooperative partner and performing the same move on a live opponent in a real fight.

Faced with these problems, Kano sought to reform koryu jujitsu and create a new martial art that would avoid these pitfalls. In making these reforms, he had an overall vision of what was wrong with traditional jujitsu and what stood in need of change.

Besides his concern with social education and rehabilitating the public image of jujitsu, Kano was interested in creating a truly combat-effective martial art. What he saw was that the martial arts of his day needed reform not at the level of technique, but of training method. By the time of the Meiji restoration, there were literally thousands of widely known jujitsu techniques, and many of these were quite effective. Kano himself was exposed to many of these techniques in the four years that he learned koryu jujitsu, but he was also astute enough to realize that there is a gulf between technique and the application of technique. In other words, a given technique might be an effective technique when considered independent of the participant; however, if it is applied poorly, it will naturally fail to have the desired effect. *Kano's project then was to switch emphasis from the techniques themselves to the people who actually apply the techniques.* In combat, the value of a technique is limited by the student's ability to apply it. It therefore makes more sense for instructors to allocate most of their concern to finding methods of training the techniques into students, as opposed to simply accumulating more and more techniques.

Consider an analogy: In combat, a rifle is only as accurate as the person shooting it. It is useless to spend countless resources developing an extremely accurate rifle if the person using it has no shooting skill. So, too, with jujitsu technique: In combat, it will prove only as effective as the ability of the student who applies it. Accordingly, Kano did little to innovate jujitsu technique; in fact, almost all the technique he taught was part of koryu jujitsu. For example, his technique syllabus of 1895 *(gokyo)* only contains about 45 throws, a small number when compared with other ryu. His truly important innovations were at the level of training method. The problem that confronted Kano was the allowing of a combat-realistic form of training that could expose students to the stress and fatigue expected in combat, without too much danger of injury.

We have seen that live training *(randori)* is an essential part of combat training. However, the problem with koryu jujitsu was that the majority of techniques had unsafe elements that made them unsuitable for daily, live training (e.g., eye gouging). If randori becomes too dangerous, students will not progress as a result of an unacceptably high rate of injury and attrition. One response to this problem is to eliminate randori altogether, which was the response of most koryu jujitsu schools. They could rationalize this response by claiming that the moves were simply too dangerous to perform live on one another. The obvious problem with this response is that students never get to apply the techniques they will need during a real fight. We are thus caught in a dilemma. On one hand, we can attain great combative realism by allowing totally free training, but we do so at the cost of unacceptably high rates of injury and dropout. On the other hand, we can make training safe and enjoyable by eliminating randori, but we do so at the cost of combat effectiveness.

Kano was much aware of this dilemma, and his solution to it is without doubt one of the truly great breakthroughs in the history of the martial arts. Noting that certain kinds of techniques were responsible for most of the injury problems associated with live training, Kano sought a middle ground between the realistic-but-unsafe extreme of all-out combat randori and the safe-but-unrealistic extreme of idealized-movement training (kata). What he did was limit the types of technique that could be applied in randori. He permitted only those that could be applied using full power on a resisting opponent in a live combat situation *but* with little likelihood of injury. This methodology of placing limits on technique has been the role model for all subsequent grappling styles and also many striking styles of fighting. In this way, the realism of live training can be incorporated without inflicting an unacceptably high rate of injury and attrition on students.

Kano's solution to the realism/safety dilemma was not seen as satisfactory by all, however. Different arts have not always agreed with the exact limits that Kano put on randori, although he was in fact quite conservative—he banned all striking, several types of throws, and many submission holds that other styles permit. There was also some concern that by removing dangerous techniques, Kano was "watering down" jujitsu and making it far less combat-effective. It was eventually up to Kano to show that this complaint was based on mistaken ideas. Nonetheless, his general solution to the dilemma found tremendous favor and success, despite some complaints and criticisms.

There is a widespread belief in the traditional martial arts that the overall effectiveness of a martial art is directly proportional to the number of techniques it has and the apparent deadliness of those techniques. So, for example, an art that contains many techniques designed to break an opponent's neck, to poke out eyes, or to invoke other instances of terrible injury or death will be viewed as a dangerous and effective martial art. This kind of attitude was quite prevalent in koryu jujitsu. Many ryu advertised their effectiveness in terms of the number and alleged deadliness of techniques they contained, and quite frankly, this is a natural belief to hold. After all, the idea of one man scratching out another man's eyes or rupturing his eardrums with a powerful slap certainly sounds intimidating.

What many people fail to realize, however, is that these dangerous moves are physical skills like any other. As such, it takes realistic practice to perfect their application, the same way it takes practice to perfect a golf swing or slam dunk a basketball. Just as nobody could hope to make it into the National Basketball Association by only practicing a basketball kata, nobody can likewise hope to master the realistic application of these deadly moves through a martial art kata. The person who uses these allegedly deadly techniques would lack any real experience in applying these moves in a realistic situation against a resisting opponent; therefore, that person has a minimal chance of success.

Accordingly, the deadly techniques favored by so many traditional martial arts have only a *theoretical* deadliness with little *practical* deadliness. Part of Kano's program was to expose this fallacy that was so prevalent in the traditional martial arts. Kano realized that the overall effectiveness of a martial art is determined by much more than the sum of its techniques and their theoretical deadliness. The other element that determines overall effectiveness is the training methodology that ingrains the techniques into the students. It was this crucial element that had been ignored in most koryu jujitsu styles. Traditional jujitsu had developed a fetish for technique as an end in itself, and thus it ignored the need for a means of training the actual technique into the students. As a result, it fell into the "deadly technique" fallacy—the fallacious notion that the effectiveness of a martial art is directly proportional to the number and apparent deadliness of the techniques it accumulates. *Therefore, Kano did not just teach technique*. He taught a training methodology that could successfully ingrain the safe techniques into his students so that they could use them effectively and confidently in a combat situation. In this way, Kano hoped to arrive at a more combat-effective martial art.

A surprising consequence of Kano's decision to rid judo of many of the dangerous techniques of koryu jujitsu is that this created a more combat-effective fighting style. This is the exact *opposite* of what most people would expect. Normally, one would think that the more deadly and dangerous techniques a martial art has, the more effective it would be. We have seen that such thinking is an instance of the "deadly technique" fallacy. Kano saw clearly that a person would be a much more effective fighter if that person trained with full power on resisting partners with techniques that can be used safely during daily training—versus someone who only performed kata on passive, unresisting partners with theoretically deadly techniques.

To see this point, we need to be quite clear as to what constitutes a "safe" technique. Safe techniques are those that can be used with full power on resisting opponents in live training sessions on a daily basis. Clearly, a large number of the techniques of koryu jujitsu fall outside this category. Strikes to vulnerable parts of the body, eye gouges, groin attacks, and the like cannot be made part of a safe, daily training regimen. In addition, there are some throws and joint locks that have a higher-than-normal risk of injury associated with their use. These, too, have to be omitted. The techniques that remain can be made part of a safe and enjoyable sparring program that will not be too far removed from the same way those techniques can be applied in a real fight.

A point that must be made clear is that "safe" does not in any way imply that the technique is ineffective. The techniques are only safe in the sense that they are used under supervision on mats *(tatame)* among students who agree to stop applying them when their partner submits. If these safety constraints are not used, these "safe" techniques can be used to maim, render unconscious, or even kill an opponent. For example, the arm-locks shown later in this book can be safely used in live training between partners if they both agree to stop applying the technique as soon as it takes effect. Failure to do so will result in a badly broken arm. Contrast this with eye gouging, or any other of the unsafe techniques of koryu jujitsu, which cannot be applied full-power without an unacceptably high risk of injury. Since students get to apply these safe techniques in live combat every time they train, they quickly become used to the subtle body/motor skills required to apply them on a fully resisting foe.

We thus arrive at the paradoxical result that a person who trains with a set of safe techniques does better in real combat than a person trained with a set of apparently deadly techniques. These were the counterintuitive and revolutionary ideas that lay behind Kano's reforms. But what was needed was a concrete, empirical test of the validity of these innovative ideas. Without this, Kano's reforms would be nothing more than theory. The acid test for this new approach to the martial arts came four years after the opening of the kodokan.

Tournament of 1886

Kano opened his kodokan judo school in 1882. This was a remarkable feat on his part. He was only 22 years old and had studied jujitsu for only four years. He opened a small school with only nine students. In time, he expanded the size of the school and changed its location several times. He was even able to recruit some of the most outstanding jujitsu fighters in Japan into the kodokan. These men refined their already high skill level by using Kano's training methods (of which randori was the most important) until the kodokan began to establish a reputation as one of the leading schools in Tokyo.

Such success did not go unnoticed. The result was a series of challenges issued to the kodokan by koryu schools and individuals. The top kodokan students (who were themselves former jujitsu students who had switched to kodokan judo) defeated all comers with relative ease. Kano had a strict set of rules and regulations in regard to these challenge matches. He wanted to avoid the undesirable image of jujitsu schools brawling in public, so all matches were to be held in the kodokan with limits on foul tactics and strikes. As such, they were more like grappling matches than true no-holds-barred fights.

Still, the ease with which kodokan fighters dispatched their opponents was quite impressive. In 1886, the Tokyo police were considering the adoption of a martial art in which to instruct officers. A well-publicized tournament was held to test the effectiveness of various styles so that one could be selected to teach the police force. In the end, it came down to the new style of judo versus some of the best known ryu of classical jujitsu. The kodokan, represented by some truly legendary figures, such as Saigo and Tomishita, decisively won 13 of 15 matches and drew the other two. Wins were determined either by ippon throws, landing the opponent flat on his back, or by submission. (As it turned out, throws were the means of victory in all the major fights; in fact, there is little mention of ground grappling or submission holds in the records.) Obviously, there were limits on the types of techniques one could use. Foul tactics were banned, and once again, it was more of a grappling tournament than a fight. This was a truly massive win for the kodokan.

Having been in existence for only four years with a youthful master, the kodokan had taken on and soundly defeated the preeminent koryu jujitsu masters of the time in a public setting. The result was almost immediate. Kano's school went from being another martial arts ryu to being the most successful school in Japan. By 1887, he had well over 1,500 students. As the fame and renown of the kodokan increased, it pushed traditional jujitsu into the background. In addition, Kano's position as a well-respected figure in the Japanese education system meant that by 1911, judo was made part of public schooling. Within a short time, judo went from being a private martial arts style to a national sport. Such was Kano's eminence and drive as a public educator and political figure that he sought international recognition beyond Japanese borders. He was made a member of the Olympic committee and sought to make judo an international art. To accomplish this aim, he sent many of his best students overseas to promote the study of judo, and in addition, he accepted many foreigners to study in Japan. In the face of this tremendous success, koryu jujitsu was completely eclipsed and in danger of disappearing altogether.

Modern Jujitsu: New Concepts, New Directions

In chapter 1, we saw the rise of a combat tradition in early Japanese history that flowered into a systematic and comprehensive approach to the art of combat. As political turmoil created a demand for combat skills, military training became a valuable commodity. In time, professional schools (*ryuha*) emerged and became sponsored by local warlords. The time and resources available to these ryuha enabled them to make significant advances in technique and training. The result was an increasingly sophisticated approach to military fighting arts that peaked in the late feudal era. When the Tokugawa shogunate brought about political stability and thus removed the need for military training, the demand for a civilian martial art increased. Various ryuha began to specialize in unarmed fighting styles. The outcome was the emergence of a specialized unarmed curriculum much closer to what we think of as modern jujitsu.

In the 17th and 18th centuries, this kind of jujitsu came to prominence in Japan. But the extreme policies of the Tokugawa shogunate produced political and cultural isolation and ultimately resulted in the decline of the Japanese ruling and military class. When this happened, classical jujitsu fell into serious decline. Jigoro Kano started a new martial tradition, kodokan judo, in which he tried to remove the specific elements of traditional jujitsu that he thought had contributed to that decline. In a series of challenge matches, classical jujitsu ryu faced off against the kodokan. The result was a series of lopsided victories for Kano's schools. Their superior training methodology and overall strategy gave them a decisive advantage in competition. In the face of these defeats, classical jujitsu fell into further decline, leaving judo as Japan's eminent martial art.

FUSEN RYU AND THE DEVELOPMENT OF GRAPPLING JUJITSU

By the end of the 19th century, judo was in an unassailable position as the foremost combat art in Japan. It had convincingly defeated all-comers in competition and enjoyed the support of the Japanese education system (as Kano himself was highly placed in that system). To the surprise of many, the kodokan received a challenge from Mataemon Tanabe, the head of a relatively small jujitsu school named Fusen ryu.

The Fusen ryu was a school with an ancient lineage. It was founded by Takeda Motsuge, who was born in 1794 and trained as a Buddhist priest from an early age. He took on the name Fusen and began the study of various classical martial arts. After his death in 1867, a lineage was formed. As to the nature of the challenge that was given to the kokodan, there is some current disagreement regarding the specific details. It appears, though, that it began as an individual challenge between Tanabe and some members of the kodokan but eventually became an interschool challenge tournament.

The idea of a challenge from yet another classical jujitsu ryu could not have worried the kodokan, as they had easily defeated the best-known jujitsu schools already. Unbeknownst to them, however, they were about to take on a different opponent from anything they had faced before. There is little reliable information about the Fusen ryu, but we do know that the grandmaster of the 1890s,

Mataemon Tanabe, had trained extensively in ground grappling and that he had made this the emphasis of his school's training. It is unclear if this was Tanabe's own doing or if this had always been the case with Fusen ryu.

Regardless, ground grappling had always been present to some extent in classical jujitsu. Experience on the battlefield showed the frequency with which real fights end with the combatants wrestling each other on the ground, even if that was not their intention. It was also an essential part of the battlefield art of capturing and restraining an enemy.

Nonetheless, it was uncommon for a school to advocate a whole system of ground grappling and practice fighting on the ground for extended periods of time, as though it were the preferred place to be in a real fight. It should be noted that in all the interschool clashes between the kodokan judo school and the classical jujitsu ryu, the outcome was decided by throwing skill. The original curriculum of technique in kodokan judo was a set of throws with no ground grappling. Kano greatly favored throws as the basis of his system, and his students were able to throw their opponents cleanly on their backs to attain victory in competition. Indeed, before 1900, there appears to have been little, if any, ground grappling in judo.

Tanabe had made note of this fact and proposed an innovative and brilliant response. He would not try to match throwing skill with the judo representatives; rather, he would take the fight to the ground, where he knew he had a massive advantage in technical knowledge and skill. In this way, he could easily take the judo players out of their preferred element and into an element where they posed little threat. Rather than win by a throw that lands an opponent flat on his back (ippon), he sought to win by submission, forcing the opponent to surrender the match from the application of a painful lock or stranglehold on the ground.

There are several accounts of what happened when Fusen-ryu jujitsu took on kodokan judo. Some claim that the challenges began with Mataemon Tanabe himself engaging in matches with senior kodokan members, culminating in an interschool challenge in which Fusen ryu soundly defeated the kodokan. In addition, there is some disagreement over the dates of the events. Most sources put the interschool match at 1900, some a little earlier, others as late as 1905. All sides agree, however, that the previously invincible kodokan experienced its first and only defeat in challenge competition by the hitherto unheralded Fusen ryu.

Most accounts of the matches agree that the Fusen-ryu representatives employed the novel tactic of sitting down as soon as the matches began, thus making the matches ground grappling duels. It is unclear whether they simply sat down on the mat or actively jumped into the *guard position* (a ground-grappling position greatly favored by many grappling jujitsu stylists; the guard position is covered extensively in chapter 7). Once on the ground, the judo representatives had little idea of how to cope with the Fusen-ryu fighters, and all were quickly defeated by submission holds. The lopsided result was a huge shock for Jigoro Kano and the kodokan. Realizing that his judo was sorely lacking in ground-grappling technique, he quickly sought to have Tanabe teach his curriculum to the kodokan students. One of the most well-known and plausible accounts of the challenge matches between Fusen ryu and kodokan judo comes from Kainan Shimomura, 8-dan in kodokan judo. In the September 1952 edition of *Henri Plée's Revue Judo Kodokan,* Shimomura wrote:

Encounters between professors of the state were the exception. However, public opinion got so worked up that in January 1891 an intergroup combat took place in which Tobari (then 3rd dan judo, he died an 8th dan) for the Kodokan opposed [Mataemon] Tanabe, expert of the Fusen-ryu school. One must not commit the error of considering the ancient jujutsu as being a priori inferior to modern judo. Straightaway Tanabe sought the combat on the ground, but Tobari succeeded in remaining standing up. After a fierce fight Tanabe won by a successful stranglehold on the ground. Tobari, bitterly disappointed by the defeat, began to feverishly study groundwork.

The year after, he challenged Tanabe again. This time it was a ground battle and once more Tanabe won. He was now famous and, in the name of the ancient schools, challenged the members of the Kodokan, and even Isogai (then 3rd dan, at the time of his death he was a 10th dan) was put in danger from his ground technique. The Kodokan then concluded that a really competent judoka must possess not only a good standing technique but good ground technique as well. This is the origin of the celebrated "ne-waza of the Kansai region." And in conclusion to all this one may well say that Mataemon Tanabe, too, unconsciously contributed towards the perfecting of the judo of the Kodokan. (Cited in *Blood on the Sun: The Odyssey of Yukio Tani* by Graham Noble.)

Effects of the Fusen-Ryu Challenge Matches

It is worth investigating the matches between the kodokan and Fusen ryu because they set the pattern for much of the modern development of jujitsu from the 20th century to the present. The single greatest feature of the Fusen-ryu victory was the adoption of an overall strategy that was wedded to a fighting technique that left opponents at a distinct and unexpected disadvantage. The idea was to take an opponent out of his area of expertise and into a situation that he was ill-prepared to deal with, while at the same time developing one's own skills in that specific area. This is exactly the strategy adopted by Mataemon Tanabe.

He saw that the training of pre-20th-century judo was woefully inadequate in ground grappling. Thus, he developed his students' skills in ground grappling to a high degree, knowing that it is a relatively easy matter to take a fight to the ground. In this way, he could rationally expect his students to rapidly put their opponents into a phase of combat that they were simply not able to cope with. This unexpected strategy succeeded brilliantly in the empirical test of open competition. The core element of this novel strategy is the idea that unarmed combat can be broken up into *phases*, each of which is quite different in character from the others. For example, fighting in a standing position is entirely different from fighting on the ground. A fighter can be proficient at one but inept in the other. In addition, fighting in the standing position is quite different when the two combatants get a grip on each other and go into a standing clinch. At that point, the control that they can exert on each other totally changes the character of the match from the situation where neither had any hold on the other.

Tanabe realized that the judo players were skilled in the standing position when they had a grip on their opponents. This is where they had been able to trounce their opposition in the previous challenge matches, such as at the Tokyo police tournament. The gripping and throwing skills honed by live training (*randori*) had given the judo representatives a decisive advantage against the classical jujitsu schools in tournaments. The mistake made by traditional jujitsu ryu was to take on the kodokan at their greatest skill—namely, gripping and throwing.

Fusen-ryu representatives saw that if they could take the fights into a phase of combat that the judo players were ill-suited to deal with, the chances of success would be much greater. Ground grappling was an obvious choice. It is easy for trained fighters to take a fight to the ground, especially if they are confident enough to simply sit down to the guard position (on their backs) and fight from there. In addition, the means of victory on the ground is via submission holds, something that most untrained people have no idea how to defend against. Tanabe's great insight, then, was this notion of *phases of combat*. It was a strategy that used these phases to take an opponent out of his comfort zone and into a phase in which he had little chance of success.

Analysis of Fusen-Ryu Jujitsu

One of the great surprises of martial arts history is that there is so little attention paid to the remarkable feats of the Fusen ryu. Few people in the martial arts community have even heard of the Fusen ryu or Mataemon Tanabe. This is strange, given the tremendous and unexpected success they had in challenge matches against the mighty kodokan judo school. A number of intriguing questions immediately come to mind when one first hears of their remarkable exploits. First, who was Mataemon Tanabe? Who trained him, and what became of him after the challenge matches? Second, had Fusen ryu always focused on ground grappling in the roughly 65 years of its existence before the challenge matches? What kind of training methods did they employ to get their students to such a high level? Third, what ever became of Fusen ryu? Why did it fade into obscurity after such a brilliant achievement?

Regrettably, there is little information available to answer these questions, and most has to be inferred from indirect sources. To this day, Mataemon Tanabe remains a shadowy figure, but there is a famous photograph of Jigoro Kano with a group of leading classical jujitsu masters, including Tanabe, around 1906. At that time, Kano was in the process of attempting to formulate a record of traditional jujitsu technique so that he could create a set of kata that would preserve that technique. Most of the jujitsu men are from well-known schools and are quite old. Tanabe stands out, looking young, strong, and fit. That he should be placed in such highly ranked company at such an age is an indication of just how highly esteemed he was. This makes it all the more strange that he should quickly fade into obscurity.

Of Tanabe himself, we know very little. It is said that he was the fourth grand master of Fusen-ryu jujitsu, which makes sense. The Fusen ryu began 60 years before these dramatic events transpired, and in that time frame, a school would have gone through approximately four top instructors. Tanabe, though, appears to have attained considerable fame and renown in turn-of-the-century Japan as a result of his exploits. He is mentioned by several other highly regarded martial artists—for example, Mitsuyo Maeda (whom we shall see later with regards to the development of Brazilian jiu jitsu).

We do know, however, that Jigoro Kano—by then the grand master of Japan's leading martial arts school and a powerful figure in the Japanese government (through the education department)—came to him to ask for instruction in ground grappling. It was a request that Tanabe agreed to, and it may well be that this action—the one that consented to reveal the core elements of Fusen ryu ground grappling—led to the demise of Fusen-ryu jujitsu. Once ground grappling was made a part of the kodokan judo syllabus, it became extremely popular. In a short time, judo became dominated by ground grappling (*ne waza*) expertise. In the period immediately after the Fusen-ryu matches, there was an explosion of interest in ne waza technique, almost to the exclusion of standing technique. This might strike the modern reader as strange since we typically think of judo as predominantly a standing, throwing art, with only a little ground grappling. In the early years of judo, before World War II and especially from 1900 to 1925, there was a tremendous emphasis on ne waza. The majority of judo matches were won and lost on the ground. In the face of this ne waza explosion, it is likely that Fusen ryu simply faded away.

As for the training methods of Fusen ryu, we can rationally speculate that they included the same element that was crucial to the success of kodokan judo, namely the practice of live training (randori). In the previous chapter, we saw that Kano's insistence on randori as the backbone of training gave his students a decisive edge in competition over their rivals, who trained solely with kata. Such live training was made possible by the removal of dangerous elements of technique so that students could train safely on a daily basis at something close to full power on resisting live opponents. The available evidence suggests that Fusen-ryu students did the same thing with their ne waza training. We can infer this by the fact that they were happy enough to engage in sporting competition with rules. Clearly they had progressed beyond the foul tactics (e.g., biting, eye gouging) and striking blows (*atemi*) that were so much a part of classical jujitsu. They had adapted to the idea of sporting competition.

As such, there was nothing to prevent them from safely engaging in randori practice. The submission holds that were so much a feature of their ground-grappling game—all their victories in the challenge matches were due to submission holds—could be made a safe part of randori training if both partners agreed to stop when a submission hold had been successfully applied. In addition, one of the most well-known Fusen ryu students, Yukio Tani (whose fascinating life we shall soon look at in detail), regularly employed randori training with his students in England, a place to where he emigrated at the turn of the 19th century. Clearly he was employing the same training methods that he learned back in Japan.

Case Study: Yukio Tani, Fusen-Ryu Representative

The history of grappling jujitsu has some truly fascinating characters who lived lives so colorful, entertaining, and instructive that some details ought to be told. One such figure is Yukio Tani. Some time around 1900 (there is disagreement as to the exact date), he came to England with his brother as part of a plan (with a Mr. Barton-Wright) to open a jujitsu school and teach technique. The school soon failed, and Tani went into partnership with William Bankier, a former strongman and showman who wrestled at Tani's

school. The idea was to display Japanese jujitsu for entertainment purposes to the English public and by so doing, become rich. Tani's brother soon left, but Yukio stayed on, going into a career as a nightclub act, wrestling all-comers for money.

What made this act so popular was Tani's appearance. He was tiny, standing only five feet tall and weighing 125 pounds. People in the club were invited to wrestle him. If they could last a few minutes, they were given a substantial amount of money; if they lasted 15 minutes, they were given even more money. The only conditions were that no striking or foul tactics be used (although it appears that more than a few tried these tactics), and interestingly, Tani also personally required that his opponents wear a Japanese *gi*, the heavy canvas jacket similar to that worn by judo and Brazilian jiu jitsu players. This enabled Tani to employ a range of grips, throws, sweeps, and strangleholds that were totally foreign to his unsuspecting opponents. The result was that the diminutive Japanese jujitsu man was able to crush almost every one of the literally thousands of opponents he faced over the many years of his act. Apparently, he averaged 40 to 50 opponents a week!

He quickly grew famous in England and became known as the invulnerable Japanese wrestler. In fact, there is even reference to him in the writings of the great playwright George Bernard Shaw (*Major Barbara*), where one character refers to having a battle in a club with the "Jap wrestler" and having his arm broken! Tani became rich as a result of his exploits and certainly raised the image of jujitsu's effectiveness in the eyes of the English. Tani fought not only the local brawlers and tough men of the nightclubs; he also fought pitched battles with many of England's best wrestlers and strongmen, most of whom were twice his size. Almost all were easily defeated by Tani's favorite techniques—armlocks and strangleholds.

Note that ground grappling and submission skills were the key to Tani's success. Quite often, he was pinned down on his back by his larger opponents; however, this would be of little consequence. Tani would simply fight off his back, then strangle or armlock them from underneath. This was a foreshadowing of the methods used by the Gracie family when they came into fame in North America. They, too, surprised many of their opponents by defeating them from underneath. Tani also employed many throws, but these did not end his matches; rather, they were simply a means of taking the fight to the ground, where a range of submission holds could be easily and effectively applied.

Many of Tani's matches and achievements are well documented. There are descriptions of his victory in a sanctioned wrestling bout with the British catch-wrestling champion Jimmy Mellor. This match demonstrated Tani's versatility as it was fought using catch-wrestling rules and without his opponent's wearing a *gi*. One cannot help but admire the courage and skill of this tiny man who night after night, for years at a time, fought the toughest barroom brawlers, wrestlers, boxers, and strongmen in the clubs of England. By day, he even wrestled the local grappling champions and his own students. All this, in a foreign country and in a culture that was hardly friendly to Asians.

Bear in mind that Tani was only 19 when he took up this lifestyle, and you can see why he is held in such high esteem. Through it all, he remained even-tempered and modest, always maintaining that he was only of average ability in jujitsu when compared with the best in Japan. Tani is believed to have trained in several styles of jujitsu, such as Tenshin yo ryu and Yoshin ryu. However, in a fascinating study of Tani's life and times, historian Graham Noble (*Blood on the Sun: The Odyssey of Yukio Tani*) talks of Tani's links to Fusen ryu.

> We know little about Tani's early training. Apparently his father and grandfather were teachers of jujutsu and he started training at a young age. So this must have been around 1890. Shingo Ohgami told me that Tani trained with Fusen-ryu groundwork specialists Torajiro Tanabe and/or Mataemon Tanabe. This is supported by information in Takao Marushima's *Maeda Mitsuyo: Conte Koma* (1997), where it is said that Mataemon Tanabe was a friend of Tani's father.

In time, Tani tired of the constant fighting and opened his own school. When Jigoro Kano came to England as part of his effort to expand kodokan judo around the world, he offered to help Tani if he would agree to teach as a judo representative in England. This was a good opportunity for Tani: Judo was by then the national martial art of Japan, and such a position carried considerable prestige. He accepted and was immediately made a black belt in judo (second dan). From that point, he taught as a judo man and helped launch judo in England. In a way, his story is representative of the fate of Fusen ryu jujitsu itself—it was swallowed up by the much bigger and better organized judo movement.

MITSUYO MAEDA: A PROTÉGÉ OF THE NE WAZA REVOLUTION

One of the most important figures in the history of grappling jujitsu was Mitsuyo Maeda (1878–1941). He was originally a highly regarded student of classical jujitsu, but like most people of that time, he eventually switched to kodokan judo. Around 1896, Maeda began judo and quickly rose to prominence in the kodokan as a result of his outstanding ability. It is interesting to note that the time that Maeda entered judo coincides with the time that followed Mataemon Tanabe's individual challenges to members of the kodokan. Judo players were already studying ne waza as a way of countering Tanabe's well-known ground skills (in this, we saw that they were unsuccessful). Maeda was in fact present to witness the kodokan team lose to Fusen ryu, which preceded the movement toward ne waza training. Maeda was highly ranked in the kodokan and was doubtless a part of the drive toward ne waza expertise.

At the time, however, Jigoro Kano was interested in exporting judo from Japan. He sent delegates all over the world to expand judo overseas with several highly ranked judo men being sent to America and other parts of the world. Maeda (and Tomita, one of Kano's first students) was sent to the East Coast of the United States to display and promote judo in 1904, but there he had mixed success. He did fight some challenge matches and win; however, he considered America unsuitable for living as a result of the strong anti-Asian sentiments that he encountered.

Thus, he began a remarkable journey around the world, not unlike that of Yukio Tani, fighting a huge number of challenge matches wherever he went and emerging the winner in all but two cases. In Europe, he took on the name "Count Comde," which is a humorous play on words. It plays on both the Spanish term for combat and the Japanese term for trouble, and it conveys the idea that he was the "prince of combat who was constantly in trouble!"

Shortly before World War I, Maeda moved to Brazil. He became involved in the Japanese government's program of overseas colonization. This was the time of colonial powers. Japan, as an emerging power, wanted to be part of the colonial elite and join nations such as England, France, and Germany. A national program of emigration to Brazil was begun, and a considerable number of Japanese made the voyage. Maeda was a major figure in this movement and an enthusiastic advocate of Brazil as a place for the Japanese to live.

In looking for land in which to house the colonists, Maeda came to befriend Gastao Gracie, a man of Scottish descent whose family had emigrated to Brazil and gained some prominence in local politics. Both men had an interest in professional fighting. Maeda had become something of a legend in Brazil, fighting all-comers in a large number of challenge matches and teaching his fighting skills to an ever-growing number of students. Indeed, "Count Comde" had grown quite rich as a result of his exploits and became an owner of a considerable amount of land. In return for the help given by Gastao Gracie, Maeda offered to teach his famous fighting skills to Carlos, the oldest of Gastao's sons. For somewhere between two to four years, Carlos learned from Maeda until Maeda, ever the traveler, moved on to a different part of Brazil.

REFLECTIONS ON MAEDA'S APPROACH TO COMBAT

In the course of his many travels, Maeda fought a vast number of fights. Some were all-out challenge matches whereas others were impromptu street fights or grappling-only exhibitions; some were sanctioned wrestling matches or were fought in a Japanese gi; others were not. This vast experience in many different environments gave Maeda a wealth of knowledge on the art of combat. His formal background was in Tenshin Shin'yo jujitsu and kodokan judo; however, it seems that he began to modify his fighting style in the face of his own practical experience.

First, Maeda faced opponents who were different from those he faced in Japan. The majority of them were Western boxers and wrestlers who presented an entirely different set of problems from those Maeda faced in Japan. For instance, the wrestlers fought without the Japanese gi jacket, and they employed a set of takedowns and ground-grappling techniques different from the ones used by the judo and jujitsu fighters, who Maeda began with. Boxers presented another problem. There was no striking in judo competition, and the strikes of traditional jujitsu were nothing like those of Western boxing. Maeda then had to learn an entirely new skill, which has since become one of the most fundamental skills of grappling jujitsu fighters when they fight in modern, mixed martial arts tournaments. It is the skill of closing the gap and getting into a safe clinch with a dangerous striker.

Once in a tight clinch, a jujitsu fighter can tie the striker up and nullify the power of his strikes; then, he can take him down to the ground where striking ability will be of little value. Maeda talks about this problem in his biography. He liked to use elbow strikes and low kicks to close the distance and get into a standing clinch. From there, he used his judo skills to launch his opponent with a throw. At that point, he would use the same strategy used by the Fusen ryu: Take the opponent to the ground, and expose him to pins and submission holds that he had no idea how to defend.

Maeda was thus executing the strategy of *phases of combat* and taking it a step further. His central idea was to take his opponents into a phase of combat in which they had no experience but in which he had great experience. Maeda's training in the kodokan during the ne waza revolution had left him with tremendous expertise in ground grappling. Boxers, on the other hand, had no expertise on the ground. Wrestlers had skill on the mat, but they were not versed in the range of submission holds that Maeda was using against them. Just like the Fusen-ryu fighters, Maeda sought to take advantage of this by taking the fight to the ground at the first opportunity. But unlike the Fusen-ryu fighters, Maeda had to deal with the problem of closing the gap against an aggressive and skilled striker, and this called for some technical innovation on his part. Maeda was among the first to prove the usefulness of phases of combat theory in open, mixed martial arts fighting against high-level opponents. In addition, he showed the great combat-effectiveness of grappling skill against dangerous strikers. His tremendous record of success left no doubt as to the usefulness of his strategy.

BEGINNINGS OF BRAZILIAN JIU JITSU

We have seen already that Maeda offered to teach jujitsu to Carlos Gracie. Maeda had created a martial arts academy where he taught what he called "jujitsu." It appears that the content of his teaching was largely a mix of classical Japanese jujitsu, kodokan judo, and his own strategy and methods of fighting that he had developed over his years of fighting. Carlos Gracie enrolled and became a student. It is unclear how long he trained under Maeda, but current estimates put it at no more than four years and probably somewhat less than this. In addition, Maeda was often traveling around Brazil at this time. It would seem, then, that a good deal of Carlos's training would have been under Maeda's top students, who often took on teaching responsibilities in Maeda's absence. What is clear from the historical record is that by the early to middle 1920s, Maeda had moved on to immerse himself in the Japanese colonization project.

In 1925, Carlos opened his own jujitsu school. He had begun training his brothers, and together they began teaching jujitsu based on Maeda's technique. It is interesting to note that Carlos was only in his early 20s when he opened his school, and he had trained for only about four years—it was a situation similar to Jigoro Kano's. As a student of Maeda, Carlos had learned the crucial underpinnings of the art that would become famous as Brazilian jiu jitsu.

(A quick note on spelling: *Jujitsu* and *jujutsu* are both considered the correct renditions of the Japanese characters. However, when jujitsu first came to the West, it was given a variety of [mistaken] spellings, as people grappled with the problem of translation and adequate representation of the Japanese language. The most common early representation of *jujitsu* was *jiu jitsu*. Since the Gracies began jujitsu training at a time when *jiu jitsu* was the most common spelling of the term, they naturally wrote down their art as *jiu jitsu*. Since then, most people have switched to the more correct *jujitsu* or *jujutsu*. Having created a tradition, the Brazilians have stuck with the old style *jiu jitsu*—hence, the spelling used in this book when referencing the Brazilian style.)

Maeda taught Carlos the excellent training methods of kodokan judo, with its emphasis of live randori and ne waza skills (remember that Maeda was a kodokan student at the beginning of the ne waza revolution in judo). He also taught classical submission holds that were not part of the judo curriculum. In addition, because Maeda had been exposed to numerous fighting styles during his travels, he did not limit his teachings to judo. In fact, in one old photograph, Maeda is shown training without the traditional Japanese gi jacket, and it reveals him using a standard control and submission technique of Western catch wrestling—a half nelson and hammer lock. Maeda was a regular competitor in catch wrestling events while in England, and there is no doubt that he absorbed what he took to be useful from these arts and incorporated them into his training and teaching.

Perhaps most important, he showed the overall strategy of phases of combat. He demonstrated how grapplers could take dangerous opponents into a phase of combat that they were not familiar with and by this means, achieve victory. Maeda created and refined the classic combat paradigm of closing the gap, getting into a tight clinch, taking the opponent down to the ground (where he could be controlled), and then finishing the fight. This crucial theme, so central to Maeda's incredible success in actual fights, was to become the guiding light behind the subsequent development of Brazilian jiu jitsu. The details remained to be worked out, but Carlos absorbed the broad vision of Maeda's teachings and moved on.

Building on the base that Maeda had given them, the Gracie brothers began full-time teaching and training at their academy and soon gained a good reputation for technical knowledge. What really advanced their reputation and stature, however, was their participation in challenge matches against other martial arts. Starting in the late 1920s and early 1930s, the Gracie brothers became confident enough in their skills to begin open-challenge public matches.

People were invited to fight them in sanctioned matches with few or no rules. It is doubtful that such matches could take place in any other place than Brazil. The unbeaten record of the Gracies in those early years quickly gained them a great reputation (and notoriety) for fighting prowess in Brazil.

It is interesting to note the crucial role of challenge matches in the history of grappling arts. Kano's judo was catapulted into the spotlight through its great success in challenge matches with the classical jujitsu schools. Fusen ryu came to the fore through its successful challenge matches with the kodokan. Yukio Tani and Mitsuyo Maeda managed to convince skeptical Westerners of the validity of jujitsu technique through open-challenge matches. The Gracies did the same in Brazil. It is unlikely that any of these people could have attained the fame and success that they did without the use of challenge matches. There is no proof quite so convincing as to the effectiveness of a fighting style as a long series of victories in fights with few or no rules. Such events settle the argument over combat technique with a conclusiveness that words can never achieve.

Over time, the Gracies came to learn a tremendous amount from these fights. As they continued to train and fight, they began to modify their technique and strategy in the face of the lessons that their experience in fighting gave them. Because of their small size, the Gracie brothers found that some of their techniques had to be slightly modified to make more efficient use of leverage, and thus require less strength to apply in combat. They also found that quite often they had to fight for extended periods on their backs, given the great size advantage of many of their opponents. Therefore, they had to greatly develop this aspect of their game.

Also, because actual fighting was their main focus (rather than pure grappling), they had to change their strategy somewhat from the way that they had originally learned it. Experience had shown them that the most common form of victory in most grappling styles—the pin—was of little significance in a real fight. People did not give up merely by being held down; thus, the concept of pinning an opponent as a means of victory was removed. In the sports of judo and wrestling, the only pins that counted were those that put an opponent's back on the ground.

The Gracies saw that often it was more advantageous in a real fight to get *behind* an opponent and control him from behind while he is facedown on the floor. This position gets few or no points in judo and wrestling, but it is potentially devastating in a real fight. Moreover, the Gracies learned that in a real fight, not all pinning positions are equal. Some present much better opportunities to strike and hurt your opponent than do others. Thus, they tried to implement a system that graded the different types of pins according to how potentially damaging they would be to an opponent in a real fight. In this way, the vast sum of real fight experience that the Gracies were building up began to be used as data in the development of a fighting system that was based on hard empirical evidence—accumulated much in the same way as a scientific project.

FURTHER DEVELOPMENT
OF BRAZILIAN JIU JITSU

Over the course of many years of research and hard-fought experience, the Gracies brought an unprecedented degree of sophistication to ground fighting.

It was based on a theory of positional dominance that went as follows: Once a fight goes to the ground, the two combatants can fall into a variety of positions relative to each other, and these positions range from very good to very bad. Between them are positions that are more or less neutral, with neither fighter having a decisive advantage.

The Gracies developed a set of skills that enable a fighter to move from position to position, escaping from bad ones and entering into and maintaining good ones. They learned that both position and control of position are the keys to victory when matches are fought on the ground. Some positions enable one fighter to unleash a torrent of unanswerable blows on an opponent whereas others make it exceedingly difficult for your opponent to control and strike you. In addition, the Gracies noted a strong correlation between positional dominance and the use of submission holds. Dominating positions tend to make the successful use of submission holds much easier: The opponent can be put under so much pressure that he is far more likely to make a mistake and unwittingly expose himself to a simple submission hold. In addition, it was found that once a dominant position was attained, it was much more difficult for an opponent to successfully apply a submission on you. To be sure, submission holds can be used from almost any position—in some cases, even disadvantageous ones. These, however, tend to have a much lower success rate, especially in a real fight where there is a constant danger of being pounded by strikes as you attempt the hold.

The constant theme that the Gracies pushed was that of advancing up the hierarchy of positions to keep increasing the pressure on the opponent. The more pressure he was under, the more likely it was that he would lapse into some kind of mistake and render himself vulnerable to a well-applied submission hold; additionally, the less likely it was that he could fight back with strikes or his own submission holds. In some cases—especially those where the opponent was much bigger, stronger, or proved to be difficult to take down—a variation of this strategy was called for. In these instances, the Brazilian jiu jitsu fighter would operate without true positional dominance from *underneath* his opponent. The idea here was to attain a position where even though you occupied the bottom position, your opponent could not effectively control and dominate you.

Borrowing from Maeda's jujitsu and judo background, they made use of the so-called guard position, whereby an opponent is held between your legs while you are on your back. As long as you can use your legs and hips to control your opponent, you have an excellent chance of working your way into submission holds while at the same time making it difficult for him to successfully strike you. Even though you do not control his body in the same way you do when pinning him from a top position, you exert sufficient control to execute many submission holds and reversals; thus, you can rationally attempt to win the fight from there. The Gracie brothers made frequent use of the guard position and developed it to a truly extraordinary degree, often catching unwary opponents from what initially looked like a weak position.

The truly innovative idea that the Gracies introduced into the grappling world was that of incorporating a point system. It was based on these features of positional dominance on the ground that could be made part of safe, daily training and competition. Points were awarded according to the degree of positional dominance that a player achieved over the course of a match. A player was rewarded with points as he worked his way up the hierarchy of positions in ground grappling. For example, if one player takes the other down to the ground where control can be achieved, he is rewarded with two points. Should he then get past his opponent's legs and into a dominating pinning position across his opponent's side, he gains yet more points and so on. If either player forces the other to submit, then points become irrelevant and the match is over—the same way it would happen in a real fight. In this way, students learn to develop the same positional movements and habits that they would use in a real fight. Their daily training is thus similar to the way that they would conduct themselves in a real fight.

These sound positional habits ingrained in the student in daily grappling training are an excellent preparation for combat. This has been shown time after time in mixed martial arts (MMA) events where Brazilian jiu jitsu fighters have been disproportionately successful, and it has also been demonstrated in the vast number of cases where they have engaged in street fights (many of them videotaped). There is no doubt that it is the success of Brazilian jiu jitsu in contemporary MMA competition that has rekindled public interest in jujitsu as a martial art. It is undeniable, however, that among jujitsu styles, only Brazilian jiu jitsu has done well in MMA combat. It is worth investigating the differences between Brazilian jiu jitsu and the older, classical forms of jiu jitsu in the light of our historical survey to explain this asymmetry.

DIFFERENCES BETWEEN BRAZILIAN JIU JITSU AND TRADITIONAL JUJITSU

Brazilian jiu jitsu was largely unknown outside of its home country until it exploded onto the world stage in the 1990s. The initial reaction to this previously unheralded combat style on the part of the martial arts community was mixed to say the least. Based on moral and aesthetic principles, some people rejected outright the whole idea of challenge matches and MMA competition, claiming that such events contravened the "spirit" of the martial arts. Others claimed that MMA events were nothing more than an interesting sideshow that had little to do with real combat, since real fights involved multiple opponents, weapons, concrete floors, and the like.

Among the many martial artists who accepted the validity of MMA fights as important evidence of combat effectiveness, a good deal of confusion arose over the nature of the most successful fighting style—Brazilian jiu jitsu. Many people saw the similarities between certain elements of traditional jujitsu and Brazilian jiu jitsu technique, particularly some of the submission holds and pinning positions. On this basis, some people misinterpreted Brazilian jiu jitsu as merely some subspecies of traditional jujitsu. This initial confusion was not helped by the shared nomenclature of the two arts

It is important to realize, however, that there are dramatic differences between Brazilian jiu jitsu and traditional jujitsu that run much deeper than the difference in spelling! The fact that Brazilian jiu jitsu has had tremendous success in MMA competition that has not been replicated by traditional jujitsu is a clear sign that Brazilian jiu jitsu has important combat and training elements that are lacking in traditional jujitsu. Few people have been able to articulate these differences in print, which has led to the persistent belief that the successes of Brazilian jiu jitsu somehow vindicate *all* jujitsu systems.

What is needed, then, is a clear statement of the differences between Brazilian jiu jitsu and traditional jujitsu. When writers approach this topic, one often hears glib references to Brazilian jiu jitsu as being a "ground-fighting style" or that it somehow makes more efficient use of leverage and technique than traditional jujitsu. Though there is some element of truth to these statements, the real differences run much deeper.

But before we examine the differences, let us begin with the common ground. First, all systems of jujitsu have a clear philosophical commitment to the use of efficient technique to defeat brute strength and aggression. Second, in bringing about this end, there are many classical techniques that date back centuries—submission holds, throws, takedowns, and so on—that are just as integral a part of Brazilian jiu jitsu as they are of traditional jujitsu. Nonetheless, the differences between traditional jujitsu and Brazilian jiu jitsu are profound, and we shall now examine them in detail.

Positional Strategy

The most important difference between the two arts is the use of a comprehensive positional strategy that is unique to Brazilian jiu jitsu. This positional strategy has its roots in the observations of real combat made by the Gracie family as they engaged in training and actual fights during the developmental years of their art. We have seen that the crucial idea is this: As two people engage in combat, there is a vast number of positions they can occupy relative to each other. Some of these positions give one combatant an advantage, others a disadvantage, and others are more or less neutral. For example, if one fighter was able to get behind his opponent, he would have a significant positional advantage and could effectively strike his opponent, who would on the contrary find it difficult to strike back as effectively at the person behind him. Thus, it makes good sense for a fighter to strive to get behind his opponent in the course of a fight. Doing so significantly increases one's ability to harm an opponent while greatly decreasing the chances of getting hurt by the opponent.

Effective control of position is also closely related to another crucial skill of all jujitsu styles—the ability to finish a fight with an effective submission hold. Traditional jujitsu has a vast array of submission holds designed to force an opponent to cease resistance or risk serious injury and possibly unconsciousness. Many of these submission holds, however, are difficult to apply effectively in real combat for the simple reason that the opponent is not under sufficient control when the hold is attempted. *The positional strategy at the heart of Brazilian jiu jitsu makes the use of submission holds much more effective because Brazilian jiu jitsu encourages the use of submission holds only when sufficient control of the opponent has been attained through dominant position.* This is a key idea that goes a long way to explaining the unrivaled success of Brazilian jiu jitsu in MMA events, challenge matches, and real fights. This positional strategy is best carried out by a grappling style of martial art. The reason is obvious enough. Once you get hold of your opponent, you can constrain his movement and thus hold him in the positions you seek. If you do not hold him, he is free to move out of any disadvantageous position you place him in.

The best place to constrain a person's movement is on the ground because most people do not move efficiently on the ground (it has to be learned) and also because body weight can be used to pin and immobilize a person much more easily on the ground than in a standing position. This is why Brazilian jiu jitsu usually advocates taking a fight into a clinch—where you can attain a dominant standing position on your opponent—and then, if appropriate, you can take the fight to the ground, where a more dominating position can be easily held and maintained.

Although Brazilian jiu jitsu has quite a large number of moves in its repertoire, they can all be placed under two broad categories

1. Those that allow a fighter to enact the strategy of advancing from one position into a more dominating one (positional moves)

2. Those that allow a fighter to finish a fight quickly and efficiently (submission moves)

In general, it is the case that positional moves lead one fighter into the opportunity for submission moves. Positional control gives one the optimal conditions for applying a submission hold while at the same time severely limiting the ability of your opponent to apply his own submission holds on you. In this way, concern over position generally precedes concern over submission.

So much for the basic positional strategy that forms the strategic core of Brazilian jiu jitsu. We need to go on now and see the other crucial differences between Brazilian jiu jitsu and traditional jujitsu.

Training Method

The second most important element in Brazilian jiu jitsu that separates it from traditional styles lies in the *training method* it employs to ingrain its positional strategy and technique into students. This is an inheritance from Maeda, who was a top student of Kano and who, as we saw, made live training (randori) the basis of his training method.

Traditional jujitsu is learned almost exclusively through kata, a prearranged set of movements carried out on a cooperative training partner. No contact is made during the simulated striking movements, and the "opponent" passively moves with the techniques. In contrast to this, Brazilian jiu jitsu has a training method much closer to that seen in judo. It is based on the performance of technique on a *resisting* training partner, who is trying his best to avoid defeat and attain victory. This is live-grappling sparring. In such sparring, students get the crucial skill of applying grappling technique on someone who is not cooperating and who is also counteracting by trying his own technique.

As you can imagine, this is far more difficult than working in prearranged katas. To ensure safety during this live-grappling sparring, students cannot use strikes on one another—although students preparing for MMA fights usually put on gloves and add strikes to the training—and they certainly cannot use eye gouging, hair pulling, groin strikes, or other such tactics that can occur in a real fight. Experience shows, however, that the grappling aspect of combat is the most crucial element of a real fight. By training this grappling technique in daily sparring sessions, students are constantly working on the most crucial element of a real fight in a way that resembles how they would actually apply it in real combat. With only minor modifications to account for the elements that creep into a street fight (e.g., foul tactics), the Brazilian jiu jitsu student can easily make the adjustment from a sparring session to a real altercation quite easily. The same positional strategy and moves, allied to submission skills honed in hard daily sparring, account for the remarkable success of Brazilian jiu jitsu fighters in real combat.

But important differences exist between the randori of judo and that of Brazilian jiu jitsu. Many grappling styles prohibit certain kinds of submission holds, yet the live-grappling training used in Brazilian jiu jitsu is remarkably free of limitations. For example, judo allows locks only to the elbow joint, along with strangleholds. Sambo prohibits strangleholds altogether whereas Olympic wrestling prohibits any kind of submission hold at all. Brazilian jiu jitsu allows virtually any form of submission hold to the joints of the body, along with strangleholds and chokes. Students thus become adept at using and defending the whole spectrum of possible submission holds. In addition, training is done both with the gi (kimono) and without. By this means, students are exposed to a wide variety of training conditions.

Point System

The heart of the Brazilian jiu jitsu training method is the use of a point system (which is also used in Brazilian jiu jitsu competition) that is designed to reflect the nature of a real fight. We noted earlier that once a fight begins, the two combatants can work their way into a number of different positions relative to each other. These positions can be arranged into a hierarchy: some very good, others very bad, and others somewhere in between. The point system of Brazilian jiu jitsu awards points to a fighter each time he advances into a better position. The better the position, the higher the reward in terms of points. But, if a fighter escapes a bad position, he is *not* given points for escape—that is simply his duty. For example, in a real fight, if you work your way into a tight, controlling position behind your opponent, it is clear that you have gained a considerable advantage. From this position, it is difficult for your opponent to successfully apply a submission hold on you and even harder for him to strike you effectively. For you, on the other hand, it is easy to move into a wide array of strikes, chokes, strangleholds, arm bars, neck cranks, and so on. This clear positional advantage would be reflected in the point system. Attaining a controlling rear position scores the maximum of four points. (The point system of Brazilian jiu jitsu will be explained in full detail in chapter 9.)

Technique Differences

Other significant differences exist between traditional jujitsu and Brazilian jiu jitsu. Unlike Brazilian jiu jitsu, traditional jujitsu has many techniques that could not be used in a sporting or live-training context. For example, many of the favored strikes in traditional jujitsu are aimed at the genitals, eyes, and other weak points of the human body; in addition, there are numerous foul tactics, such as biting, hair pulling, stomping, and the like. Brazilian jiu jitsu completely lacks all such techniques. In fact, every technique of Brazilian jiu jitsu can be used in sanctioned sporting MMA matches.

In addition to the removal of technique that cannot be practiced at full power on a resisting opponent, there has been wide-scale revision of technique on the part of Brazilian jiu jitsu stylists. This was due partly to the small size of many of the most influential members of the Gracie family. Lacking size and strength, they were forced to look for the most efficient, effective use of leverage and biomechanics to get techniques to work in their favor. The result has been some significant revisions to traditional techniques. For instance, Brazilian jiu jitsu has a clear emphasis on technique that makes use of so-called gross-motor movements. These are movements that involve large muscles of the human body, and they are strongly contrasted with fine motor movements, which involve delicate and precise manipulation of small-muscle groups (such as hand and finger movement). Swinging a baseball bat would be an everyday example of a gross-motor movement. Threading a needle is an example of fine motor movement.

Many of the core techniques of traditional jujitsu involve fine motor movement. For example, many of the standing wristlocks, finger locks, and eye pokes—which are so prevalent in traditional styles of jujitsu—require precise finger placement. However, fine motor movements are hard to accomplish under the kind of stress and strain found in real combat. Think of how difficult it would be to thread a needle when your heart is pounding and when you are in the midst of a massive adrenaline burst. In the heat of combat, gross-motor movements are far easier to perform. For this reason, many of the core techniques of traditional jujitsu are either totally absent in Brazilian jiu jitsu, or greatly downplayed.

When Brazilian jiu jitsu is compared with traditional jujitsu, it soon becomes clear that Brazilian jiu jitsu is much closer in form to other grappling arts than it is to traditional jujitsu. This is not surprising when one looks at the lineage of Brazilian jiu jitsu artists. Maeda, the Japanese fighter who taught Carlos Gracie, was for a time a student of a traditional jujitsu. However, he became a student of Jigoro Kano's judo at age 18, and it was in judo that he really excelled, rapidly working his way up the ranks of the kodokan seniors. Such was his skill level that he was selected by Kano as a representative of judo to be sent to North America. This was an honor meted out only to the best kodokan teachers and fighters, and it clearly shows just how highly regarded Maeda was by his peers and teachers.

Maeda had been heavily influenced by Kano's training methods, which were centered on live sparring (randori) and by the influx of ground-fighting technique that entered into judo as a result of the tournament loss to the jujitsu of the Fusen ryu. We should note that judo is quite different today than it was before 1925, when it was much less restricted by rules and referee intervention. Ground grappling (ne waza) was far more prevalent than it is now. Indeed, ground grappling dominated judo so much that Jigoro Kano instituted wide-ranging rule changes in 1925 to prevent ground grappling from completely dominating judo.

Since then, numerous additions to the rules and regulations of judo have progressively eroded the amount of ground grappling allowed in judo competition. This is due to a range of factors. First, Kano definitely had Olympic aspirations for his sport (which were eventually realized in 1964), and concerns about spectator interest may have caused him to limit ne waza. The result has been a lack of interest and training among judo players in ground grappling, since the current rules of judo make it unlikely that extensive training in ne waza will pay any dividends.

But there is one important exception to this general trend. One particular branch of judo—kosen judo—has consistently avoided the pressure to emphasize standing-throwing technique over ground grappling. In kosen judo, ne waza almost always determines the outcome of the match. If there is any martial art that Brazilian jiu jitsu most resembles, it is doubtless pre-1925 judo, which today is seen only in the few kosen judo organizations still in existence. The only traditional style of jujitsu that Brazilian jiu jitsu has close links with is Fusen-ryu jujitsu, which was itself a direct forebear of kosen judo. It appears, however, that Fusen-ryu jujitsu largely died out after being assimilated into judo. The similarities, then, between kosen judo and Brazilian jiu jitsu are far greater than those between traditional jujitsu and Brazilian jiu jitsu.

DECLINE AND FALL OF THE GRAPPLING ARTS

Grappling styles of jujitsu are based on live training, control, and dominance on the ground, in addition to the use of submission holds to end a fight. We have seen that they came into prominence in the late 19th century. They rose to a peak in the early 20th century with the rise of ne waza training in judo, the beginning of kosen judo, and the exploits of individuals such as Yukio Tani, Mitsuyo Maeda, and the Gracie brothers. In addition, other grappling styles, such as Western catch wrestling—a professional wrestling style based on a rich and complex set of grappling skills that include submission holds—reached a peak at this time. The modern Russian grappling art of sambo had its roots in this time period as well, when a group of grappling experts trained in Japan under Kano and returned to Russia. Combining their knowledge with the extensive tradition of wrestling in Russia, they created a formidable grappling style of their own. Just when the grappling arts seemed destined to bloom, a series of events undercut the tremendous progress that had been made and thus greatly reduced the popularity and prestige of the various grappling styles.

In 1925, Jigoro Kano, disturbed by what he saw as an unhealthy trend toward ne waza in judo, instituted the first set of rule revisions that favored the use of standing-throwing technique over ground grappling. Players would be penalized if they repeatedly tried to drag their opponent straight down to the mat without attempting to throw. Over time, more and more such restrictions were put in place that made it increasingly difficult to use ground grappling to win a match.

In the post–World War II era, these restrictions got even worse. As judo became an Olympic sport with spectator demands, there was increasing pressure to severely limit "boring" ne waza and focus on the more crowd-pleasing throws. Judo became more and more a test of gripping and throwing skill with less and less focus on ground grappling and combat in general. In time, a widespread view developed that judo had little to do with fighting. The result was that judo, despite its prestige as an Olympic sport, fell into disfavor as a fighting art in the public view.

Sambo became the national grappling style of the Soviet Union. The political tensions between communism and the capitalist West, however, meant that sambo never got any real exposure in the Western nations until after the fall of the Berlin wall. Even among martial artists, it was virtually unknown until the 1990s.

Professional catch wrestling, a fascinating and effective grappling style with many unique submission holds, was ultimately (and unfortunately) overtaken by the development of fake professional wrestling with crowd-pleasing, "worked" matches. The great skills of the old-time catch wrestlers were not needed once the outcome of the "fight" was predetermined. Professional wrestling slowly descended into the farcical comedy that it has become today. Nowadays only a tiny number of genuine catch wrestlers remain.

Amateur wrestling, on the other hand. received a tremendous boost with its early inclusion in the Olympic Games. However, all the really combative elements, such as submission holds, were removed. This created a public perception that amateur wrestling was merely a sport, one not to be taken seriously as a martial art or fighting style. It was not until the 1950s that this erroneous perception was overturned with the great success of many amateur wrestlers in MMA competition.

Brazilian jiu jitsu did well in its native land. The Gracie family expanded over time and created a large network of family members who were all involved in the project of expanding and refining their art. They continued their great run of success in MMA competition, but their fame was limited to the borders of Brazil. Because Asia was taken to be the home of fighting arts, Brazilian jiu jitsu remained unknown until the grappling revolution of the 1990s.

The result of these events was that in the post–World War II era. the grappling arts fell into serious decline as *combat arts*. They came to be viewed either as interesting and fun sports (judo and wrestling), farcical entertainment (professional wrestling), or they were simply ignored or just plain unknown (sambo and Brazilian jiu jitsu). The Asian striking arts came to totally dominate the martial arts after World War II. Karate, kung fu, kenpo. taekwondo, and even ninjitsu became hugely popular. Each was backed up by exposure in popular cinema productions, and in time, *martial* arts eventually became synonymous with *striking* arts.

A barrage of action movies that exhibited exciting striking techniques in well-choreographed sequences enhanced the public's image of the great fighter as a great *striker*, easily crushing his opponents with a few well-placed blows. Lacking any means of testing the actual effectiveness of the various combat styles, people largely assumed that this bias toward striking arts was the result of their innate superiority. A general assumption began to permeate the mind-set of both the general public and the martial arts community—that success in combat was to be attained through prowess in striking ability.

Memories are short, however. If people had been made aware of the success of grapplers, such as Tani and Maeda, against strikers in open competition, they may have been less quick to form such conclusions. In the space of the four decades following World War II, grappling arts became increasingly overlooked as combat arts.

RESURGENCE OF THE GRAPPLING ARTS

In the 1990s, MMA competition was introduced to both North America and Japan, and it was done so with an unprecedented degree of public exposure. The idea was to have the various martial arts face off against each other with few rules or restraints. In the cauldron of open combat, people could see the relative merits of the many different approaches to martial arts. These events became some of the largest pay-per-view events in history. To say that their effect on the public's view of real combat was eye opening would be an understatement. In a short time, the misconceptions about real fighting that had developed in the decades of the post–World War II era were shattered.

People were shocked to see hallowed theories of combat repeatedly fail when put to the test. Competitors who had expected to blast their opponents with deadly strikes proved unable to dispatch them before being rapidly locked up in a clinch and invariably taken to the ground. Once on the ground, few competitors had the necessary skills to perform well, and most proved unable to defend themselves when put in vulnerable positions. Ironically, when they were put in dominant positions, most even lacked the skills to maintain and exploit their positional advantage.

The exception to this rule, however, was the grapplers, especially those skilled in Brazilian jiu jitsu. They were able to get to the clinch, and from there, they actively looked to take the fight to the ground, knowing full well that few people had the expertise to offer much resistance as soon as the fight went to the mat. People were stunned at the ease with which jiu jitsu fighters wrapped their opponents up and took them to the ground. The Brazilian fighters quickly gained an aura of invincibility that made them the envy of the martial arts world.

Mixed martial arts events became dominated to a truly extraordinary degree by Brazilian jiu jitsu. In the United States, Royce Gracie totally dominated the early Ultimate Fighting Championship events; Renzo Gracie did the same in the World Combat Championship (WCC) and Martial Arts Reality Superfight (MARS) events; and Ralph Gracie was undefeated in the extreme fighting events. In Japan, Rickson Gracie breezed through the competition to win two consecutive vale tudo tournaments.

These early MMA events had a number of features that made them a particularly valuable and interesting part of martial arts history. First, they were as close to a real fight between the various styles of martial arts as could be allowed in a publicly sanctioned sport. There were long time limits, bare knuckles, no weight categories, and *very* few rules. None of the fighters really cross-trained, and almost every competitor came from one fighting style. As a result, there was a genuine clash of styles in those early MMA events. It was an arena where one could see a man trained only in boxing take on another man trained only in karate.

In this environment, the Gracies and their students employed the same phases of combat strategy that had served Fusen ryu and Maeda so well almost a century earlier. The Gracies used it with a polish and sophistication that immediately took them to center stage of the martial arts world. Their opponents were shocked to see the Gracie-trained fighters working effectively off their backs in what appeared to be hopeless positions and winning fights with unanticipated submission holds. The success of Brazilian jiu jitsu was as surprising as it was complete.

DEVELOPMENT AND CHANGE IN MMA COMPETITION

In time, the nature of MMA events began to change. Because of the lack of rules, there were some rather brutal fights. These tended to occur when two fighters met each other whose enthusiasm was much greater than their skill level. American audiences were not used to the image of one man holding down another man and brutally hitting him. It did not square with the general public's image of a clean fight—an image of both men standing up as they fought and stopping when one went down. To a public raised on the Western boxing ethic of not hitting a downed fighter, it appeared brutal and sadistic. A strong political movement developed to ban MMA fights in North America unless drastic changes were made to the rules. At the same time, other spectators demanded more nonstop action. Quite often, the early MMA events had long periods of ground grappling, which some people found boring. Fights would often degenerate into draws with little activity on either side. To keep the action going, rules were implemented to prevent long periods of inactivity.

As a result of these demands, most MMA events began to introduce short rounds and shorter time limits. At the end of a round, the two fighters would stand up, and prolonged inactivity would result in a referee intervention that resulted in both fighters standing up. Weight categories were also introduced at this time to prevent the tremendous size differences that characterized many early MMA fights. If fights went the distance, a judge's decision would determine the outcome. If a fighter appeared to be in trouble, the referee could stop the fight and declare a winner. Gloves became compulsory. They enabled strikers to hit full power without fear of breaking their hands, a common problem in early MMA fights. In addition, it made grappling more difficult, since grapplers lost much of their grappling sensitivity when their hands were gloved.

The general result of these rule changes was to greatly increase the importance of striking in MMA events. Fighters could now hit harder without fear of injury. Knockout victories became much more common, and there was now much more time spent in the standing position, since the beginning of every round saw the return of the fighters to their feet. Many fighters sought to convey the image of greater aggression by striking as much as possible, knowing that this would work to their advantage if the fight should go to a judge's decision.

In the face of these crucial changes, a number of important trends emerged. The first attempts at cross-training began to appear. This was the idea of training in a number of different disciplines to accomplish the following objective: have sufficient expertise in every aspect of a fight to avoid getting into serious trouble while at the same time having some area of specialty where one tried to attain victory. For example, a kickboxer might train diligently in ground grappling in order to survive long enough on the ground to last to the end of a round. He could then resume the fight where he wanted it—back on his feet where his striking skills could come into play. In addition, he could spend time learning to defend takedown attempts and thus avoid the whole ground game as much as possible and keep the fight in the phase where he felt most comfortable.

In the early days of MMA, many fighters looked on Brazilian jiu jitsu as a riddle to be solved. They studied it intently until they were no longer taken by surprise by its strategy and tactics. Wrestlers learned to avoid the submission holds that had wreaked havoc in the early MMA events. This enabled them to use their excellent takedown skills to take their opponents quickly to the ground where they could use their great strength and athleticism (often combined with considerable size advantage) to pound them from a top position and eventually win via decision or a referee's stoppage. Strikers even learned to defend takedowns and break out of clinches. In this way, they could keep the fight in a standing position as much as possible, where their striking skills would be most effective. Thus, the increase in skill level as a result of cross-training, along with the rule changes, allowed wrestlers and strikers to experience much greater success in MMA competition. The trend came full circle when jujitsu and submission fighters had to cross-train in striking and wrestling so as to keep abreast of the changes in MMA. These developments have led to the emergence of three basic types of fighters in contemporary MMA events.

Submission Grapplers

These are fighters who base their game on the use of positional control on the ground as a means of setting up highly efficient submission holds to end a fight. It was this approach to combat that proved so dominant in the early MMA events and continues to be one of the most popular and successful approaches today. We have seen that the most well-known advocates of this approach were Brazilian jiu jitsu fighters; however, many other grappling styles employ a similar strategy.

The guiding idea with these fighters is to take the fight to the ground so that they can assume the kind of control necessary to restrain a wildly resisting opponent before applying a submission. Although most submission grapplers prefer a top position on the ground, they will often accept a bottom position, because many of their favorite submission holds can be successfully applied from underneath their opponent.

What was impressive about the submission grapplers in early MMA competition was the efficiency of their victories. Quite often, they challenged and defeated opponents far larger than themselves. This was possible because they were comfortable working underneath their opponents. The submission holds they employed were also highly efficient; they applied a large amount of force against a weak part of their opponent's anatomy. Such victories were bloodless and made a favorable impression of victory without the brutality.

The chief weakness of submission grapplers has been their lack of takedown and striking skills. These weaknesses were not exposed in early MMA events since few of the fighters had any idea how to defend a takedown or break out of a clinch. As a result, even rather poorly executed takedown attempts were almost always successful. On the occasions when submission grapplers faced skilled wrestlers, they were able to take advantage of the wrestlers' lack of knowledge of submission holds and gain many impressive victories. In time, however, strikers came to learn takedown defenses, and wrestlers learned how to avoid many of the most important submission holds. In addition, the rule changes greatly increased the amount of time spent in the standing position in each match.

From then on, there were no easy victories for the submission grapplers. Even so, submission holds still account for a high percentage of victories in MMA competition. The beauty of submission holds is that they can end a fight at any given time, just like a knockout punch. On many occasions, a fighter has been totally dominated, only to quickly apply a submission hold and snatch victory. In this sense, a fighter trained in submissions always has a chance of victory. All he needs is for his opponent to suffer from a lapse in concentration so that he can end the fight. Because of the tremendous efficiency of submission holds, they can be successfully applied on much larger opponents. Most of the great instances of a smaller man defeating a larger man in MMA competition involved the use of submission holds as the means to victory.

"Ground and Pound" Fighters

Wrestlers are noted for their tremendous skill in takedowns, defending takedowns, and controlling position on the ground. Once it became obvious that takedown and ground-grappling skills were crucial in real fights, wrestlers began to enter MMA tournaments in large numbers. In the early days, the wrestlers had mixed success and failure. They had many good attributes, great athleticism and conditioning, and unmatched skill in takedowns; however, they lacked any real knowledge of submission holds. The result was that they could not finish the fight efficiently. In addition, they were vulnerable themselves to such holds and often fell victim to them. Once wrestlers learned to avoid the submission holds of submission grapplers, they performed much better.

In time, the use of small, four-ounce gloves became mandatory in MMA events. These allowed fighters to hit hard for long periods of time without fear of harming their own hands. Shorter time limits and the use of judges to decide the outcome of a fight that went the distance also meant that wrestlers could take an opponent down (using their superior takedown skill) and gain any kind of top position. From there, they would look to pound their opponents with their fists while simultaneously avoiding submission holds as best they could. Since the wrestlers were almost always larger, stronger, and more athletic than their opponents, this strategy of taking opponents to the ground and pounding them for long periods of time often worked. It was almost always enough to win a judge's decision if the fight went to the time limit—and quite often, it resulted in a referee's stoppage.

The chief weakness of this approach is that it almost always requires the fighters to have greater size, strength, and athleticism to attain victory. There are no cases of a smaller, weaker man using this strategy to defeat an opponent. Also, such fighters can only win if they gain a top position. If they should be taken down themselves or swept over into a bottom position, "ground and pound" is no longer possible, and defeat normally ensues. There is also a constant danger of submission holds that can always catch the unwary or tired off guard.

"Sprawl and Brawl" Fighters

When MMA events were first held in North America and Japan, many people were stunned at the poor performance of martial artists who specialized in striking with fists and feet. In match after match, they were quickly bundled up in a clinch and taken down to the mat. Defeat soon followed. Quite often, striking without gloves caused the fighters to break their hands, which resulted in an inability to continue. Within a short period, people became somewhat dismissive of the combat effectiveness of the striking arts. But this assessment was premature. Once gloves were introduced and once rule changes were created that greatly increased the time spent in the standing position, striking became much more important.

Strikers also learned from their early failures that defending the takedown and breaking out of clinches were absolutely crucial if they were to succeed in MMA competition. What they learned was the classic wrestling defense to takedowns—the sprawl (see chapter 4). In time, they used this knowledge, along with escapes from the clinch, to make it far harder to take them down. At the same time, they also learned ground grappling in enough depth to survive long enough to get the referee to stand them back up and return the fight to their favored position. The pattern of such fighters is to sprawl in defense to takedowns and break out of clinches so as to escape from any prolonged grappling situations.

Takedown attempts can be tiring. As strikers' opponents become progressively fatigued with each failed takedown, they become sloppier and easier to hit effectively with hands, knees, and feet. In the clinch, strikers can take a heavy toll on their opponents with knees and elbows before breaking free. After each sprawl and clinch-break, strikers can look to knock out their opponents or at least severely hurt them and thus look to win a judge's decision. Since strikers are wearing gloves, they can hit at maximum power throughout the match without fear of hurting themselves, which was not possible in the early, bareknuckle MMA events.

The main problems associated with this strategy toward MMA events, however, are the excessive reliance on gloves, referee intervention, judge's decisions, and short rounds to keep the fight standing. Such fighters do well if their opponent is weak on takedowns, but a takedown expert who can keep someone down will always prove a problem for such "sprawl and brawl" fighters. Such an approach is unlikely to succeed against a larger opponent.

Most fighters in contemporary MMA fall into one of these three categories. Given that the vast majority of martial artists have most of their expertise in one style—and, hence, one approach to combat (striking, submissions, or takedowns)—it is unsurprising that they begin with one area of expertise. They then add on at least enough skills in the other phases of combat to survive. Because most of their skill is in one area, the result is a natural bias toward that area of expertise—thus, our three basic categories of an MMA fighter.

But the early days of MMA are over. No one style totally dominates. On any given day, any one of the three main approaches to MMA combat can emerge victorious. All competitors need skills in all three of the main phases of combat to succeed. *Completeness* is the great virtue of the modern competitor.

Underlying Theory and Strategy of Modern Jujitsu

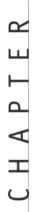

Too often, martial artists obsess over the accumulation of techniques without ever attaining an overall strategy to guide how those techniques are applied in the course of a fight. For example, let's assume that all I have is a set of techniques, each isolated from the other. Any time a given technique fails to end the fight, I would have to begin all over again and hope that the next technique that I apply will bring victory. What fighters need is a background strategy that they can follow over the course of the fight. *Technique is used merely to realize that strategy.*

One of the great failings of most traditional martial artists in early mixed martial arts (MMA) events was a lack of overall battle plan. Most had no more than a vague notion of blasting their opponent into defeat. This invariably proved far more difficult than they had anticipated. In contrast, the jujitsu fighters had a clear overall strategy that involved getting into a tight clinch as soon as possible and taking the fight to the ground. Once on the ground, they put into operation a direct positional strategy that gave them a clear idea of where they wanted to be, relative to their opponents. All of their technique was designed to carry out their overall battle plan. *Thus, at every given moment of the fight, they knew precisely what they ought to be doing and how they could do it.* This was in strong contrast to their opponents, who often lacked any idea of what to do during the course of the fight, especially when things went awry.

The importance of an overall strategy cannot be overstated. A lack of a clear and flexible fight strategy will quickly become apparent in any fight that goes beyond a minute's duration. When a fighter lacks an overall fight strategy, he inevitably proceeds in the manner of a blind man, stumbling from one moment to the next, trying desperately to make sense of the action unfolding in front of him. Just as deadly is a lack of a secondary minute-by-minute, second-by-second, positional strategy that gives a fighter a clear sense of direction on how to move and what to do to his opponent at any particular moment. *Lack of strategy always leads to inaction, confusion, and a sense of hopelessness when things go wrong.* This is fatal in a real fight.

Many fighters fell victim to lack of direction in early MMA events. Often, fighters who were trained in martial arts that only practiced striking in the standing position would be taken quickly to the ground. Once on the ground, they had no idea what they should do. A sense of despair soon set in. They swung between fits of desperate flailing and complete inaction. These fighters were strong, well trained in their chosen arts, and mentally tough and experienced. They certainly did not give up because they were weak or cowardly; they gave up because they had no idea what they should do. Once this occurred, they simply stopped moving. Inaction is fatal in a fight because it allows an opponent to completely dominate events without resistance.

A combat strategy gives a fighter a clear sense of direction throughout the fight, which in turn gives the fighter a sense of hope, no matter how bad things get. As long as a fighter has this sense of hope, he will keep going.

COMBAT STRATEGY OF JUJITSU

The classical jujitsu of old Japan appeared to have no common strategy to guide a combatant over the course of a fight. Indeed, this was one of Kano's most fundamental and perceptive criticisms of the classical program. The lack of strategy may have been because classical empty-hand jujitsu was considered a last resort when a warrior had lost his weapon, rather than an independent fighting style. Even Kano's radical changes did not involve a clear statement of a grand combat strategy. The principal strategic element he emphasized was the notion of *kuzushi*, keeping an opponent off balance so that he could be easily controlled and thrown. Along with kuzushi he added notions such as "minimum effort, maximum effect" and various other interpretations of *ju* (gentle, soft, or flexible). However, this is far from a complete and specific fight strategy.

Only with the rise of Fusen-ryu jujitsu, and the first era of jujitsu challenge matches with Tani and Maeda, does a clear fight strategy emerge among jujitsu fighters. This strategy was perfected over time by the Gracies, and it rose to prominence in contemporary MMA events. This strategy has two main elements. First, there is the overall strategy. We have seen that the overall strategy is based on the notion of single combat being divided into three phases, each of which has a set of skills that are independent of each other, which means that a fighter can be good in one phase but poor in the other two. Mataemon Tanabe was the first to show that by taking a highly skilled opponent out of his favored phase and into a phase where he was less skilled, he could be easily defeated. Tani, Maeda, and the Gracies adopted this overall strategy and added to it over time. Maeda applied it in the case of MMA fighting, and Tanabe applied it only in submission grappling tournaments.

The Gracies added a tactical strategy of positional dominance to this overall strategy of phases of combat. It is the second strategic element in modern grappling jujitsu, and it has been an essential part of the dominance of modern jujitsu in contemporary MMA. It has been so successful that it is now the standard modus operandi for all fighters in MMA events when a fight goes to the ground. The central theme here is to attain a position from where you can attack your opponent while his ability to counter is severely undermined. This execution can be done while in a standing clinch, but it is easier on the ground—hence, the preference that most contemporary jujitsu fighters have for ground grappling.

Thus, jujitsu fighters carry two strategic elements with them.

1. An overall strategy that keeps the fight in a phase where they have a skill advantage over their opponent.

2. A tactical strategy that works for positional dominance, which continually strives to place them in a position where they can attack their opponent far more easily than their opponent can fight back.

The ideas that underlie these two crucial strategic innovations of modern jujitsu have proven highly successful in MMA competition. At this point, let's examine each significant component in detail.

PHASES OF COMBAT

Experience has shown unequivocally that single combat can be effectively divided into three principal phases. These phases are divided by the degree of body contact and control that the two combatants have over each other, and they have proven to be the most important factors in determining the behavior and tactics of the two fighters in the course of a fight.

If neither fighter has any body contact or grip on the other, then the two fighters are free to move as they please. They will move, strike, evade, and shoot toward their opponent at will, since nothing constrains their movement. We can refer to this first phase of combat as the *free-movement phase*, since its greatest feature is precisely the freedom of movement enjoyed by both fighters.

The moment the two fighters get a grip on each other, however, the nature of the fight changes. Once body contact and grip is established, the movement of one fighter is constrained by the other. They are no longer free to move about as they please, but they must now take into account the movement, grip, and body position of each other so that they can decide how to move and act. This second phase of combat is referred to as the *clinch,* a term commonly used in all combat styles to refer to a situation where two fighters have a tight, controlling grip on each other in a standing position that severely constrains movement.

The third major phase of fighting occurs when a fight goes to the ground. This phase happens in almost every serious fight, especially once a fight enters the clinch phase. This third phase is called *ground combat,* and it is entirely different from the first two phases (as so many people have regrettably discovered at their own expense). Skill on the ground has repeatedly been shown to be the most important factor in determining success in MMA competition. Even those fighters who prefer the other phases of combat must know enough ground-fighting technique to survive and regain their footing. So much for the three distinct phases of combat. At this point, we must go on to see exactly how knowledge of these three phases can be used to overcome and defeat an opponent.

The crucial idea in the phases of combat theory is that of taking an opponent into a phase in which he is least skilled, relative to your own skills. As a fighter, I would stand the greatest chance of success when I take my opponent into a phase of combat in which I am more skilled than he is. For instance, if I can keep a fight on the ground (my strength), then it would not matter if my opponent were a far better boxer, since boxing skill is of little value on the ground.

The key is to determine the phase of combat in which you have the greatest skill advantage and to endeavor to keep the fight in that phase. The fact that most people are by nature weak in ground combat has created a natural bias toward ground combat on the part of jujitsu fighters. However, if two skilled jujitsu ground fighters meet each other in combat, the one who is stronger in the standing position would be well advised to keep the fight there, since that is where he has the greatest skill advantage.

Consider an analogy: Ordinarily, we would not think of a 13-year-old girl as having any chance of victory in single, unarmed combat with the heavyweight boxing champion of the world. But what if circumstances changed and the fight were to take place in the ocean? Say you learn that the girl is a national swimming champion and that the boxer cannot swim and is terrified of water. Who would you bet on now? Clearly, the fight is entirely different when the overall context of the fight is changed in this way. This is exactly what happens when the theory of phases of combat is put into operation. By taking the fight into a phase or context where my opponent is weaker than I am, I can negate his strengths and exploit his weaknesses. So then, let us clearly divide and describe the three phases of combat.

Free-Movement Phase

The free-movement phase is where all MMA matches and many street fights begin, with both fighters on their feet, with no grip on each other. The lack of contact and grip allows them to move freely—hence, the name. Such freedom of movement allows fast footwork, shooting, and striking; it is unsurprising that these skills are the most important in this phase of the fight.

Standing Clinch

Once a fight begins, it almost always goes into a clinch. Interestingly, most street fights *begin* in a clinch (rather than free movement), with grabbing, shoving, and holding. The fact that the fighters hold each other restricts their movement. A distinct set of skills is required to do well in the standing clinch position, and these skills are different from those required in the free-movement phase. The skills that are crucial in this phase of combat include attaining and breaking a grip; off-balancing an opponent and keeping one's own balance and posture; striking in the clinch; takedowns appropriate to clinch fighting; standing submissions; and so on.

Ground Combat

Almost no fights begin in this phase; however, they almost always end up there. Going to the ground totally changes the nature of the fight. Movement in a supine position is very different from movement in a standing position, and it requires extensive training before it becomes natural. Great control is possible on the ground because bodyweight and the ground itself can be used to pin an opponent and confine his movements. This makes possible the use of many highly efficient submission holds. The key skills in ground combat are the application of submission holds, the ability to work your way out of inferior positions, and the skill to move into increasingly dominating positions.

Theory of Phases of Combat

The following is the theory of phases of combat in the clearest possible terms.

1. Unarmed, single combat can be divided into three main phases. Each phase can be differentiated from the others by the degree of body contact and by the control the two fighters have on each other.

2. The nature of combat in each phase is distinct from the other phases. Each phase has a different set of skills appropriate to it. This means that it is possible (in fact, likely) that a fighter will be highly skilled in one phase, but weak in the others.

3. Fighters can develop skills that allow themselves to take a fight into a phase in which they are strong and the opponents are weak, and thus they can maintain control of the fight.

4. Taking a fight into a phase of combat where one fighter has a higher skill level than the other creates a great imbalance between the two fighters, and it greatly increases the probability of victory for the fighter who can dominate in that phase of combat.

RANGES OF COMBAT

In the modern era of martial arts, the theory of ranges of combat has gained great credibility and acceptance. The idea is that when two people fight, there is always an optimal attack that is dependent on the current distance between them. For example, there is a range at which kicking is the most effective means of attack; as the two combatants move closer to each other, punching becomes the optimal offensive tool; as they approach still closer, hand-trapping skills take over until range decreases again; at that point, grappling attacks become the best means of attack. Such a theory has considerable intuitive appeal. It simply makes sense to consider different methods of attack as linked to range and distance. After all, the legs are longer than the arms, and that reach advantage certainly seems relevant in certain combat situations.

There are two basic approaches to the use of range as the basis of a theory of combat.

1. We can first divide range into elements based on *distance*. For example, the most popular practice is to talk of short, medium, and long range. This method has the advantages of simplicity and flexibility.

2. We can also divide range into elements based on *technique*. For example, one often hears reference to kicking range, punching range, trapping range, and grappling range. However, this method of defining range via technique is rife with problems, as we shall soon see.

However appealing the theory of ranges may appear in principle, actual experience in MMA events has revealed serious inadequacies with the theory. Under actual combat conditions, range has proven to be seriously incomplete as the core element of a general theory of combat. Regardless of how cherished a given theory may be, if it clashes with the hard facts of experience, a serious theorist must be prepared to revise it, or even abandon it for a new theory that matches up better with experience.

In only one of the three phases of combat has range proven to be an important factor—the free-movement phase. As long as the two fighters have no contact with each other, range and distance always play a crucial role in determining their choice of attacks and defense. A theory of combat, however, that is relevant to only one of the three phases of combat is incomplete. Range is not only incomplete as the basis of a theory of combat; it has serious shortcomings even within the one phase of combat to which it is most relevant. One of these shortcomings is that every category of technique (such as punching, kicking, trapping) has different applications at different ranges. For example, there are long-range kicks (side kicks) and short-range kicks (stomping front kicks). In addition, there are long-range punches, such as jabs and rear crosses, as opposed to short-range hooks and uppercuts. The knee strike is often thought of as a close-range technique, but the flying knee strike can be used effectively from outside range. The division, then, between "kicking range" and "punching range" is just too simplistic. Every category of technique has myriad applications at different ranges. To say that I am currently in "kicking range" is thus thoroughly unhelpful. In light of these considerations, one can see that correlating a technique with a given range can actually be limiting for a fighter. For example, by thinking of a given range as a kicking range, a fighter consciously or unconsciously blocks out the many other attacking options available at that range. Such thinking can lead a fighter into a dangerous false sense of security. In understanding a given range as only a kicking range, a fighter could overlook the danger of other forms of attack at that range. This problem was common for traditional martial artists in the early MMA tournaments.

Many people versed in striking arts thought they would be safe from grappling attacks at the ranges typically thought of as kicking and punching ranges, since "grappling range" was generally understood to be a close-range skill. In fact, this assumption was clearly not the case. Grapplers consistently demonstrated an ability to cover long distances far more quickly than people expected, shooting toward their surprised opponents and entering into a clinch or takedown. They quickly dispelled the idea that grappling was a serious possibility only at short range by repeatedly attacking with grappling technique from longer range. This is why the term *free movement* was used to describe that phase of the fight where neither one has a grip on the other. It is intentionally vague. Too often people try to characterize some aspect of combat too tightly. They describe some situation as "kicking range" or "grappling range," which creates a limiting mind-set in a fighter. It predisposes him toward whatever technique has been used to define that aspect of combat, and it often blinds him to the danger of his opponent's using some other technique that is supposedly inappropriate for that range.

Something that quickly became obvious in MMA combat that has still not been sufficiently understood in the martial arts community is that range could not be used by fighters to control an opponent. Despite many attempts, no one has successfully used range and distance as a tool to control the pace and tempo of the fight. On the contrary, the typical pattern of fighting in MMA events is for fighters to be able to close distance almost at will. One of the central themes derived from contemporary MMA fighting is that although range cannot be effectively used to control an opponent, body contact can.

The best way for a fighter to control an opponent is to utilize the body contact and superior position, which is possible in the clinch and ground grappling. Although it is almost impossible to prevent an opponent's moving quickly through the various ranges toward you, it certainly *is* possible to control him in the clinch. In this position, you can slow the pace of his offense, recover the initiative, and go on the attack, either by breaking the clinch and resuming the fight on the feet, or by taking him to the ground. Thus body contact and positioning, not range, has proven to be the key factor in the controlling of an opponent and the tempo and direction of a fight.

What finally enabled strikers to do well in MMA competition was not control of range (no one ever did this successfully) but learning to block takedowns and break out of clinches. They learned how to use body contact and control through defensive grappling techniques (such as sprawling, clinch-breaking, shot-blocking) to prevent being easily taken down and to keep the fight in a standing position. Thus, range by itself never proved to be an independently useful strategic concept, even in the one phase of combat it is most well suited.

Actual experience in MMA combat has clearly shown that it is not range that determines the techniques and tactics that a fighter employs; rather, it is the style of combat in which the fighter trains that determines the strategy. For example, a grappler seeks to grapple at all ranges, shooting into takedowns from long range, locking up a tight clinch at close range. A boxer favors punches at all ranges—straight jabs and crosses at long range, hooks and uppercuts at shorter ranges. A strong kicker favors kicks at all ranges. *In other words, fighters employ the techniques in which they have the most expertise, not the ones that are supposedly best for a given range.* They constantly seek to push the fight in a direction that favors their skills. This is the lesson of actual experience.

One might be tempted to ask the following: If the theory of ranges is really so incomplete and inadequate as the basis of a theory of combat, why did it become prevalent for so long before the reemergence of MMA combat? It appears that the overrepresentation since World War II of standing striking arts—where range really does play a crucial role—gave people the false impression that it could serve as the basis of a *complete* theory of combat. As long as a fight is kept in the free-movement phase (as is the case in boxing, kickboxing, and most forms of striking arts), range plays a massive role in the strategy of a fighter. Because the advocates of range had never been regularly exposed to situations where they were bundled up in a clinch or taken to the ground, they conceived all combat to be dominated by the free-movement phase. This ignorance explains the shock and consternation among so many martial artists when MMA reemerged: It became painfully obvious that free movement was only one of several phases of combat—and indeed, in the early MMA tournaments, it was not even an important one.

Our discussion of the limitations of range as the basis of a theory of combat is an important one. Range has long been posited as the cornerstone of combat theory. As long as a fight remains in the free-movement phase, range is indeed a truly crucial concept. Range does determine much of a fighter's behavior in this phase of combat. Yet fighting is so much more than just the activities associated with the free-movement phase. Once movement becomes constrained in the clinch or on the ground, a whole new set of considerations come into effect. As such, range is (at best) an incomplete theoretical basis of combat. Such considerations as these point to a need to revise our understanding of unarmed combat. We need to move away from a theory of range and toward a theory that comprises different phases of combat. MMA events have consistently shown that the most important factor in determining the direction of a fight is not careful observance of range, but the ability to keep your opponent in a phase of combat where he is least likely to be a threat. The most important elements that separate combat into different phases are the degree and type of body contact and control the fighters have attained.

When two fighters come into contact by gripping each other, their movements become constrained. They are no longer free to move as they wish without taking their opponent's grip into account. This constraint becomes even more pronounced when a fight goes to the ground, since there is a greater degree of body contact with each other and with the floor. Once on the ground, movement becomes *very* constrained, especially for the man underneath. The nature of the fight changes completely once body contact has been established because both fighters find their movements constrained by the other. Striking someone effectively while tied up in the clinch is different from striking someone in a normal boxing situation. It changes still more once the fight goes to the ground.

Unarmed combat, then, can be effectively divided into different phases. In each phase, the nature of the fight changes significantly. The criterion for dividing combat into different phases is the relative freedom of movement the fighters have, which is based on the amount and type of contact, grip, and position each has on the other. As discussed previously, combat normally begins in the free-movement phase, without either person's having any grip on the other. Once contact and grip is established, movement becomes constrained, and the fight has entered the clinch phase. Should the fighters fall or one take the other down, the fight enters the ground-fighting phase. These three basic divisions have proven to be the most pertinent in determining the course of real combat. Thus, the most important consideration at any stage of a fight is not what range an opponent is in, but what degree of constraint through body contact, grip, and position the two fighters have exercised on each other.

HIGHEST MANIFESTATION OF PHASES OF COMBAT THEORY

Our historical survey of modern grappling approaches to jujitsu has revealed that jujitsu schools have used the phases of combat theory in a similar way. Starting with Fusen ryu, jujitsu practitioners have sought to take opponents into a phase of combat that opponents were ill-prepared to deal with. This objective was always done by taking the fight to the ground, and the reasoning behind this decision was simple and rational. First, most martial arts concentrate on the standing position as the focus of most of their techniques, which is natural enough because all fights begin in a standing position. Since most fighters are well trained in the standing position, it certainly makes little sense to fight them in their strongest phase when fighting them at their weakest phase puts you at a much more advantageous position.

Second, it is almost inevitable that a serious fight will end up on the ground. Once a fight begins, the pressure the two combatants exert on each other is usually strong. The chances of their losing balance, either by accident or by design, is quite high. This fact has been shown in innumerable real fights, and the sheer inevitability of ground combat makes it a sensible area to focus on.

Third, fights tend to be won and lost on the ground to a greater degree than any other phase of combat. This is because an opponent can be controlled and dominated far more readily on the ground than in a standing position. As a result, one fighter can pin the other fighter and severely punish him with strikes and submission holds. If the other fighter does not know how to escape, the chances of evading a fearful beating are slim indeed. Thus, the cost of being dominated on the ground is generally much higher than any other phase of combat.

Fourth, inferiority in strength, size, and athleticism is less of a handicap on the ground than in the other phases of combat. This is because movement on the ground is not a natural skill, but a learned skill. If a larger opponent has not learned the skills of movement on the ground, he stands less chance of success than in a standing position, where people are much more comfortable (since we spend most of our daily lives and physical activity in a standing position). For these and other reasons, the jujitsu schools focused on the ground as the best phase of combat to dominate their opponents.

One result of the historical trend toward ground combat has been that people have mistakenly assumed that the jujitsu fighter should *always* seek to take the fight to the ground. In fact, this is not the case. There are times when ground combat is not the wisest choice. Remember, phases of combat theory states that a fighter should seek to stay in whatever phase of combat he has the greatest imbalance of skills over his opponent. This does not exclusively mean the ground. If both my opponent and I are strong on the ground, but he is weak on his feet while I have moderate skills on my feet, then it makes more sense to keep the fight in the standing position. Thus, the idea is not always to head blindly for the ground; rather, a fighter should keep the fight in whatever phase he has the higher skill advantage over his opponent.

The highest manifestation of phases of combat theory is thus the well-rounded fighter who can excel in all three phases of combat. A fighter with a complete range of combat skills can take an opponent out of his favorite phase of combat and into a phase in which the opponent is uncomfortable and unlikely to succeed. This ability to feel comfortable in all phases is a mark of a well-rounded athlete.

A fighter well versed in all three phases of combat does not necessarily show any marked favor toward any one phase, but he will adjust in response to the preference of his opponent. Of course, it is natural to favor one phase over the others. We all have our strengths and weaknesses, and most of the great MMA fighters of today have an area of specialty in one phase. Nonetheless, it is not acceptable to be totally unprepared in any one phase of combat, since a skilled and well-rounded opponent seeks to keep you in that phase and thus nullify your strengths and expose your weaknesses.

An interesting development in current MMA events is the success of many fighters who are not particularly strong in any one phase of combat but who are moderately skilled in all three. Often, these well-rounded fighters have been able to defeat fighters who are far superior to them in one phase of combat but weak in the other two. Such matches are often fascinating to observe. The specialist works hard to keep the fight in his favorite phase while the all-rounder constantly tries to shift the fight into another phase, where he knows he can dominate the action. If the specialist can succeed in keeping the fight where he wants it, he is assured of victory; if not, the all-rounder, even though his skills are not exceptional in any one phase of combat, can attain victory via the opponent's weakness. Battles such as these are an excellent demonstration of the theory of phases of combat in operation. The outcome of the fight is therefore largely determined by the judicious use of strategy.

POSITIONAL CONTROL

We noted earlier that modern grappling approaches to jujitsu employ strategy at two separate levels. There is an *overall strategy* based on phases of combat—the grand battle plan, as it were. Once the two fighters begin the match, however, they use strategy at another level, a strategy that guides their actions minute by minute, second by second, throughout the course of the fight. This is the concern to constantly strive for superior position over their opponent—their *positional strategy*.

At any given moment in a fight, the two fighters occupy certain positions relative to each other. Some of these positions give one fighter a considerable advantage over the other, allowing him to attack more readily and successfully than the other can. Other positions are neutral, offering neither fighter any real advantage. Still others are disastrous, giving the opponent a considerable advantage in offensive possibilities. These positional concerns become especially important once the two fighters lock up in a clinch and go to the ground. Should one fighter attain a really dominant position, he can attack with virtual impunity while his hapless opponent can only think of escape. If an opponent is not skilled in grappling, the chances of his escaping unscathed from a dominant position are remote.

Indeed, in early MMA matches, the establishment of a strong, dominating position was nearly always enough to finish a fight. The fighters of that time simply lacked the grappling skill to get out before unacceptable damage was done to them. The current generation of MMA athletes are much better trained in grappling jujitsu skills and theory. As a result, they are much better equipped to avoid or escape dominating positions and resume the fight.

To clarify the theoretical underpinnings of positional strategy, we can offer clear definitions of the terms *dominating position* or *inferior position*. A dominating position is any position that allows one fighter to control the body and movement of an opponent in such a way that the fighter can attack with strikes and submission holds with greater efficiency than the opponent can. Obviously, an inferior position is simply the opposite of this.

Note, however, that domination comes in degrees. Some dominant positions are simply more dominating than others, and there are *many* dominant positions. The mounted position (chapter 6), knee-on-belly position (chapter 6), side-control position (chapter 6), and some versions of the headlock (chapter 5) are all examples of dominating positions, though this is by no means an exhaustive list. Of these, the mounted position and the rear-mounted position are often considered more dominant than the others because an opponent can be struck and submitted from those positions with greater ease. We can also understand a *neutral position* as one in which neither fighter has any intrinsic advantage in attacking with strikes and submissions over his opponent. Good grapplers typically work within a strategy that emphasizes controlling an opponent by attaining good position. Once a good controlling position has been attained, the opponent can be put under severe pressure with strikes and grappling technique. This intimidating pressure almost always forces the opponent into error and greatly increases the likelihood of a submission hold being successfully applied on him.

The advantage of this workmanlike approach to combat is that it greatly increases the likelihood of a fighter's success when well applied. Fighting is a game of chance. There is always a chance of victory and a chance of defeat, no matter what respective skill level exists between the two fighters. The strategic fighter constantly looks to stack the odds in his favor. *This is best done by striving to put oneself in a position where one can easily attack an opponent while his ability to strike back is severely undermined.* This is a high-percentage approach to fighting, and it has proven its effectiveness countless times in MMA combat.

Without doubt, there is something rather callous about such an approach to fighting. Usually, we are raised with a sense of a "fair fight" in which the two opponents square off with an equal chance of hitting each other. The idea of putting yourself in a position where you can hit while your opponent cannot certainly runs counter to the notion of "fair fighting." However, the central concept behind jujitsu as an approach to fighting is not fairness, but *efficiency*.

Link Between Positional Skill and Submission Skill

We have noted the great importance of controlling your opponent both in the standing clinch and on the ground. One of the best ways to do either is to attain a dominating position. By this means, a smaller person can control a larger person for long periods. Merely holding someone down, however, does not make the opponent surrender the fight. *What is needed is a way of forcing the fight to end, of making an opponent give up.*

For most people, the way to make the fight end is for the winning fighter to pound the opponent with feet and fists. This time-honored method certainly works well; the problem, however, is that the opponent is usually pounding away, right back at you. If he is larger, stronger, or more athletically gifted than you, then there is an excellent chance that *you* will be the one forced into surrender and defeat. We have seen that a much more rational strategy is to place yourself in a position where you can attack at will while your opponent's attacks are severely impeded. Imagine a fight where your opponent has his arms tied behind his back. This would make your fight easy indeed. By attaining a truly dominant position on your opponent, you are essentially working on that very principle of restraining your opponent and gaining a decisive advantage, just as you would if his hands were tied.

Once you are in a dominant position, it is time to end the fight. Most people do this by smashing their opponent with strikes, which is highly effective. Another less bloody and more efficient method is the use of *submission holds*. These are potentially injurious holds that threaten the opponent with broken limbs or unconsciousness. Unlike strikes, these offer the opponent the chance of bloodless surrender, and thus they have a more humane element to them. On the other hand, they can be used to cripple an opponent in ways that are far more damaging in the long term than are strikes.

Submission holds therefore offer the jujitsu practitioner a great degree of flexibility in the way that they treat an opponent. A vast number of submission holds exist in jujitsu, and they can be applied from virtually any position, at any point of an opponent's body. Experience has clearly shown, however, that it is generally safer to work your way into a dominant position *then* look to apply submission holds. *The chances of a submission hold being successfully applied are much higher when done from a dominating and controlling position.*

Too often fighters attempt submission holds from inadequate positions. They quickly find that it is easy for their opponent to counter and retaliate in a heavy-handed manner. It is much safer to work oneself into a solid position; at that point, the opponent can be controlled sufficiently enough to allow a smooth and easy entry into a hold that will force the opponent to surrender or face severe injury or unconsciousness.

Hierarchy of Positions

We have seen that once two fighters get a grip on each other, the nature of a fight changes. This is due to the control they can now exert over each other's movement. *A key point here is that the degree of control each fighter can exert over the other is dependent on the positions each holds over the other.* Many positions exist that two fighters can work into once they come into grips, and the amount of control and dominance these positions offer comes in degrees. Some positions have far greater potential for controlling an opponent. The many possible positions in a grappling fight—whether in a standing position or on the ground—can thus be arranged in a hierarchy based on the degree of control over an opponent that they offer. This hierarchy starts at the bottom with positions that are clearly inferior. They are positions that allow an opponent to easily control and dominate your movement, nullifying your offense while greatly facilitating his offense. We then work our way up through less inferior positions until we come to neutral positions. These do not offer any intrinsic advantage to either fighter. From there, we come into the dominant positions that allow decisive control over the opponent's movement.

Jujitsu fighters constantly look to work their way up this hierarchy of positions. As control over the opponent increases with each positional advance, the likelihood of finishing the fight with strikes or submission holds (or a combination of both) greatly increases. This highly effective positional strategy is a relatively recent advent in the history of jujitsu. The early systems of jujitsu, as we saw in our historical reviews, were basically a last-ditch system of combat on the battlefield that formed only a small (and not important) part of a warrior's battlefield training. Only with the rise of an autonomous unarmed system of combat did attempts at a comprehensive strategy begin to emerge in jujitsu. With Fusen ryu, we see the first successful use of an overall strategy that guides the techniques of jujitsu in ways that were as revolutionary as they were successful. Mataemon Tanabe and Yukio Tani were the pioneers who successfully used this strategy to promote the efficiency of their art. Maeda then expanded the application of this approach to the MMA arena, using it in several fights with stunning success. It was the Gracies, heirs to Maeda's teaching, who took the strategic element of these new grappling approaches to jujitsu to a new level. They refined and perfected the idea of a positional control that we have been examining, and at this point, we can now clearly state the theoretical core of this new approach to jujitsu.

The most efficient manner in which to fight is to place yourself in a position where you can attack your opponent far more easily than he can attack you. You can best complete this objective by controlling and dominating his movement. Most sports require you to master the movements of only your own body to be successful. The combat grappling arts, such as jujitsu, require you to become the master not only of your own movement but also that of your opponent—a far more difficult and complex task. But it does allow you to choose the best means of controlling and finishing a fight. The following sections cover examples of various fighters' grappling tactics.

Renzo Gracie Versus Maurice Smith: Rings Tournament Japan

Renzo Gracie, a specialist in his family's well-known form of grappling jujitsu (Brazilian jiu jitsu), was clearly favored on the ground. In addition, he had demonstrated good skills in the standing clinch in his previous fights. His opponent was Maurice Smith, a former world champion in various forms of kickboxing and a winner of the K1 kickboxing tournament (the highest achievement in his sport).

Smith had made a successful transition to MMA by studying ground grappling with another great MMA fighter, Frank Shamrock. As a result, he won several tremendous fights over highly ranked grapplers and gained a fearsome reputation as a knockout artist. Smith clearly had a massive advantage in standing-striking skills, along with a considerable size advantage. This was to be a classic matchup of striker versus grappler, with both of the competitors at the top of their respective fields.

As it turned out, Renzo Gracie was able to take the fight immediately to the ground with a successful takedown. Smith tried gallantly to employ his grappling training to hold Renzo at bay and get back to his feet, but the skills of the specialist ground grappler quickly proved too much for Smith. Renzo worked his way easily into a dominant pin from across-side and applied a side triangle-lock (yoko sankaku jime) combined with an armlock (ude gatame) to force the tap-out in a short time. This was a great example of two top-ranked fighters with strengths in different phases of combat. Each knew the other's strategy and strengths, and each knew what had to be done to attain victory. The outcome was decided by one fighter's quickly taking the fight into a phase that created a dramatic imbalance in skill level. Once there, Renzo's masterful knowledge of submission holds gave him the means to efficiently end the fight.

Renzo Gracie Versus Kikuta: Pride Tournament Japan

Renzo Gracie took on the formidable Japanese fighter Kikuta early in Kikuta's career. Kikuta was a former judo player who had made the jump to MMA. In time, he became a world champion in submission grappling at Abu Dhabi and also won the prestigious "King of Pancrase" title. He had tremendous size, strength, and takedown skills. On the ground, he lacked the submission skills of Renzo Gracie, but it was on the ground that he expected to punch his way to victory, given his size advantage and positioning skill. This match was thus to be a classic encounter of "ground and pound" versus the submission specialist as neither fighter was considered to be strong in free-movement striking. Kikuta, however, had a clear edge in the standing clinch as a result of his strong judo background and his size. On the ground, both men were good, but in different ways. Gracie was strong on submissions and could play the top or bottom game equally well; Kikuta favored the top game.

As the fight progressed, it quickly became apparent that neither man was interested in the free-movement phase. The fight was largely spent in the clinch position. Kikuta scored a number of impressive takedowns into top position but was quickly locked up in Renzo's guard. At no stage was Kikuta able to punch effectively inside the guard, nor could he improve his position on the ground or gain any form of submission hold. This particular fight had no set time limit. After nearly an hour of struggle, Renzo was able to lock on a tight guillotine choke in the clinch and drop to the guard position with the choke still in place, thereby securing a remarkable victory against a much larger, stronger, and highly trained opponent.

What is interesting about this fight is the way in which phases of combat theory was utilized by both fighters. Neither felt capable of winning the fight in the free-movement phase, so this phase was not used at all by either fighter. Both fighters were fine grapplers, on the ground and in the clinch, and both fighters sought the same phases of combat; however, each used a significantly different positional strategy within those phases. Renzo sought the bottom position, a rational choice given Kikuta's size and great takedown skills, and Kikuta sought the top position, also a rational choice given his desire to win by striking on the ground. What made the difference was Renzo's ability to fight from underneath, utilizing the guard against his larger opponent (who dominated the takedowns) along with exercising his superiority in the use of submission holds. This advantage gave him the ability to finish a fight without time limits.

Thus, both fighters sought the same phases of combat (clinch and ground) but approached those same phases in different ways by operating with a different positional strategy. Kikuta sought to go to the ground in top position and pound his way to victory; Renzo sought to go to the ground but play the bottom position and patiently wait for the opportunity to attack his bigger and stronger opponent with a submission hold. The fight was thus an interesting example of the interaction between phases of combat strategy and positional strategy.

Maurice Smith Versus Mark Coleman: Ultimate Fighting Championship

This epic fight is often regarded as one of the best MMA fights on record. It pitted two truly excellent fighters with different styles against each other in a clash for the heavyweight crown of the UFC that was to become an MMA epic. Smith, as we saw earlier when discussing his fight with Renzo Gracie, was a superb kickboxer who had picked up fairly good ground-grappling skills when he switched to MMA events. He was to face the formidable Mark Coleman, a world-class freestyle wrestler who was immensely strong and aggressive. Coleman had a considerable size advantage and was famous for his "ground and pound" game. No one had ever given Coleman any serious problems up to this point, and he was expected to win easily.

The fight began as expected. Coleman easily took Smith down using his great wrestling skills and attained a top position inside Smith's guard. Smith showed great poise as he weathered the initial storm of Coleman's attack. He successfully tied up Coleman on the ground and controlled the big man's strikes. On the few occasions that Coleman advanced into a superior striking position, Smith was able to quickly recover and put him back in the guard position, from where he could exert sufficient control to prevent any serious damage.

As the fight wore on, Coleman became fatigued. Soon the barrage of strikes slowed, then finally stopped. Smith, on the other hand, was just coming into his game. He used his new grappling skills to regain his feet and take the fight into the free-movement phase where he had a clear advantage. Coleman was at this point so tired that his takedowns were no longer effective. Exploding into the fight with punches and kicks, Smith totally took charge of the action, landing strike after strike on the exhausted Coleman. When time ran out, Smith won a unanimous and well-deserved victory that was as remarkable as it was unanticipated.

The strategic element of the fight was most interesting. It pitted the "ground and pound" strategy versus "sprawl and brawl" strategy. Coleman sought the ground phase to nullify Smith's striking skills, and as long as he had energy, he was successful. His positional strategy, however, was too suspect against the wily Smith. He was never able to maintain a really dominant position long enough to pound his way to victory, and he became frustrated and exhausted by Smith's intelligent use of the guard position. His lack of submission holds meant that he could not finish the fight efficiently.

Smith, on the other hand, clearly sought to simply survive on the ground. Once he had tired his opponent out, he could take the action into his favored phase, on the feet. From there, he avoided all of the exhausted Coleman's takedowns, blocking shots and sprawling on top of the big man. This enabled him to keep the fight in the free-movement phase where he could pepper Coleman with strikes and go on to win.

Strategically, the fight is interesting in that it shows the need for a more sophisticated positional strategy and submission holds if the fight is to be won in the ground phase. It also demonstrates the idea of a fighter learning enough about an unfamiliar phase of combat to survive and escape from it so that he can return to his favored phase and attain victory.

The fight also marked an important turning point in MMA history. Early MMA had been so dominated by ground grapplers that many had assumed that striking arts were ineffective. Smith's victory clearly showed that striking skill could be used to win matches at the highest level, provided it was combined with a sound knowledge of the technique and strategy of the ground game. Thus, Smith used the phases of combat theory to suit his own game by taking the fight back into the free-movement phase and winning a brilliant victory.

An interesting footnote to this story is that Coleman's career went into a temporary slump after this fight. He took time off and learned a sound positional strategy based on improving position on the ground after getting a takedown. In this way, his "ground and pound" game became much more effective. As a result, Coleman came back in grand style, showing off his new-found strategic knowledge and skills to win the prestigious Pride Grand Prix event. Rather than simply pounding away from any top position, he sought to get to a truly dominating position and hold it. This allowed him to punish his opponents much more effectively and thus give him the title.

So much for our analysis of the strategy and tactics of modern jujitsu and contemporary MMA combat. The genesis of phases of combat and positional dominance—beginning with Fusen ryu and working up through the exploits of Maeda, the Gracies, and contemporary MMA fighters—has revealed the extent to which *strategy* forms the backbone of modern approaches to single combat. We need to go on now and reveal the core techniques that allow a fighter to put this grand strategy into operation.

Free-Movement Phase

In the previous chapter, we saw that combat can be divided into three main phases, each separated by the degree of body contact and control the two fighters have on each other. Mixed martial arts (MMA) fights always begin with the two combatants' squaring off with each other on their feet in the same manner as boxers. Neither one has any hold or grip on the other; they are thus free to move about as they please and to choose whatever attacking or defensive movements they wish. Some fighters look to strike with fists and feet; others look to aggressively close the distance and tie the other fellow up in a clinch; some look to go immediately into a takedown to the ground. This free movement phase of combat is the one that most people are familiar with. It is close to what they see in boxing and wrestling matches, and it is characterized by the movements and skills that the average person typically associates with "real fighting."

The free-movement phase of fighting comprises two basic approaches, each quite different from the other.

1. Some fighters have outstanding striking skills in the standing position. This ability gives them an excellent chance of achieving victory by knockout or referee's stoppage, provided that they can keep the fight in the free-movement phase. They consider the free-movement phase as a desirable state to be held onto as long as possible. Fighters who use this approach must ensure they are not wrapped up in a tight clinch and controlled or taken to the ground. They must work on the skills of knockout striking, breaking out of clinches, and resisting takedown attempts to keep the fight in the free-movement phase. This approach to fighting can be dubbed "sprawl and brawl," since sprawling on top of an opponent to defend the takedown is the most common and effective means of keeping the fight in the standing position. Users of this approach to the free-movement phase consider striking skill as an end in itself, a direct means to victory through knockout or decision.

2. Other fighters see the free-movement phase as an obstacle to be passed. They look to spend as little time as possible in this phase since it represents a time of danger. Rather than get into a battle of strikes in which there is a risk of being hit and even knocked out, they look to close the gap into a clinch or takedown. This is the tactic of both "ground and pound" fighters and submission fighters (jujitsu fighters generally fall into the submission category). The key skills for this approach are the ability to close distance and clinch in addition to shooting into takedowns while evading and blocking strikes. Those who use this approach to the free-movement phase consider striking only as a means to setting up takedowns and the clinch.

Which approach to the free-movement phase you opt for depends on the skills and attributes that both you and your opponent have. Obviously, if you are stronger than he is in striking skills, then it makes good sense to opt for the first approach, to remain in the free-movement phase. If you feel yourself to be outclassed as a striker, then the second choice, to leave the free-movement phase as soon as possible, makes good sense.

VICTORY IN THE FREE-MOVEMENT PHASE

The most crucial means to victory in the free-movement phase lies in superior striking ability. If you can hit harder, faster, and more accurately than your opponent can, while at the same time taking fewer hits and preventing him from taking you into another phase of combat, then you stand an excellent chance of victory on your feet. In an MMA tournament (and also in a street fight), you must be able to strike while defending takedown attempts. This is the crucial difference between striking in a boxing or kickboxing match and striking in a real fight. In the former, you can commit to full-power punching and kicking without fear of takedowns, since these are illegal in boxing and kickboxing. The problem confronting strikers is that fully committing to striking opens you up for takedowns. The result is that strikers must be much more cautious in their offense in MMA than in normal boxing matches. Strikers must limit the duration of their striking combinations (short combinations are the order of the day in MMA), and they must also work hard on their takedown defenses if they are to avoid being quickly and unceremoniously dumped to the ground by a quick grappler.

Because a fight will go to the clinch quickly once striking begins, most MMA striking specialists use the head as the primary target for punches in the free-movement phase. Fighters execute little body punching since they simply do not have the time to work the body as if it were a boxing match. Kicks also tend to be focused on the legs and not the body; there is much less chance of being grabbed and taken down with a low kick than a high kick. In general, fighters tend to use high kicks only late in the match when their opponents are tired or hurt and are therefore less likely to counter. When a fighter works with powerful, chopping kicks to the opponent's legs, with quick, strong punches to the head in short combinations, while at the same time defending takedowns, a striker can present himself as a *very* formidable opponent. As a result of following this strategy (along with significant changes in the rules), far more fights are being won in the free-movement phase than was the case in early MMA competition, when strikers tended to use the same tactics they would in a boxing or kickboxing match. This assumption, combined with a total ignorance of the crucial ground-fighting game, had spelled disaster for specialist strikers in early MMA competition.

ESSENTIAL SKILLS FOR THE FREE-MOVEMENT PHASE

We have made careful note of the fact that each phase of combat has its own set of skills that are quite different from the skills required in the other phases. It is this fact that allows a fighter who is strong in one phase to be defeated by another fighter who can keep him out of his strong phase of combat and place him in his weak phases. Unsurprisingly, the skills that make for a great fighter in the free-movement phase revolve around mobility and speed, since this is made possible by the freedom of movement enjoyed by both fighters. Whether the fighter is a striking specialist who wants to keep the fight in the free-movement phase or a grappler who wants to quickly get into a clinch or takedown, mobility and speed are the two attributes that lie behind the techniques and skills appropriate to the free-movement phase of combat.

Stance and Motion

The most important foundational skill in the free-movement phase of combat is without doubt the ability to maintain a solid fighting stance while moving quickly and efficiently around, away from, and toward your opponent. Because little glamour is associated with this skill, people tend to overlook it and not practice it nearly enough. Poor stance and motion skills quickly become apparent when you begin to fight. Your opponent will have little difficulty in striking you or taking you down when your stance and motion is flawed. Most people can hold a stance easily enough when asked to; this skill, however, is not enough. You must be able to hold a stance while moving fluidly into attack and defense under the pressure of live combat—this ability is much more difficult to acquire, and it requires constant drilling and practice.

Stance

The most efficient stance for combat in the free-movement phase of combat is without doubt the standard boxer's stance. This stance is more or less standard in Western boxing and in most styles of kickboxing. It allows for good protection of the head from punches and kicks along with good offensive striking potential. In addition, it permits rapid movement in any direction for both offensive and defensive purposes. Of course, small differences exist in stance among fighters in arts such as boxing, kickboxing, and MMA. Some fighters crouch more than others, others stand more erect. Some fighters stand slightly more square to their opponents, others more side on. Small variations in stance are certainly acceptable. However, the core ideas behind an efficient fighting stance—the hands up to protect the head, the feet slightly more than shoulder-width apart, the weight evenly distributed on the balls of the feet, the rear heel slightly off the floor, the chin tucked down, the elbows in, the knees bent—these are common to all. See figure 4.1.

Motion

The ability to move freely and efficiently while maintaining good balance and stance is one of the most crucial skills a fighter must master. Footwork allows a fighter to evade his opponent's attacks in an efficient manner. In addition, it carries a fighter into a range that he can enter into his own attacks. It is no exaggeration to say that without good motion skills, a fighter is little more than a punching bag. He can be struck at will and has little hope of successfully returning fire.

Fighters must be able to move quickly in any direction at a moment's notice. To do so, they must be in good stance. *Therefore, you can see then that stance and motion are linked skills.* If one is lacking, so will the other. Many students show a strong preference for showy techniques, and they have disturbingly little interest in practicing foundational skills such as stance and motion. This is a great pity, since it is the foundational skills that are really the most important to learn. They prove to be far more useful in a real fight than any of the more exciting-looking moves.

A general rule of thumb in basic motion drills is that a fighter should move with the foot that is in the same direction to where he wishes to move. For example, if you wish to move forward, step with your forward leg first, then your rear leg (figure 4.2). If you want to move right, the right foot moves first, the left follows (figure 4.3). At all times, your feet should brush the floor as you move, and your weight must be carried on the balls of your feet. Do not let your weight rock back onto your heels because any movement then becomes difficult.

Figure 4.1 Stance, front view *(a)* and side view *(b)*.

Range and Distance

Earlier, we talked about the inadequacies of range as the basis for a complete theory of combat. Range proved to be seriously incomplete, as it did not pertain to the clinch or ground phases of combat. This does not mean that range and distance are irrelevant or unimportant in combat. In the free-movement phase of combat, range and distance are crucial concepts. When two fighters square off, there is always a distance between them. This distance or range varies as the two fighters move around each other and attempt to launch attacks. *Controlling and policing that distance is a crucial combat skill that often determines the course of the fight in the free-movement phase.*

The problem, however, is that the major theories of range and distance have not proven useful in actual MMA competition. We saw that certain theories of range define the use of range via technique. For example, there is the kicking range, punching range, elbow range, and so on. Actual experience, however, has clearly shown that once two fighters are close enough to hit each other with any form of offensive technique, it is useless to talk of a given range as being appropriate only for one category of techniques.

Figure 4.2 Forward movement.

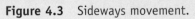

Figure 4.3 Sideways movement.

Consider the knee strike. Most people think of the knee as a close-range weapon, yet one of the most successful means of knockout victories in MMA is the flying knee strike, which launches from long range (or kicking range). The free-standing knee strike has also been used successfully by fighters. They strike at each other at what appears to be punching range. In addition, knee strikes are used with great success in all the variations of the clinch and, indeed, on the ground as well. You can clearly see, then, that it is pure folly to talk about a range that is suitable for only the knee strike, since experience shows the ease with which it can be applied at all ranges. Considerations such as these point toward the need for a new theory of range, one that can be of use in a real fight and that is in accord with the observable facts seen in MMA competition. This is what we shall try to offer now.

A New Theory of Range and Distance

Everyone agrees that range and distance are crucial concepts in the free-movement phase of combat. Experience in MMA competition has shown, however, that range and distance change so rapidly in the course of a standing fight that they are exceedingly difficult to control. If a fighter closes the distance with determination and commitment, the fight always ends up in the clinch and free movement will be lost. In addition, there is no way to predict which techniques will be used at any given range, since every category of technique has many variations, each of which can be used at any range. *The only concept of range and distance that has proven useful in MMA competition is the basic division between contact and noncontact range.* By this, we mean that if a fighter can reach out and physically touch his opponent, then he is at a range where he is close enough to successfully engage in offensive technique. In other words, if you can touch your opponent, then you are close enough to strike him or take him down. If you cannot touch him, then any offensive technique is useless. You will have to use some form of movement to take you forward into contact range, where you can successfully apply offensive technique.

The concept of contact versus noncontact range is loose. It does not try to specify a range at which a given technique is appropriate (we have already seen that this is impossible), nor does it try to divide ranges into short, medium, and long. Experience has shown that range changes so quickly in the free-movement phase of combat that such a division is not helpful. Our new concept of range enables a fighter to know that if he is far enough away from his opponent that neither one can reach out and touch the other, he is safe from attack. He has sufficient warning to evade and counter whatever form of offense his opponent attempts.

Our simple concept of range and distance does not attempt to limit a fighter to certain types of attacks at certain ranges. It recognizes the fact that once contact is possible, then any form of attack is possible—from kicks, punches, elbows, knee strikes, and takedowns. If contact cannot be made with your opponent, then the chance of an attack's being successful are quite low.

Because it seems to say little about range and distance, such a simple concept of range seems open to obvious criticisms. There is a reason for this—there is not much that *can* be said. Previous theories of range tried to legislate too heavily, and they quickly came into conflict with the observable facts. Another criticism is that there are different ways in which I can reach out and touch my opponent. If I reach out with my lead leg, I can touch him sooner than if I reach out and touch him with my lead arm. Which method is correct? The truth is that the small difference in reach between lead arm and lead leg is not significant enough to matter. Remember, range and distance change with tremendous speed in a real fight; thus, small variations in distance are unimportant.

So then, we have put forward a new theory of range and distance. It is exceedingly simple, and it deliberately avoids dividing range and technique into categories that are of no use in actual combat. Its simplicity makes it easy to apply even under the stress of combat, and it has proven itself a reliable guide to successful application of technique without limiting a fighter's options.

Example of Range and Technique: Jose "Pele" Landis

An instructive way to analyze the question of range as the basis of strategy and technique selection is to look at a concrete example drawn from contemporary MMA competition. Jose "Pele" Landis, a distinguished MMA fighter from Brazil, is an apt example of a fighter who demonstrates the limitations of classical theories of range and distance in real fighting.

Pele came from a background in Muay Thai kickboxing and Brazilian jiu jitsu. The former is a style that strongly emphasizes knee strikes from many positions and ranges. Pele's natural body type—long legs and flexible hips—made him ideally suited to the use of the knee as a striking weapon. In MMA events around the world, Pele made the knee strike the basis of his offense, often catching unwary opponents from the unlikeliest of angles and positions. In both the free-movement phase of combat and the clinch, Pele was without doubt one of the most dangerous and unpredictable fighters in MMA, largely as a result of his uncanny use of the knee strike.

One might ask, then, what was the basis of Pele's successful use of the knee strike? According to classical theories of range and distance, it ought to be due to the fact that Pele was an expert at controlling distance and range, since there is supposed to be a range at which the knee strike is the optimal weapon. The fact is, however, that Pele used the knee strike at *all* ranges. Range was not the relevant factor in predicting how he would attack. Rather, his training background and body type made him unusually suited to knee strikes, and it was these factors that made him continually select the knee strike as his weapon. It did not matter whether his opponents were at short, medium, or long range, or at "kicking range," "punching range," or "grappling range," or at any other distance for that matter. Pele would look to score with some variant of the knee strike.

Position and Angle

We have seen already the degree to which positional skills are stressed in the overall strategy of the jujitsu fighter. People normally think of positional skills in the ground-fighting phase of combat and, to a lesser degree, in the clinch phase as well. However, position does play a role in the free-movement phase of combat. The guiding idea in the free-movement phase is to seek a position that gives you some kind of offensive and defensive advantage. In effect, this means you must create some kind of angle between you and your opponent that gives you a better position from which to launch your strikes and takedowns, while at the same time limiting your opponent's ability to do likewise. This constant effort to create an advantageous angle on your opponent is a key skill in the free-movement phase of combat.

If you stay directly in front of your opponent, you will be directly in front of his main offensive striking weapons and will suffer accordingly. In addition, it is much easier for him to block any takedown attempts you make. Instead, you can use good footwork skills to take you out to an angle that limits your opponent's offense and makes his defense more difficult (once again, note the importance of footwork and motion). One particularly useful angle is to circle around his lead hand. This takes you away from his power hand and leg (the rear arm and leg) and makes takedowns much safer and easier (figure 4.4).

Punching

There is no doubt that punches are the most effective form of striking weapon in the free-movement phase of combat in current MMA competition. The vast majority of knockout victories are the result of powerful hand strikes. Not only are punches the means to quick victory in the free-movement phase, they also set up the entries into clinches and takedowns that take the fight into other phases of combat. *Mastery of basic punching skills, then, is crucial to any jujitsu fighter, regardless of which phase of combat he prefers to fight in.*

It is important to note, however, that punching in an MMA setting is quite different from punching in a boxing match. Many people mistakenly assume that because the punching movements of MMA appear similar to those of Western boxing, the two are identical. In fact, the two are different in subtle but

Figure 4.4 Angling away from a strike.

important ways. The biggest differences between punching in a boxing match and in an MMA match is that in the latter, takedowns are legal and clinches will not be broken apart by the referee.

Remember, the rules of boxing limit the fight to the free-movement phase of combat. This is not the case in MMA. A boxer need not be concerned about fighting in the clinch and takedowns, since these are not part of boxing. Accordingly, he can focus on the use of his hands as weapons with no regard for other dangers. He need not worry about kicks, knees, elbows, throws, and takedowns. As a result, he can totally commit to his punching attacks and defense. The MMA fighter, on the other hand, must concern himself with all of these other dangers, since they are all legal in MMA. Because of this fact, some important differences emerge between the punching strategy of a jujitsu fighter in an MMA fight and a boxer in a boxing match.

In MMA competition, for example, punching combinations tend to be much shorter than in boxing. A fighter has only a short time to punch before his opponent closes the distance into a takedown or clinch; thus, long combinations are out of the question. MMA fighters also show a strong preference for straight punches with longer reach, such as the jab and cross. If you are close enough to use shorter-range punches, such as the hook and uppercut, then you are close enough to clinch, which limits the use of these types of punches in the free-movement phase (although they are used much more in the clinch). Lastly, the head is almost always the target in MMA fights. In a boxing match, there is sufficient time to work the opponent's body as a prelude to attacking the head. As a result, punching attacks to the body are much more common in a boxing match. In MMA, body attacks are done mostly in the clinch, rather than the free-movement phase.

Figure 4.5 Jab.

Jab

The jab is the workhorse punch in MMA, just as it is in boxing and kickboxing. Try to visualize it as we take you through it stage by stage: From a fighting stance, throw the lead hand out in a straight line, turning the palm down as you extend out. Be sure to bring the fist back in the same straight line that it went out, returning to your fighting stance. Keep your chin tucked to the shoulder of the arm that launches the jab. Do not push the jab out. Let the punch snap out by staying relaxed. See figure 4.5.

Though the jab is not intended to be a power punch, it can hit an opponent with surprising force if a fighter snaps it out with assistance from the lead shoulder and hip, while at the same time taking a small step forward with the lead foot. This takes the fighter into striking range and adds weight to the strike. The rear hand needs to stay high to defend the fighter's face from counterstrikes. The fighter needs to throw the jab with force and commitment; a lazy jab can be strongly countered by a skilled striker.

The main target of the jab is the opponent's chin. Also, remember that the main functions of the jab are the following:

1. To gauge the distance between you and your opponent
2. To harass, intimidate, and hurt your opponent throughout the free-movement phase of combat
3. To set up other strikes in short combinations. For example, fighters can follow the jab with the straight-right cross or a rear-leg roundhouse kick. These are simple but highly effective combinations that work well in MMA.
4. To distract an opponent long enough to set up either a takedown or an entry into the clinch to take the fight out of the free-movement phase

Cross

The rear cross is the power punch of MMA. It is responsible for more knockout victories in the free-movement phase than any other punch. Again, try to visualize it as we take you through the movements: From a fighting stance, the rear hand snaps out in a straight line as your rear hip and shoulder rotate in the same direction. Push off your rear foot to add further impetus to the blow. Do not wind up the punch and thus telegraph your intentions to your opponent. Let it snap straight out from your stance without any unnecessary movement. See figure 4.6.

Because a large percentage of your body weight is involved in the punch, tremendous power can be generated when a fighter executes this move. Do not, however, try to use muscular strength to generate power. To do so only serves to tighten you up and slow the punch. Relax and let your moving body weight do the work. Make sure that your lead hand stays high to protect your face. Usually the rear cross is set up by a jab; however, there are times when the rear cross can be the first blow thrown. Often, it is good to follow the rear cross with the left hook, as there is a natural flow between these two strikes.

The rear cross is also an excellent counterstrike. Fighters can use it to counter an opponent's roundhouse kick or knee strikes. One of the best times to throw the rear cross is immediately after a change in level. An opponent will often take the change in level as a prelude to a takedown attempt, and he will drop his hands to defend the takedown. This gives an excellent opening for the rear cross. Remember that the main target of the cross is the chin, jaw, and face.

Figure 4.6 Rear cross.

Figure 4.7 Hook.

Figure 4.8 Uppercut.

Hook

The hook is another punch that utilizes body weight in motion to generate tremendous power, and it is best done with the lead hand. The idea is to dip a little and lean slightly out to the lead side. Picture its execution: Without dropping your lead hand, raise your lead elbow, and snap your hips inward, turning in sharply on the ball of your lead foot. Your lead punching arm should be bent sharply, with the palm facing you and with your lead elbow the same height as your fist. The punch should not be a wide, looping motion, but a short, snappy one (figure 4.7). Immediately return to your fighting stance, unless you are throwing the punch as part of some combination. Be sure to keep your rear hand high to block any counterstrikes to your face. The primary target of the hook is your opponent's jaw and chin, though the whole side of his head works just as well.

The hook is a powerful knockout weapon, as it often comes in unseen by the opponent. It is a great counterpunch that works especially well just after you have evaded an opponent's punch by slipping away or changing levels. It can be used to great effect on your opponent's body, especially to his liver—a damaging shot, indeed.

Uppercut

The uppercut is a powerful blow when you are close to your opponent. It relies on exploding your body weight upward to generate great knockout power.

From a fighting stance, dip a little and bring your lead shoulder and hip slightly forward. Do not drop your lead hand before the punch. In a short, snappy motion, turn your palm to face you, and rip your uppercut between your opponent's hands up to the chin (figure 4.8). Return to a fighting stance, unless you are going to the next step of a combination.

The uppercut can also be thrown successfully with the rear hand. Utilize the rear hip and shoulder to add even more power to the blow. The uppercut is an excellent counter to the opponent who changes level into a takedown. Time his level change, and launch the uppercut with commitment straight to the chin, catching his forward movement and generating great power.

Kicking

In the early days of MMA competition, kicks were of little value. In fact, they often were detrimental to the users, since they made kickers vulnerable to takedowns that put them on the ground and at the mercy of ground grapplers. In time, however, kickers learned to defend takedowns, and kicking has become an important skill in the free-movement phase of combat.

Roundhouse Kick

Undoubtedly, the most important kick is the roundhouse kick. Indeed, it can safely be regarded as the "king of kicks" in MMA competition. It is responsible for more damage, knockdowns, and knockouts than any other kick by far. The roundhouse kick that is utilized by contemporary jujitsu fighters in MMA is derived from the kickboxing style of Thailand, Muay Thai. The fighter utilizes his hip weight and leg weight to smash his shin (rather than his foot) into his opponent's leg, upper body, or head. It is generally best to throw the roundhouse kick with the rear leg, as this makes for much more powerful strikes.

To throw the rear-leg roundhouse kick, execute the following moves: Step forward with your lead foot, and open your hip a little by turning the lead foot in the same direction you are kicking. Whip your rear leg around in a manner not unlike that of a soccer kick; utilize the weight and power of your hips by rotating on your supporting foot so that your heel turns toward the opponent. Make contact with the lower half of your shin. See figure 4.9.

Relax as you throw the kick. Do not think that by tightening up and using your muscles that you are adding power. You are not. Relax and think of your leg as a whip. Also, do not simply attack your opponent with *only* the

Figure 4.9 Roundhouse kick.

rear-leg roundhouse because he can easily (and strongly) counter with a rear cross. Set it up first with your hands. Throw a jab to cover your opponent's eyes, then smash the kick to his thigh.

During a match, if your opponent is stunned or utterly fatigued, the roundhouse is a great way to finish the fight. If this is the case aim for the head. Keep in mind that it takes some practice to ready the shins for the kind of impact they must take in a real fight. But by kicking the heavy bag for long periods of time, your shins will harden and be ready to absorb the impact.

The lead leg can also be used to throw the roundhouse kick. The best way to do this is to switch stance just before you kick so that your lead leg becomes your rear leg. Skip your lead leg back, and bring the rear leg forward, changing your feet in one quick motion. Now you can throw the lead leg with real power, since it has now become the rear leg. The best target for the lead-leg roundhouse kick is the inner thigh of your opponent, a painful blow that opens him up for other strikes and also for takedowns. Remember that one of the best times to use the roundhouse kick is immediately after breaking a clinch and returning to free movement. Your opponent will be distracted and thus open for strikes.

Case Study in Effective Kicking in MMA: Bas Rutten

There have been many strong kickers in MMA, but few could match the kicking prowess of the Dutch kickboxing specialist Bas Rutten. Rutten came from a background of Muay Thai kickboxing, and in addition he had learned solid grappling skills while fighting in the Pancrase circuit in Japan. Rutten's specialty was a lightning-fast roundhouse kick, thrown with tremendous power to the legs, ribs, liver and, in some cases, head. At the time, the problem for strikers in early MMA competition was their fear of being taken down. Rutten, however, was confident enough in his ground-grappling skills to throw his kicks with total commitment without worrying about going down to the mat, since he knew he had sufficient skill to survive there. He used only the simplest kicks (roundhouse and front kicks) and in such a way that his opponents had a difficult time countering him.

Figure 4.10 Knee strike.

Knee Strikes

The knee strike is a truly punishing weapon that can be employed in a vast number of situations. Many knockdowns and knockouts have resulted from the use of the knee in the free-movement phase of combat.

Flying Knee

The flying knee is one of the most powerful strikes that one human being can use on another, short of employing a weapon. It utilizes the whole weight of the body, along with a hard striking surface to inflict genuine knockout power.

Starting from a fighting stance, step in briskly toward your opponent and hop on your supporting leg, taking your body off the ground. Thrust the knee and hip of your other leg straight toward your opponent, looking to hit the chin or upper body. Be sure to keep your hands high to cover your face and prevent an effective counter. See figure 4.10.

The flying knee is an excellent way to cover the distance between you and your opponent and get safely into a clinch. It is also a great way to finish a stunned or retreating opponent.

Free-Standing Knee

Most people think of the knee as the striking weapon of choice in a clinch, but it is also effective in the free-movement phase when you are not gripping the opponent at all. In this case, you must be sure to keep your hands up to prevent counterpunches.

To execute the free-standing knee strike, use your lead hand as a distraction by thrusting it toward your opponent's face, and put your other hand up in front of your own face. Lean back so that you can thrust your hips forward to add power to the knee strike. Aim for the jaw, the upper body, or the thigh.

In MMA, there is always the danger of a takedown. Many fighters are therefore wary of throwing free-standing knees to their opponent's body since these are often countered by a leg grab and takedown. Instead, they focus on the head as a target, which forces the opponent to defend his vulnerable head, rather than simply absorb the impact to the body and follow with a takedown. One of the best times to use this strike is just as your opponent changes levels into a takedown. Several notable examples of knockouts in MMA matches have happened in just this manner. The free-standing knee is also an excellent counter to a strong punching attack. When this assault happens, cover your head as your opponent punches, and drive your knee straight into his abdomen.

Evasion and Blocking

It is one thing to be able to hit a target, but remember that your opponent will be attempting to hit you back. It is crucial, therefore, that you learn the skills of avoiding strikes to minimize the damage that you take in the free-movement phase of combat. Evasive skills allow you to avoid strikes without contact. These are easy on your body and require proficient motion skills. Blocking allows you to safely *absorb* impact (rather than avoid it), and it requires sound conditioning and stance skills.

Evasion

The most simple and effective form of evasion is simply not to be there when a strike comes toward you. When your opponent launches a kick or punch, use footwork skills to skip back a step and avoid the blow. Do not skip back too far, as this will prevent a counter attack. Go back just far enough to avoid the strike, then look to come back with your own attack. Do not continue to retreat in a straight line because your opponent will eventually run you down. If you must continue to retreat after your initial backward movement, do so in a circle to confound his attacks.

Another form of motion that is useful in evading punches is slipping your head to the outside of incoming punches (figure 4.11). To do so allows you to easily counterattack with strikes and takedowns. Level changing underneath an opponent's hands is also a means of avoiding punches, and it sets up takedowns quite efficiently as well.

Figure 4.11 Evading to the outside.

Figure 4.12   Covering block.

Blocking

A different approach to nullifying a striking attack is to safely absorb a blow by taking it on a part of the body that can handle the impact. Obviously, a hit in the face is a painful and unpleasant experience. However, if your face is covered by your arms, the experience can be made more manageable. The forearms and shins, both hard and insensitive areas of the body, make the best blocking surfaces. They are used to cover up and protect the weak areas, such as the jaw, face, neck, ribs, abdomen, and thighs. Blocks are especially useful in MMA for fighters who want to enter into a clinch from the free-movement phase. The idea is to safely absorb a few blows, then walk forward into the clinch, grabbing the opponent's upper body and controlling him.

Covering block.   The covering block is one of the best ways to protect the head from punches, elbows, and kicks. Raise your hand to the back of your neck, and raise the elbow of that same arm high, as you tuck your chin and take the impact of your opponent's strike on the outer arm (figure 4.12). Keep your other hand high to protect the other side, should your opponent combine his strike with others. As with all blocks, *do not reach out to the incoming strike*. Let it come to you and take the impact close to your head.

Palm block.   The palm block (figure 4.13) is used to nullify your opponent's jab. The idea is to use the palm of your rear hand to catch the incoming jab in front of your face. Note that the palm block is used only on the jab: it is insufficient to stop a rear cross. Do not reach out too far to intercept the jab. Let it come to you and block it around relatively close to your face (but not so close that your own hand will be driven into your face). A good idea is to fire out your own counter jab every time you catch an opponent's jab. Do not merely block all the time—you must throw a blow in reply to your opponent.

Double-forearm block.   The double-forearm block is an effective way to protect the upper body from kicks and punches. From your fighting stance, turn toward the incoming blow as you simultaneously step away from it slightly. Bring your forearms together and tuck your chin, crunching your upper body inward, like a turtle retreating into a shell. Take the impact on the forearms (figure 4.14).

Shin block.   The shin block is the standard means of blocking a roundhouse kick to the thigh. When your opponent attempts to kick your leg, raise that leg up and outward so that his kick makes impact on your shinbone. This may sound painful, but it is much better than taking it on the thigh. You can combine this block with the double-forearm block to further solidify your defense.

Shooting Into Takedowns

There is no doubt that shooting into takedowns from the free-movement phase was the skill that most radically changed people's attitudes toward real fighting

Figure 4.13 Palm block.

Figure 4.14 Double-forearm block.

in the early days of MMA competition. Before the advent of contemporary MMA, most people thought it would be relatively easy to knock out anyone foolish enough to attempt a takedown. Others lived with the belief that nobody was capable of taking them down. This all changed quickly when people witnessed the first MMA events. It became clear that the shoot into takedowns was far more difficult to defend than most people had anticipated. It proved to be the nemesis of most striking attacks.

Whenever fighters committed to punches and kicks, they became open to takedowns. This vulnerability made even the best strikers wary of hitting their opponents, and it drastically reduced their effectiveness. It was not until strikers learned the grappling skills of defending takedowns, breaking out of clinches, and surviving on the ground that they became confident enough to throw their strikes with power. The key points for the jujitsu fighter to bear in mind when preparing to shoot in on his opponent are the setup for the shot and the level change that precedes every shot into a takedown.

Setups

There are several ways to set up takedowns.

1. Motion: Retreat backward to get an opponent moving in toward you. Lower your level, then shoot as he moves into you. This will create a combined velocity that makes it difficult for your opponent to successfully resist the shot.

2. Angle: Step out to one side to create an angle on your opponent. A wise angle to work with is the one in which you step outside your opponent's lead hand. This position puts you in a relatively safe place (his weak side and blind spot) and makes the shot easier.

3. Range: Step into contact range, thus giving your opponent the opportunity to strike. As he commits to strike, lower your level and shoot into the takedown.

4. Striking: By attacking your opponent with strikes, you preoccupy him with defense and thus make the task of shooting into a takedown much easier. The jab is the best strike to set up shots, but fighters have also used the rear cross and various kicks with some degree of success.

Level Changing

The ability to lower one's level as the prelude to a shot is a truly crucial skill for the jujitsu fighter to master. All the main shots, especially those to the legs, are preceded by a change in level. If you fail to change levels properly before your shot, the chances of a successful takedown are slim. By lowering your level, you drop into a stance that enables you to propel yourself forward at high speed, underneath your opponent's defenses and into his hips and legs. This makes for quick and efficient takedowns that are difficult to defend. The guiding idea is to drop into a stance that is similar to a sprinter's stance, which makes it easy to shoot forward by driving off your rear foot and penetrating into your opponent's hips and legs (figure 4.15a). You can even fake level changes to confuse an opponent and make him nervous.

A way to ensure that you are changing level correctly is to keep your lead shoulder directly over your lead knee as you lower your level. If your lead shoulder goes too far forward, it becomes easy for your opponent to snap your head down to the mat and ruin any chance of a takedown. If your posture is too upright as you change your level, you can be knocked straight back. Keep your lead shoulder directly over your lead knee, and all will be well (figure 4.15b).

Double-Leg Takedown (Morote Gari)

Of all the methods used to take an opponent down in MMA, the double-leg takedown is probably the most commonly used. It allows you to control your opponent's legs and hips, and it allows for quick and efficient takedowns as a

Figure 4.15 Level changing.

result. The key to any well-executed double-leg attack is the preliminary level change that puts you in a solid position to penetrate under your opponent and get through to his legs.

To perform this move, take a quick step forward with your lead foot between your opponent's feet, pushing off your rear foot. As you shoot, be sure to keep your elbows close to your body. Do not reach out too far to grab your opponent. Grab directly behind both his knees as your shoulder hits your opponent's lead hip, as shown in figure 4.16a (be sure that your head goes to the outside of your opponent's lead hip). This means that you shoot under his weaker punching hand, which makes it far more difficult for him to strike you effectively as you shoot in. You can skip your lead knee off the mat if you wish. Your rear leg steps up to the outside of your opponent and allows you to drive across him as you lift and pull on his legs (figure 4.16b). Try to avoid staying down on your knees. Seek to get up to your feet and drive. The result is a solid, driving tackle that puts most opponents on their backs in a short time (figure 4.16c).

Figure 4.16   Double-leg takedown.

Head to the Inside Single-Leg Takedown

Another popular takedown is the single-leg takedown, which has many versions, but the one shown here is particularly appropriate for MMA competition. Single-leg attacks are extremely useful for attacking a left-handed fighter whose opposite leg is forward. Once again, the key to good execution is an efficient change of level before the takedown begins.

To perform this move, step your lead leg just outside your opponent's lead leg, and drop to your knees as you penetrate under his defense (figure 4.17a). Your two knees go down to the floor on both sides of your opponent's lead foot. At the same time, your lead arm whips around your opponent's lead knee, and your rear hand grabs him at the heel (figure 4.17b). Press your head firmly against your opponent's lead leg at the inner thigh, then push forward with your head and pull with the hand on your opponent's heel to take him straight down (figure 4.17c).

Head to the Outside Single-Leg Takedown

An alternative to the double-leg takedown is the head to the outside single-leg takedown. This can be a little easier to accomplish since you focus your attention on the leg that is closest to you. Change levels just as you would for a double-leg takedown (figure 4.18a). As you go down and forward, shoot your lead hand between your opponent's legs and hook it around his lead knee. Both your knees land on either side of your opponent's lead foot as you lock

(continued)

Figure 4.17 Single-leg takedown, head to the inside.

Figure 4.17 *(continued)*

Figure 4.18 Single-leg takedown, head to the outside.

both arms deep around his lead leg at the knee (figure 4.18b). Having gained this preliminary control position, reach with your inside hand to the back of your opponent's other knee, blocking it from moving backward (figure 4.18c). Drive forward into your opponent's hip for the takedown (figure 4.18d). Be sure to keep your head and neck tight to the hip of your opponent to prevent the guillotine choke being used against you.

Blocking a Shot and Sprawling

A crucial skill in the free-movement phase of combat is that of blocking a shot and sprawling. In early MMA events, few fighters had this skill. The result was that most fighters went down easily when their opponents shot in for a takedown. This move allowed grapplers to totally dominate the matches, and it gave little opportunity for strikers to utilize their skills.

In time, however, fighters learned to defend takedowns, and the game changed considerably. When takedowns fail as a result of good defense, the fighter who attempts the takedown is often put in a vulnerable position and can be easily attacked. The key to defending the most common takedowns, leg attacks, and high dives is to either block the initial shot with the hands or forearms, or failing that, get one's hips and legs back and away from the opponent by sprawling heavily on him.

Blocking a Shot With Hands, Forearms, and Underhooks

When your opponent shoots in for a takedown, he needs to lower his level just before the shot. As he does so, lower your own level to match his, then block his shoulders or collarbones with your hands or forearms to stop his incoming momentum (figure 4.19). Quickly move away and return immediately to a fighting stance. Look to counter with strikes as he struggles to regain his stance. This is an excellent time to drive a knee strike into him.

Figure 4.19 Blocking a shot with forearms.

One final method of blocking a shot that has proven effective in MMA competition is the use of underhooks. If your opponent locks around your waist or legs, dig one of your arms under his, and lift up as you push your hips back. This detracts greatly from his offense and gives you considerable control of his body.

Sprawling

Whenever your opponent shoots in, he is looking to pull in your legs or lower back (or both) to take you down. You can prevent this by lowering your hips and sprawling your legs back (figure 4.20). Make sure your back is arched. When performing this move, always remember the following: *do not lock your hands around your opponent's waist!*

To do so is to allow a simple counter. As you sprawl, you want your opponent to bear all your weight. Avoid putting your knees on the ground as well because doing so takes weight off him. After you sprawl, do not simply stay in front of your opponent. He may recover after the initial failure and still take you down. Instead, look to spin around behind him and to put yourself in an attacking position. If you do not favor ground fighting, get up and move away; look to counter with strikes as your opponent rises.

Figure 4.20 The sprawl.

Case Study in Takedown Defense: Chuck Lidell

Among professional MMA fighters, few have proven so adept at defending the takedown and keeping the fight in the free-movement phase than Chuck Lidell. Lidell came from a strong background of wrestling, which gave him the experience and taught him the techniques to counter takedowns by blocking and sprawling. In addition, he was highly skilled in breaking out of tight clinches and getting back into the free-movement phase. By combining these skills with powerful strikes honed by kickboxing training, Lidell was successful in punishing fighters who attempted to take him down. He would either sprawl heavily on top of them as they shot in, or he would tie them up in a clinch. He would then seek to either break the clinch or stand up out of the takedown and return to free movement, where his powerful striking skills could be used effectively against his increasingly tired opponents.

Lidell had many keys to his success. First, his use of short striking combinations never rendered him vulnerable to takedowns, and second, he had a genuine knockout power that made him a threat every time an opponent attempted to shoot. In addition, he made intelligent use of counterattacks when his opponents failed to take him down, never mind the fact that his proficient defensive wrestling skills made him exceedingly difficult to take down in the first place.

FREE-MOVEMENT DRILLS

We have seen many of the most important skills in the free-movement phase of combat. These techniques form the basis of a jujitsu fighter's arsenal in this phase of combat, and they have been highly effective in actual MMA competition. It is one thing to see and practice these techniques; it is another, however, to successfully apply them under the stress of combat. So that the student can be successful in the correct implementation of these techniques, combative drills prove to be useful. We now cover a few of the important ones in detail.

Shadow Fighting

Shadow fighting is among the most important drills for developing the skills and attributes required of fighters to succeed in the free-movement phase of fighting. Most people are familiar with the notion of shadow *boxing*. This is shadow *fighting*. The ideas are similar, but there are important differences. The main difference is that the jujitsu fighter practices solo with all the techniques used in the free-movement phase—stance, motion, punches, kicks, knees, elbows, blocks, evasion, shots, sprawling, and so on. Remember, jujitsu and MMA encompass many more techniques than does boxing.

Jujitsu fighters therefore do not merely shadow *box* with their hands, but they shadow *fight* with their whole body. They move about just as they would with an opponent. For instance, imagine an opponent in front of you, trying to strike you and take you down. Counter his attacks as you attempt your own attacks. Make sure you use the full range of techniques in the free-movement phase. Set a timer for five-minute rounds, and work at a good pace. Really imagine an active, aggressive opponent as you move about with fluidity and grace.

Equipment Training

A jujitsu fighter can sharpen his skills in the free-movement phase in the same way as boxers and kickboxers do through the use of equipment. Use heavy bags, focus mitts, speed bags, kicking shields, and Thai pads to develop the power and speed of your strikes. Be creative in your use of equipment. Do not merely stand in front of the target and bang away thoughtlessly. Imagine a live opponent hitting back. Have your partner move and swing at you as you try to hit the shields that your partner holds.

Sparring

As your skills develop, you will need to go up to the next level, which involves sparring with a live opponent. Nothing else prepares you for combat as well as live sparring does. Let us get something straight from the start, though: *This does not mean that you and your partner attempt to knock each other out every time you train!* The idea is to work *with* your partner, not against him. As you spar, look to apply your techniques with a degree of contact appropriate to your training requirements and skill level. Obviously, if you have a professional fight coming up, you will need to work harder and with greater severity of contact. If you are just starting out or have no fights on the horizon, work at a much more relaxed pace. Flick out the punches and kicks, looking to place them accurately and time them well. Move smoothly and evade your opponent's attacks as early as possible.

Remember: *You are not boxing or kick boxing!* Practice entering the clinch and shooting into a takedown. It is best to work with partners whom you can trust so that training does not quickly degenerate into a brawl. Quite often, it is a wise idea to split your live sparring into either striking sparring or grappling sparring, where you focus on attacking and defending striking attacks (just like boxing or kickboxing) or you omit strikes and simply focus on takedowns and defending takedowns (just like wrestling). It is probably fair to say that grappling sparring is less hazardous and more fun, as few people enjoy being hit repeatedly in the face. It can also be done on a daily basis much more easily than striking sparring.

Clinch Phase

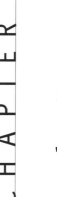

We have been stressing the degree to which unarmed, single combat is divided into phases. Each phase has a set of attributes and skills that are required for success. It is quite possible (indeed, common) to have the attributes and skills to excel in one phase of combat but totally lack the attributes and skills required for the others.

The rapid transition of a fight from one phase to the next is the great hallmark of real combat. One such transition that occurs rapidly in most fights is the transition from the free-movement phase of combat into the *clinch phase*. In general, we can define the clinch phase of combat as any form of solid grip that a fighter has on an opponent that gives him some form of control over his opponent's movement. Even a grip on your opponent's wrist, for example, is a form of clinching, since it gives you a small degree of control over his movement. When we think of a clinch, however, we usually think of it as a grip that affords much greater control than a simple wrist grab. Thus, we normally understand a clinch as a solid grip on the opponent's head or upper body (or both) with a high degree of body contact. This type of clinch allows you to control an opponent's movement and tie him up to negate his striking ability. In this chapter, we shall concentrate on the powerful, controlling clinches that have proven so important in mixed martial arts (MMA) events.

To begin, let's first examine the number of differences that exist between the free-movement and clinch phases. The most obvious difference is the degree of control over an opponent's movement that is made possible by gripping him. The free-movement phase of combat is always a neutral phase. If two fighters of equal skill face each other in the free-movement phase, then each has an equal chance of attacking the other because neither man has direct control over the other man's movement. Imagine a different situation where one fighter has his hands tied behind his back. Obviously, this handicap places him at a huge disadvantage, especially as the other begins to attack.

A dominant clinch works in much the same way. By attaining a dominating clinch position, one fighter can tie up his opponent's arms and body in such a way as to severely reduce his ability to attack and defend himself. Thus, it is in the clinch that we begin to see the influence of the positional strategy that has proven so important in the development and success of modern grappling approaches to jujitsu. It is here that the key idea begins to emerge of working into a position that allows a fighter to attack an opponent while undermining the opponent's ability to retaliate.

Another change that occurs when a fight switches from the free-movement phase into the clinch phase of combat is that submission holds begin to play a significant role. A number of submission holds can be effectively employed in the clinch, either in the standing position or as part of a takedown. Once the clinch is established, the nature of striking also changes quite radically. In the free-movement phase, you are free to use whatever strike you feel is appropriate for the situation. In the clinch, you are limited to whatever is possible within the constraints of the specific clinch that you are locked up in. These subjects will each be discussed in detail throughout this chapter.

THE CLINCH AS AN INTERMEDIARY PHASE OF COMBAT

When most people think about MMA fighting, they think of two major components: the standing position, where strikes and takedowns are the order of the day, and the ground game, where positional skill and submission holds prevail. To think in these terms is to completely overlook one of the most crucial aspects of real fighting, the battle that occurs in the clinch.

The clinch is a fascinating aspect of the fight game. It combines the characteristics of both the standing position and ground game into one phase of combat. People often think of themselves as either a ground fighter or a standing fighter. Standing fighters tend to emphasize striking skill above all else whereas ground fighters emphasize positional and submission skills. This artificial divide, however, is broken down in the clinch. In the clinch, the characteristics of both the standing game and the ground game merge. Success in the clinch is a strange combination of striking, balance, grappling, positional, takedown, and submission skills. Too often people think of the grappling skills that have taken center stage in contemporary martial arts as pertaining only to the ground phase of combat. To do so is to totally overlook the crucial role of grappling in the standing-clinch position.

To fully appreciate the role of the clinch, keep in mind that it is relatively rare for fights to go directly from the free-standing phase to the ground phase of combat. This transition only occurs when one fighter is either knocked to the ground by strikes or taken down cleanly. Far more common is a situation where the two fighters lock up in a clinch as they strike or when one fighter defends a takedown and they then progress into a clinch.

Once a fight goes into a clinch, it almost always progresses in one of two possible directions: First, the clinch can be broken and the fight returns to the free-movement phase. Second, the fight goes to the ground. Technically, a submission hold can be applied in the clinch (although these almost always end up on the ground), and a knockout can occur as well. In the majority of cases, however, the fight will either return to free movement or go to the ground; it depends on the intentions of the two fighters and their relative skill in carrying out those intentions. As such, the clinch usually plays the role of intermediary between the free-movement phase and the ground phase of combat.

A range of techniques allows a fighter to take either direction when using the clinch, and we shall look at some of them in this chapter. This use of choice is what makes the clinch such a vital phase of combat. In other words, control of the clinch allows control of the direction of the fight. Should you desire a return to free movement, having skill in breaking a clinch will allow you to do so. Should you desire a ground fight, having skill in takedowns from the clinch will allow you to do that as well.

FOUR USES OF THE CLINCH

Why would someone attempt to take a fight into the clinch phase of combat? Fighters have four main reasons to do so, and all four are constantly seen in MMA fights.

Effective Use of the Clinch in MMA: Randy Couture

Some fighting styles emphasize clinching skills much more than others. For example, Muay Thai kickboxing involves striking in several specialized clinch positions. Judo is largely concerned with throws and takedowns from clinches that involve gripping the jacket *(judogi)* that all judo players wear. However, no fighting style pays more attention to clinch work than Greco-Roman wrestling. Because no holds below the waist are permitted, players are forced to focus entirely on upper-body wrestling.

Randy Couture was an international-level exponent of Greco-Roman wrestling before turning to MMA competition. He put his Greco-Roman skills to great use in all his fights, combining them with solid striking skills and groundwork to wreak havoc with many of his opponents. Couture used the clinch to negate the dangerous striking skills of boxers and kickboxers, tying them up and keeping them off-balance so that they were unable to strike effectively. In addition, he would use the clinch to set up takedowns from where he could take the fight to the ground with himself in top position. Other times, Couture would use the clinch to tire and frustrate his opponents. In this way, he could control the tempo and course of the fight, keeping it in the standing position until he decided that it was time to go to the ground.

Although many fighters are adept at one particular aspect of the clinch game, Couture was unusual in that he was strong at almost all of them. This made him a tough opponent who could often control the tempo and direction of the fight. If he wanted to keep the fight standing, he would simply tie his opponent up in the clinch. If he feared a powerful striker, he would do the same. Any time he wanted to play the ground game, he could employ a strong takedown attack from the clinch. If he wanted to box with an opponent, he could break the clinch and return to free movement.

A proficient clinch-fighter, then, has the ability to dictate the direction that a fight goes in. Because the clinch often plays the role of an intermediary phase between the standing position and the ground fight, you can control which phase of combat will occur next when you control that intermediary phase. This ability was one of the keys to Couture's great success in MMA competition.

1. *As a means of negating the offense of a dangerous striker.* Most people are familiar with this kind of clinch work, since it is so common in the sport of boxing. Whenever one boxer finds himself in trouble, he usually tries to lock up his opponent in a tight clinch to prevent his being punched. In this case, the clinch plays a negative role, but negative in the sense that it negates the opponent's striking attack. The main users of such tactics in MMA are fighters who prefer grappling attacks. They actively seek to avoid a striking match in the free-movement phase and thus go immediately to the clinch.

2. *As a means of setting up strong striking opportunities.* The clinch can also be used much more offensively. Many proficient clinch fighters actively seek various kinds of clinches that allow for strong clinch-striking attacks—knee and elbow strikes are especially favored. For example, once a fighter attains a solid neck clinch, he stands an excellent chance of landing heavy blows on his opponent. Striking in the clinch, however, is a different business from striking in the free-movement phase. Remember: Expertise in one is no guarantee of expertise in the other.

3. *As a means of setting up takedowns more safely.* One of the great dangers of shooting in on an opponent from long range in the free-movement phase of combat is being countered by a heavy sprawl. This puts you underneath your opponent in a situation where he can lock a tight, front headlock and strike you. In addition, there is great danger of your opponent's running around behind

you and taking your back. On occasion, fighters are even knocked out by knee strikes as they attempt to shoot in on their opponent's legs. Concerns such as these make many people think it is much safer to get to the clinch first and then attempt takedowns, rather than risk an all-or-nothing shoot for the legs.

4. *As a way to keep the fight in a standing position and frustrate takedown attempts.* This tactic is used by anyone who does not want to go to the ground. People who prefer striking attacks usually engage in this tactic. If you can tie up an opponent in a firm defensive clinch, then you can make it difficult for him to complete a takedown.

Case Study in Defensive Clinching Skills: Pedro Rizzo

One apt example of a fighter who made excellent use of defensive clinching skills to aid his game was the Brazilian fighter Pedro Rizzo. Skilled primarily in Muay Thai kickboxing, he needed a means of keeping a fight in the standing position where he could utilize his strong punches and kicks. Rizzo centered his defense on an effective sprawl, along with an aggressive use of the over-under clinch. Whenever an opponent attempted a takedown, Rizzo would sprawl back and look to underhook the opponent's arms at the first opportunity. This underhook control made it tough for an opponent to complete the take-down. From there, Rizzo would stand up into an over-under clinch, which can be used in a defensive way to make it hard for your opponent to successfully take you down. Once in the over-under clinch, Rizzo would keep his hips back and stay in solid balance, then break the clinch to resume in his favored free-movement phase. Using this tactic, he negated the takedowns of many of his opponents. It simply tired them out. Rizzo could take advantage of their fatigue later in the fight and knock them out with solid punches.

TWO APPROACHES
TO FIGHTING IN THE CLINCH

Not all fighters look on the clinch phase of combat in the same way. Many fighters, especially those from a grappling style of combat, view the clinch as a great opportunity to negate their opponent's striking offense while opening their own offensive possibilities. As such, they consider it a safe haven from dangerous strikes, and they try to secure and maintain the clinch as quickly as possible. Quite often, such fighters use the clinch as a way to set up takedowns and take the fight to the ground.

However, a second way of looking at the clinch is to see it as a last chance to keep the fight in the standing position. This view tends to be the one of fighters whose specialty lies in striking in the standing position. The primary effort of this type of fighter is to break out of clinches at the first opportunity and return the fight to the free-movement phase. What is interesting about these two different approaches to the clinch is that they both recognize two essential facts:

1. The clinch plays the role of an intermediary phase of combat, somewhere between the free-movement phase and the ground-fighting phase.

2. The clinch is largely unavoidable in a real fight. If two combatants are serious about fighting each other, they will almost always end up in a clinch in a short time. In a real fight, fighters face a tremendous forward pressure, which is often a shock to those who are not used to it. This makes it almost inevitable that they will quickly run to each other and clinch.

VICTORY IN THE CLINCH

Fighters can work an effective clinch in several ways to attain victory in unarmed combat. Two direct means to victory are in the clinch phase of combat. The first of these is with strikes. Quite often, a skilled clinch fighter can put his opponent in a vulnerable position and knock him out with knee or elbow strikes. Several successful contemporary MMA fighters specialize in just this kind of method. Another method is the use of submission holds that force one fighter to surrender or else face serious injury. A less direct means of victory in the clinch is for a fighter to use clinching skills to wear an opponent down physically, as the clinch can be a physically demanding phase of combat. This tactic makes an opponent easier to deal with in the other phases of combat and thus clears the path to victory. Quite often, it is also possible to gain significant points in the clinch to then earn a coveted judge's decision.

KEY SKILLS FOR THE CLINCH

We have maintained that each separate phase of combat has a set of skills that are appropriate to it and that allow one fighter to dominate another fighter in that phase. Of course, this does not mean that there is *no* overlap in skills between the different phases. Nonetheless, the empirical evidence is clear in showing that the skills of one phase are not even close to ensuring success in the other phases. The clinch phase is no exception to this rule. A unique set of skills that we shall now look at are essential to success in the clinch.

- Basic clinch positions and grips *(kumikata)*
- Transitions from one type of clinch to another
- Entering a clinch
- Off-balancing the opponent *(kuzushi)*
- Takedowns from the clinch
- Submission holds
- Striking in the clinch
- Breaking a clinch and escaping

Clinch Positions

Approximately six types of clinch have proven the most effective in MMA competition. We must note immediately that these clinches can be ranked according to the degree of control and domination that they offer over an opponent. Some of the clinches are neutral in so far as they do not offer any intrinsic advantage over your opponent. In other words, these clinches are symmetrical in that you and your opponent have the same grip on each other; therefore, your opponent has access to exactly the same moves that you do. Two examples of neutral clinches that are important in MMA competition are the collar-and-elbow clinch and the over-under clinch.

Collar-and-Elbow Clinch

To lock up your opponent in a collar-and-elbow clinch, place one hand behind your opponent's neck at the collar (you can also grip higher up on the crown of the head). With your other hand, grip his arm at the elbow (figure 5.1). Your opponent will probably grip you in the same way, creating a neutral clinch, but you can give yourself a slight advantage by pushing the hand on the elbow inside your opponent's arm and placing your hand on his biceps. This gives you the advantage of inside control, which makes it easier for you to open up your opponent so that you can enter for strikes and takedowns. At the same time, it also helps negate your opponent's striking and takedown attacks.

Figure 5.1 Collar-and-elbow clinch.

Over-Under Clinch

The over-under clinch is undoubtedly the most common form of clinch in MMA competition. It is a neutral clinch; both fighters have symmetrical position and can thus attack each other with exactly the same moves. Skill and size determine who dominates the action in this clinch.

One arm is hooked under your opponent's arm, with the other wrapped around your opponent's arm. Your head is always placed on the same side as your overhooked arm; it allows you to control your opponent's powerful underhook by placing a lot of weight on it (figure 5.2). You should be chest-to-chest with your opponent; you can lock your hands around his waist if you wish. This is referred to as an over-under bodylock, which offers yet another set of possible attacks. Although there are many offensive options from this clinch and the bodylock, the problem, however, is that your opponent has access to those same options. In addition, the over-under clinch is a superb defensive position and thus highly favored and difficult to attack. Once they have been secured, other clinches offer a definite advantage over an opponent. Naturally, these advantages come in degrees.

Double-Underhooks Clinch

Whenever two proficient clinch fighters get into the chest-to-chest position, they typically look to secure double underhooks. This clinch position offers a definite measure of dominance by offering a tremendous amount of control over your opponent's lower back, hips, and upper body. This move occurs when you successfully get both your arms under both your opponent's arms. Additionally, this clinch makes it easy for you to drop quickly to your opponent's legs for double- and single-leg takedowns, and it also cuts down your opponent's offensive options.

Thus, the double-underhooks clinch is the first of the dominating clinches; however, it is probably the least dominating. It occurs quite often and is relatively easy to attain. Just like the over-under clinch, you can lock your hands and perform a bodylock on your opponent for additional control (figure 5.3).

Figure 5.2 Over-under clinch.

Figure 5.3 Double-underhooks clinch.

Neck Clinch

The neck clinch is something of a misnomer. The grip is really on the crown of the head, rather than the neck. To perform this maneuver, place one hand on the crown of your opponent's head, then place your other hand on top of the first. Squeeze your elbows together, and pressure your forearms into your opponent's collarbones (figure 5.4). Stand up on your toes, and try to keep your opponent's head lower than yours.

The neck clinch is popular in Muay Thai kickboxing. It offers many opportunities to hit your opponent with devastating knee and elbow strikes, while off-balancing him by jerking his head around then stepping back to the side. This move is responsible for *many* knockouts in MMA competition, usually as a result of strikes with the knee to the chin. In addition, it is an excellent setup for guillotine chokes. One of the best times to lock up a neck clinch is just after your opponent attempts a shot and fails (as a result of your defensive sprawl). As he attempts to get back up, he is *very* vulnerable to the neck clinch followed by knee strikes.

Rear Clinch

The rear clinch is a useful clinch that offers excellent opportunity for attack and control. In this case, you are behind your opponent with your hands locked around his waist, under one or both of his arms (figure 5.5). There are other variations of grip, but the waist grip is simple and effective. Because you are

Figure 5.4 Neck clinch.

Figure 5.5 Rear clinch.

behind your opponent, it is difficult for him to strike you effectively. Your opponent is largely limited to foot stomps and backward elbow strikes.

You do need to be wary of several submission-hold counters (we shall look at some later). However, you have many of your own attacks, so be aggressive in this position. Many excellent examples of the standing rear clinch have occurred in MMA competition, and they all provide opportunity to go straight for rear choke holds.

Front-Headlock Clinch

The front headlock is undoubtedly the most dominant means of locking up your opponent in a standing clinch. This grip is tight and controlling. It offers many great opportunities to strike, take down, and submit your opponent, while leaving almost no opportunity for your opponent to do the same to you. It is probably fair to say that the front headlock, both in the standing position and down on the mat, has been responsible for more knockout and submission victories than any other clinch by far. Once a fighter attains the front headlock, it is easy for him to rain knee strikes into his opponent's vulnerable head and face. The front headlock also provides close proximity for guillotine chokes, in addition to effective takedowns for controlling positions.

The front headlock can be attained in two basic ways. *Proactive* front headlocks are the result of deliberate efforts to snap your opponent's head below your own so that you can lock him up in the headlock. *Reactive* front headlocks are a defensive reaction to your opponent's attempt to take you down. As you sprawl on top of him, you lock up a front headlock.

In both cases, however, the lock is the same (figure 5.6). You must control your opponent's head and one of his arms. After wrapping your arm around your opponent's head, grab his chin. Your other hand grasps his elbow and pulls it outward. Be sure to keep your head on the side of the trapped arm, and keep your own elbows back and in tight to your ribs. You can keep your hands in this position, or you can lock them together for additional tightness.

Figure 5.6 Front-headlock clinch.

Transitions Between Clinches

As they grapple with an opponent in the clinch, fighters must look to progressively work their way into better positions until they can strike with ascendancy, take the opponent down, or make him submit. It is almost always the case that you begin in a neutral clinch, since these are the easiest to attain. From there, you must work into a more dominant one. Thus, the skill of flowing from neutral clinches to dominant ones (and then on to still more dominant ones) is a truly vital skill.

Collar-and-Elbow Clinch to Rear Clinch

From the collar-and-elbow clinch, it is possible to make a quick transition to your opponent's back. One of the best and simplest means of doing so is to use a *duck-under*. The idea is to quickly duck under your opponent's arm and pop up behind him in the rear clinch (figure 5.7). Done properly, this move is a great way to efficiently get into a solid attacking position.

Figure 5.7 Transition from collar-and-elbow clinch to rear clinch.

Over-Under Clinch to Double-Underhooks Clinch

Probably the most commonly used transition from a neutral clinch to a dominant one is that from over-under to double underhooks. The idea is to maneuver the hand of your overhook arm under your opponent's arm and thus get both of your arms underneath those of your opponent (figure 5.8). This move is relatively risk-free, and it takes little effort, hence its popularity. A skilled opponent, however, will immediately recognize the danger as you begin to swim your hand under his arm. He will probably react by swimming his other arm under yours. In this way, he can prevent you from securing double underhooks, and he can also maintain the neutral over-under clinch.

Figure 5.8 Transition from over-under clinch to double-underhooks clinch.

Quite often, this series of moves can create a protracted battle for superior position. Each fighter wants to get the advantage of double underhooks, and both attempt to swim their arms under their opponent's arms. The opponent reacts by doing the same so that neither can achieve the double underhooks. This kind of upper-body battle for control is called *pummeling*, and it is quite common in MMA competition. But it can be a tiring experience. We shall look at pummeling drills later in this chapter. They are essential for developing the skills and attributes required to be a proficient clinch-fighter.

Neck Clinch to Front-Headlock Clinch

The neck clinch is one of the very best clinches from which to unleash strikes on your opponent, especially knee and elbow strikes. However, though dominating it is better to transition to a front headlock if possible, since this offers even more control and submission and striking possibilities. The easiest way to make that transition is to throw a knee to the midsection. Most people react by bending at the waist to avoid the full impact of the knee. This inevitably brings the head down and makes it easy to throw on a front headlock. Even without throwing the knee, by merely cranking or snapping the head down and to the side, you will have little difficulty in getting the head down far enough to lock up a front headlock on your opponent (figure 5.9).

Entering a Clinch

If you watch a boxing match, you will often see that as two boxers launch their attacks, they invariably end up in a clinch. The same is true of almost all street fights. Two opponents begin with blows and quickly end up in a clinch. Indeed, most street fights start with the two protagonists so close to each other that many of the fights actually *begin* in the clinch. One might conclude from this observation that the clinch is a totally inevitable element of a real fight. There is certainly a lot of truth to this, but it is surprising how easily a totally unskilled fighter can enter a clinch if he is determined to do so. Often he will need to wade through a barrage of punches, but in most cases, he can eventually get to his goal. Nonetheless, it is important to know how to enter a clinch properly so that you can get there without submitting to too much damage.

Proactive Clinch Entries

One of the best ways to enter the clinch is to distract the opponent with some preliminary strikes. Whenever you throw a strike, your opponent must react in some way; otherwise, he gets hit. He is forced to block, move, or counter. These preliminary strikes therefore serve as a distraction so that you can follow up, close the distance, and safely enter into a clinch. When your opponent reacts, he will be preoccupied and unable to fight. At that time, you can quickly close distance and clinch.

One proactive method of clinching is to stand in front of your opponent, just out of contact range, thus keeping at a safe distance. Quickly lower your level—this leads your opponent to think you are about to shoot. Instead, come back up, and throw a quick jab to your opponent's head, stepping in as you do so. This move takes you closer to your opponent, and at the same time, it forces him to react defensively. Keep driving forward into a tight clinch.

Reactive Clinch Entries

Another means of entering a clinch is to use your opponent's aggressive forward movement as the way to close distance and clinch. Whenever an opponent comes forward to strike you, the distance between you is shortened so that it becomes easier to step into the clinch. However, you will need to cover up and block the incoming strikes, then lower your level slightly and step in, finally locking your opponent up in a clinch.

One of the most common forms of reactive clinch entries arises when an opponent shoots into you with the hope and intention of taking you down. As you sprawl in reaction to his takedown attempt, you both come up into a clinch. A particularly appropriate form of clinch here is the neck clinch. As you sprawl out on top of your opponent, wait for him to come back up. As he rises, lock up a tight neck clinch. It becomes easy now to throw strong knee strikes into him as he tries to get up. This kind of clinch work has been responsible for many knockout victories in MMA competition. It is doubtless one of the best ways to aggressively counter takedown attempts.

Figure 5.9 Transition from neck clinch to front-headlock clinch.

Off-Balancing *(Kuzushi)*

One of the most important skills in clinch fighting is that of off-balancing an opponent. This is the act of using your grip on your opponent to move him in such a way that he momentarily loses his balance. This skill is often overlooked by many fighters, yet it is the surest way to dominate an opponent in the clinch. Effective kuzushi allows you to overcome a larger and stronger opponent. There is a finesse and feeling to the skill of off-balancing that comes with constant practice. It is difficult to teach in words, and it must be experienced to be really understood.

It is no exaggeration to say that all takedowns, strikes, and submissions in the clinch phase of combat are easier to accomplish if they are preceded by off-balancing your opponent. The reason for this is simple. When people are taken out of balance, their preoccupation is recovering their balance and posture. This makes them vulnerable to strikes, submissions, and throws. Analysis of all the combat sports that allow fighting in the clinch quickly reveals that they all strongly emphasize the art of off-balancing an opponent as the setup for offense in the clinch. The founder of judo, Jigoro Kano, made kuzushi the *basis* of his modifications to classical jujitsu. He often demonstrated a profound understanding of kuzushi in his written word and his technique. His analysis of kuzushi remains to this day the best outline of the guiding principles that lie underneath the art of destroying an opponent's balance.

The guiding principle we speak of is that of lessening the degree of effort needed to throw an opponent, which is a clear attempt to act according to the maxim of "minimal effort, maximum effect." Acting on such a principle is what allows a smaller, weaker man to overcome a larger, stronger opponent. Efficient rationalization of physical effort is precisely the direction that Kano sought.

When it is explained to them in this way, most people can make sense of the abstract idea of kuzushi. However, they have a difficult time in applying the actual principle in a practical way as they grapple with an opponent. Thankfully, fighters can subscribe to some guiding rules of thumb that go a long way in directing a student during the long process of developing strong off-balancing skills. One useful beginning is to push when being pulled by your opponent and to pull when being pushed. Following this simple rule can immediately allow you to effectively interfere with your opponent's posture and balance.

Let's now divide off-balancing technique in the clinch into two basic kinds: linear and circular.

Linear Methods

Linear methods of off-balancing an opponent are usually performed from a collar clinch, neck clinch, or front-headlock clinch. By far the most common and effective means of linear off-balancing is the snapdown. The idea is to push straight back into your opponent to get him to push back. If he does not push back, he will be off-balanced straight backward. As you feel him pushing back into you, suddenly reverse direction and snap his head down toward your feet. Make sure your own feet move back so that you do not snap him into a takedown. Make sure you snap the head down, rather than slowly pull it down. Quite often, your opponent will try to regain his balance by quickly straightening back up after the snapdown, which makes it easy to off-balance him backward as he stands back up. It also makes it relatively easy to drop your level and shoot in for his legs, thereby securing a quick takedown.

Circular Methods

Circular methods are typically performed from upper-body clinches, such as the over-under clinch or double-underhooks clinch. The idea here is to rotate your opponent by pulling on one side of his body and pushing on the other. You can pull with either your underhook arm or overhook arm as you step back with the leg on the same side as you pull with. Your opponent will then be circled around and must therefore step to regain balance. You can take advantage of this momentary lapse of balance to strike or move into takedowns and submissions. A similar kind of off-balancing is done with the neck clinch. The idea is to jerk your opponent down and to one side as you step back with your leg on the same side toward the direction you are pulling your opponent. This move takes him off-balance and open to knee strikes.

Takedowns From the Clinch

Takedowns in MMA competition can be divided up into many categories. One of the most basic divisions is between takedowns that come out of the clinch and takedowns that come out of the free-movement phase as a result of shooting in on your opponent. Takedowns in the free-movement phase are almost always shots to the opponent's legs or hips whereas takedowns in the clinch often involve the upper body. This very reason is why Greco-Roman wrestlers, whose sport is centered on upper-body throws, have done so well at clinch fighting in MMA tournaments. Each kind of clinch has its own kind of takedown, appropriate to that specific clinch, and we shall examine some of the more effective takedowns that are used regularly in contemporary MMA. An important concept in clinch takedowns, however, is that of off-balancing the opponent as a precursor to the takedown. You will find it *much* easier to throw or take somebody down if you first take him out of balance. Constantly seek, then, to off-balance your opponent and to take advantage of this when throwing him or taking him down.

Over-Under Clinch to Inside Trip (Ouchi Gari)

The over-under clinch begets many takedowns. The problem, however, is that your opponent has exactly the same offensive possibilities as you do, since the over-under clinch is symmetrical. The key to a successful attack, then, is to take your opponent out of balance so that you can get through his defenses and take him down.

One of the best takedowns from the over-under clinch is the inside trip. This move has the advantage of being relatively safe, yet highly effective. From an over-under clinch, pull your opponent around you with your underhook arm so that he is forced to step toward you to regain his balance (figure 5.10a). This move widens your opponent's stance, making the execution easier. You may lock your hands in a tight bodylock as well. Step the foot of the leg that is on the same side as your underhook arm inside his legs, then sweep your foot along the mat in a circle around your opponent's foot (figure 5.10b). Drive your body weight into your opponent, forcing your weight into him. You can even drop your overarm down to the knee of his other leg, pulling it into you. This move takes your opponent straight to his back with you landing between his legs.

Figure 5.10 Inside trip takedown from over-under clinch.

Double Underhooks to Outside Trip (Kosoto Gaki)

One of the most effective takedowns in MMA competition is the bodylock from double underhooks, combined with an outside trip. Having secured double underhooks, lock your hands around your opponent's lower back (figure 5.11a). Pull his hips in tight while keeping your hips tight to his hips (figure 5.11b). There is some danger here of your opponent's countering with a headlock throw, so keep your hips low and tight to your opponent's hips. Step outside his leg, and hook it at the calf or even lower (figure 5.11c). Sag your hips into him as your arms pull his lower back in and down. Your opponent's posture will break backward, and you can step forward into a dominant top position as you land (figure 5.11d).

Rear Clinch to Rear Trip (Tani Otoshi)

Whenever you get behind your opponent, you have many opportunities to take him down. One of the simplest and most reliable methods is the rear trip *(tani otoshi)*. This move takes minimal strength and is difficult to stop. Hold your opponent's hips with both hands. Some people like to perform a bodylock around the waist (figure 5.12a). Squat down and extend a leg behind both of your opponent's legs (figure 5.12b). Pull his hips tight to yours, and trip him over

Figure 5.11 Outside trip takedown from double underhooks.

your extended leg. Land on your side (not flat on your back) alongside your opponent (figure 5.12c), and quickly get up on top of him.

Front Headlock to Cross-Ankle Pick

We have seen that the front headlock is one of the most dominating clinches in existence. Fighters can utilize many takedowns from this position, each of which is difficult for your opponent to resist. One particularly effective takedown from the front headlock is the cross-ankle pick.

From the front headlock (figure 5.13a), place your head deep under your opponent's trapped arm, then reach out with the arm that was around your opponent's arm. Use it to grasp your opponent's ankle (figure 5.13b). Do not grab high on the leg. As you pull on the ankle, drive across and under your opponent. This move puts your opponent under tremendous pressure and will eventually take him straight to his back. Keep driving and pulling on that ankle until you put your opponent in a tight pin, flat on his back (figure 5.13c). Retain your grip around your opponent's head throughout the move, with your hand on his chin.

Submission Holds

One of the great features of jujitsu is the use of submission holds in the clinch. Only a select few martial arts have this feature—judo, sambo, shootfighting,

and a few others. Submission holds add a new element to fighting in the clinch, an element that is lacking in many of the arts that emphasize clinch fighting. We can divide submissions in the clinch into two basic categories.

1. Standing submission holds. By far the most commonly seen example of standing submission holds is the guillotine choke. It has ended many MMA fights, and it remains one of the best ways to attack an opponent in a standing-grappling situation.

2. Submission holds that start in a standing position but finish on the ground. Most of the really effective standing submission holds that have proven successful in competition begin with the two fighters locked in a standing clinch. One fighter applies the lock by jumping into position and using the lock as a form of a takedown. It ends with both fighters on the ground and with the submission hold securely locked on. The flying guillotine is an excellent example of such a move. Another fine example is the rolling kimura lock *(ude garami)*, shown on pages 121-123.

As with all attacks in the clinch, the prerequisite to the successful use of submission holds in the clinch is sound off-balancing (kuzushi) and a solid working knowledge of the various clinches. By locking an opponent in a tight, controlling clinch and then taking him out of balance, the transition to a submission is much easier.

Figure 5.12 Rear trip takedown from rear clinch.

Figure 5.13 Front headlock to cross-ankle pick.

Collar-and-Elbow Clinch Into Standing Guillotine

The surest way to enter into a guillotine from the standing position is to utilize a snapdown. There are several types of snapdown, but the one from the collar-and-elbow clinch is one of the fastest and most efficient.

From the collar-and-elbow clinch, maneuver the hand that is on your opponent's elbow inside his arm to his biceps (figure 5.14a). This places your two arms inside your opponent's arms and gives you a slight positional advantage. From there, drive the forearm of your arm around your opponent's neck into his collarbone and push into him. As he begins to push back, snap his head down by jerking both arms down and forward, simultaneously stepping your feet back (figure 5.14b). This move takes your opponent's head down below yours, allowing you to quickly wrap an arm around your opponent's neck and apply a guillotine (figure 5.14c). Fighters use several ways to lock up a guillotine choke; each has its respective advantages and disadvantages. The method shown here, the figure-four guillotine, is particularly tight and quick.

Figure 5.14 Collar-and-elbow clinch to standing guillotine.

Front-Headlock Clinch Into Flying Guillotine

The front headlock is truly one of the dominant clinches. It can be used to set up many powerful strikes and takedowns, and it is equally useful in setting up submission holds, which mostly involve choking attacks to the neck. The flying guillotine is a submission hold that has been used with tremendous success in MMA competition. In fact, it is one of the favorite moves of Renzo Gracie. As such, the flying guillotine can be used in many situations; here we look at its application as part of an attack from the front-headlock clinch.

However you find yourself in a front headlock, either as a result of defending a shot to the legs by your opponent or as a result of a snapdown on your opponent, you can go straight into a flying guillotine. The key is to get a tight initial grip on the neck and arm of your opponent. To do so, grab the wrist of the arm that encircles your opponent's neck, and pull it through toward the armpit of your opponent's trapped arm (figure 5.15a). Bring both hands up toward your sternum. Place your leg around your opponent's waist and lightly jump up (figure 5.15b), locking your legs around his waist in a closed-guard position, as shown in figure 5.15c (the guard position will be seen again in the ground-fighting sections of this book in chapters 6 and 7). From here, arch your back and squeeze tightly on your opponent's neck, keeping your head close to your opponent's head.

This move puts a tight choke in place that is difficult to defend when properly applied. It does not matter whether your opponent falls to the ground or stays in standing position as you apply the choke. The flying guillotine works equally well in both cases.

Rear Clinch Into Rear Naked Sleeper Choke (Hadaka Jime)

Once you get behind an opponent, you can attempt the sleeper hold, a highly effective stranglehold often used in MMA competition. You have two basic choices in applying the sleeper hold from the rear clinch. First, you can jump onto your opponent's back, lock your feet around his waist, then apply the hold (figure 5.16). Second, you can pull your opponent backward and down to the mat, placing both feet in his hips to stabilize your position (but do not lock your feet if you go the ground!), then apply the hold. Although both moves are regularly used in competition, it is probably fair to say that the latter is a safer option to use because it minimizes the danger of being hurt, should your opponent slam himself backward to attempt an escape.

The sleeper hold is also an effective way to end a fight, both in competition and in a street altercation. It renders your opponent unconscious in a matter of seconds, provided he doesn't submit. To lock it in place, reach around your opponent's neck from behind, until your elbow is right under his Adam's apple. Place your hand on the biceps of your other arm. Your other hand slides over the top of your opponent's head, down to the back of the head (figure 5.16c). Squeeze your elbows together, keeping your head close to his. This maneuver prevents blood from getting to your opponent's brain; it forces him to submit or risk unconsciousness.

All strangleholds work on this principle of cutting off blood to the brain. As such, they are dangerous. Make sure that you practice them with caution in the presence of a qualified instructor. Most important, when they take effect, stop immediately. Release your partner as soon as he signals submission by tapping the mat or your body.

Figure 5.15 Front headlock to flying guillotine.

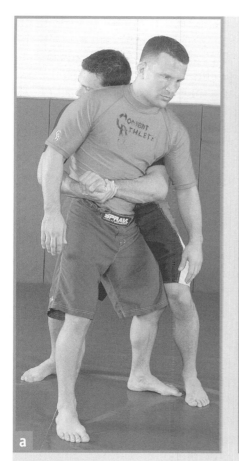  

Figure 5.16 Rear clinch to rear naked sleeper choke.

Striking in the Clinch

Most fighting styles that emphasize the use of strikes to win fights only use striking technique in the free-movement phase of combat. In fact, in striking combat sports such as Western boxing, kickboxing, and many forms of karate, striking ceases once a clinch is locked up, which is largely due to the limitations placed on striking methods in these sports. In boxing, for example, only the fists may be used to strike the opponent. Once the arms are tied up in a clinch, punching becomes difficult; hence, there is little chance for clinch fighting, even if it were within the rules. The same is true of the kicks utilized in Western kickboxing.

The result is that many people think of using the clinch as a way to prevent someone from striking you. To an extent, this is true. If a clinch is held tightly, it can certainly prevent someone from punching and kicking you. However, if specialized clinch-fighting technique is used, effective punching in the clinch is possible. If knee and elbow strikes are used (some MMA events prohibit elbow strikes), then striking in the clinch can be *very* effective.

Indeed, an ever-increasing number of victories are now being won in variations of the clinch in MMA matches. The keys to effective striking in the clinch are the following:

- *Appropriate selection of clinch.* Some clinches are more suited to striking attacks than others. In MMA matches, the majority of knockout victories in the clinch are undoubtedly won in the neck clinch and the collar-and-elbow clinch. The reason for this tendency is that both these clinches allow a fighter to control an opponent's head in such a way that powerful knee and elbow strikes can de directed to the jaw. The beauty of these clinches is that they allow solid control of an opponent by controlling a part of the anatomy (the head) that is crucial to movement. The old adage "where the head goes, the body follows" is important in clinch fighting. At the same time, these clinches allow sufficient space between you and your opponent so that you can generate maximum force in utilizing a striking technique. The result is a high knockout rate.

- *The attainment of a dominant clinch.* If you are locked up in a position where your opponent has a dominant clinch on you, then your chances of successfully striking him are low. To strike your opponent, you must attain at least a neutral clinch. If possible, attain a truly dominant clinch to aid your striking attempts.

- *Off-balancing your opponent.* The more you can keep your opponent off-balance, the easier it is to strike him, and the harder it will be for him to strike back and defend himself. You must constantly look to keep your opponent in a state of confusion by disrupting his balance because then his attention will be focused on recovering his balance. As a result, he becomes unable to strike you while at the same time being open to your own strikes.

- *Appropriate striking method.* The clinch requires its own striking methods that are quite different from striking in the free-movement phase of combat. In general, the knees and elbows are the most efficient means of striking in the clinch. (Headbutts are also highly effective; however, they are banned in most contemporary MMA tournaments.)

Case Study in Clinch Fighting: Vanderlei Silva

Few fighters in MMA have had the success in clinch fighting as experienced by the Brazilian superstar Vanderlei Silva. Silva has a relatively simple clinch game that has proven highly effective. It is centered on two types of clinch, the over-under clinch and the neck clinch. He uses the over-under clinch whenever he finds himself in trouble, either from a strong punch attack or takedown attempt. Having stopped the attack, he begins to throw heavy knees into his opponent's abdomen to create space. He then breaks the clinch, and during the transition from the clinch, he looks for opportunities to strike.

It is with the neck clinch, however, that Silva has had the most success. Coming from a background of Muay Thai kickboxing, where the neck clinch is strongly emphasized, Silva constantly looks to secure both hands on the opponent's head and neck when-

ever a takedown fails. By sprawling out on top of a takedown, Silva often forces his opponents to get back up to their feet. As they do so, their head level is low, which makes it easy to quickly clamp on a tight neck clinch as the opponent struggles back up. At this moment, Silva simply throws powerful knee strikes into the jaw of the opponent. These strikes often result in knockout or heavy damage. This is by far the most common means of knockout victory in the clinch phase of combat. It relies on a sound combination of a wise clinch selection and a vulnerable target. In other words, the neck clinch is a dominant clinch and thus a superb means of setting up strikes, especially when the opponent is off-balanced and preoccupied with getting back up, thus being unable to effectively defend himself.

- *Creating space in which to strike.* One of the keys to effective striking in the clinch (and one that few people understand) is the delicate balance between control and the creation of space. When you lock up an opponent in a tight clinch, you can control his movement. The tighter the clinch, the more control you have over him, and the more difficult it becomes to strike you. Unfortunately, however, the same is true of you. The tighter you hold him, the harder it is for you to hit him effectively—since now you lack the space required to hit effectively. To strike with power, you need to create space between you and your opponent. This task is done in different ways, depending on what type of clinch you have.

A special note must be added to this section on striking in the clinch. In MMA events, a high percentage of successful strikes happen immediately after a clinch breaks. When this happens, your opponent becomes distracted by the change in phase and is thus vulnerable to a quick strike. Fighters should constantly look for the opportunity to hit just as the clinch breaks during the transition back to free movement. This is a time when most people have their hands down, and they are tired off-balance, and unsuspecting.

Striking in the Over-Under Clinch

We have noted the fact that the over-under clinch is by far the most commonly used form of clinch in MMA competition. We have also noted that it is a neutral clinch, insofar that both you and your opponent have the same position and thus the same offensive options. As such, the over-under position does not offer dominant striking opportunities. This does not mean, however, that you cannot strike effectively in this position. It simply means that an opponent of roughly equal skill level and size can strike you just as easily as you can strike him. One of the prime reasons that many MMA fighters use the over-under clinch is to prevent the opponent from striking effectively. This reason alone should tell you something about the difficulty of striking in this particular clinch. But because it is so common and because so much time is spent there, it is worth looking at striking options, even if the over-under clinch is not the best place to engage in striking.

The most common striking method is to use your overhook arm to strike your opponent in the ribs. Hit him with a hook punch. Keep your arm sharply bent, and get your hips behind the blow. This move may not necessarily knock anybody out, but it does punish him over time and make life in the clinch unpleasant. Knee strikes are also wise options. The best way to do them in the over-under clinch is to lift his underhook arm at the elbow with your overhook arm. This maneuver opens his ribs to knee strikes. You can also look to throw a knee strike over his overhook arm and hit his face. This skill is especially important when your opponent brings his head down.

Striking in the Neck Clinch

The neck clinch is one of the best for striking an opponent. If your two arms are inside your opponent's arms, locked around the head and neck, you can often knock your opponent out. The key is to first create space in which to throw a knee strike to the jaw.

To do this, explosively straighten your arms out so that your opponent is thrown out at arm's length while you still have control of his head. Skip your legs into a lunge position with one knee back (that will be the leg you throw the knee strike with, since the rear leg can generate more power). Now there is sufficient distance to smash a knee to his jaw. Be sure to pull your opponent's head down into the strike to add power while at the same time jerking him off-balance. As soon as the strike lands, return to a tight neck clinch with your opponent's forehead pressed into your chest and arms. Repeat the process as necessary.

In some MMA events, elbow strikes are allowed, and the neck clinch is a great platform to use these. Hold on to the head with one hand, and use the other arm to whip elbow strikes into your opponent. This technique is much easier when your arms are inside your opponent's arms, so apply elbow strikes when the opportunity arises.

Striking in the Front-Headlock Clinch

The front headlock is without a doubt one of the best positions for a fighter to lock up an opponent so that he can strike with impunity. Many knockouts and referee's stoppages have occurred in this clinch position—more than any other, in fact. Therefore, it is no exaggeration to say that a tight front-headlock clinch is as dangerous as the mounted position is (we shall look at the mounted position in the ground-fighting chapters, chapters 6 and 7). The front headlock is also much easier to attain than the mounted position, and this ease applies to both the standing position as well as the ground game.

But what makes the front headlock so dangerous is the fact that your opponent's head is tightly controlled in a position that places it directly in the path of your knee strikes. His head is ultimately immobilized, and thus it takes the full brunt of the strikes. At the same time, your opponent has little opportunity to defend the incoming blows since movement and arm position is totally controlled. The fighter can perform knee strikes that hit directly on the top of the opponent's cranium and consequently do catastrophic damage in short order.

Although it is certainly possible to strike from the front headlock in the standing position, it is much more effective to take the front headlock to the mat before you begin striking. This adjustment creates a much more stable platform from which to deliver your blows. To take a front headlock from the standing position to the ground, you simply throw your legs back and sprawl out. Another method is to step back with both feet, and lower your level by sagging your hips down and circling your opponent down to the mat.

Breaking Out of a Clinch

For every type of clinch, fighters have a number of methods of escape. The key is to select the correct escape for each type of clinch. We shall now look at some of the more effective means of breaking out of the main clinches that are utilized in MMA competition.

Breaking Out of a Collar-and-Elbow Clinch

The collar-and-elbow clinch is easy to enter into and is thus one of the most common forms of a clinch. It is important for fighters to have a quick and simple form of escape so that they can get out before their opponent can control them and go on the offensive. One of the best escapes is a simple *outside Russian*.

When your opponent grabs you behind the neck, grab his arm at the wrist and triceps as shown (figure 5.17a). Push his arm across and control it by hugging it to your chest as you circle around toward the arm you are grabbing (figure 5.17b). His hand will slide off your neck. Do not let go of the elbow, but continue to push it across and control it. Your opponent no longer has a grip on you, and you can easily back away now and return to the free-movement phase (figure 5.17c).

Figure 5.17 Escaping collar-and-elbow clinch.

Breaking Out of an Over-Under Clinch

The over-under clinch is almost certainly the most common clinch in MMA. One of the best ways to get out of it is the *forearm post*. In this clinch, most of your opponent's control over you comes from his underhooking arm. It is thus this arm that you must control to get out.

Place the hand of your overhook arm on the forearm of your opponent's underhook arm, close to the elbow (figure 5.18a). Push down. This negates his grip on you. Start to move slightly away from him; pull your underhook out (figure 5.18b), posting the underhook arm on your opponent's chest to push away and escape (figure 5.18c).

Figure 5.18 Escaping over-under clinch.

Breaking Out of a Double-Underhooks Clinch

We now come to the question of breaking out of dominant clinches. This feat is always more difficult, since dominant clinches give your opponent more control of your body than do neutral clinches. One of the best ways to escape the troublesome double-underhooks clinch is the *chin post*.

As your opponent locks up a double-underhooks clinch, place both hands under his chin and push (figure 5.19). At the same time, sag your hips back and away from your opponent. This maneuver breaks even the strongest lock around your body. This move is also particularly useful when you are pinned against a fence or the ropes (or in a street fight, against a wall), or when you are locked up in a tight bearhug.

Figure 5.19 Escaping double-underhooks clinch.

Breaking Out of a Neck Clinch

The neck clinch is one of the most intimidating clinches to be caught in. Your opponent can fire a barrage of knees and elbows at you while throwing you about and destroying your balance. One natural response to this predicament is to lower your level and attempt to duck out from under the neck clinch. This move may work on occasion, but it is more likely that a skilled clinch fighter will connect with a powerful knee strike as you attempt to duck out, which will usually result in a knockout or heavy damage. For this reason, avoid trying to duck out from the neck clinch! A much better alternative is the *cross-chin post*.

When locked in a tight neck clinch, you want to stay as upright as possible so that you can defend knee attacks. Reach up and over your opponent's arms with one hand, and place your palm on his chin, thumb down (figure 5.20a). Push across his face, over both his arms, turning his jaw away from you and destroying his ability to hit hard. As his head moves away from you, reach up

Figure 5.20 Escaping neck clinch.

with your other hand and place it on the crown of his head, pushing it toward the floor, bringing the other hand up to the crown of the head to assist (figure 5.20b). Your opponent is now bent over himself whereas you are upright. This puts you in an excellent position to throw your own knee strikes (figure 5.20c) or, if you prefer, to lock a front headlock or guillotine choke.

Breaking Out of a Rear Clinch

Skilled grapplers often work their way behind their opponent, knowing that this position affords them considerable positional advantage. They seek to lock their hands around their opponent's waist for control, then they look for takedowns or submissions. One useful way to get out of this potentially danger-ous situation is to attack your opponent's arms in a tight lock, which goes by several names in different grappling styles. Often, it is referred to as *kimura, keylock, double wristlock,* or *ude garami.*

When your opponent locks his arms around your waist to control you, look down to see which hand is on top of the other. This is the arm you will attack. Begin by lowering your hips then moving out and away from your opponent. This maneuver makes your base more solid and lessens the danger of your being picked up and slammed as you attempt the move. Grab the wrist of your opponent's uppermost arm—if you are attacking his right arm, grab the wrist with your left hand (and vice versa)—then place the wrist of your other arm under the elbow of the arm you are attacking. Push his wrist down, using your wrist under his elbow as a fulcrum (figure 5.21a). Thread your hand under his elbow, and grab your own wrist. This move puts you in position to perform the

(continued)

Figure 5.21 Escaping rear clinch.

Figure 5.21 *(continued)*

lock (figure 5.21b). Break his grip around you by pushing his wrist down with both hands and lowering your hips. Turn around to face your opponent, maintaining the lock on his arm. This position puts great pressure on his trapped arm.

Having broken the lock and turned around, you now have a choice. First, you can continue holding the lock. Jump toward your opponent, placing one foot deep between his legs (figure 5.21c). Sit down, and roll your opponent cleanly over you and into the same lock on the ground (figure 5.21d). Aid the move by flicking your opponent over with the foot you placed between his legs (figure 5.21e-g). Your second choice is if you wish to avoid fighting on the ground. In that case, you can simply let go and return to the free-movement phase.

Breaking Out of a Front-Headlock Clinch

We have seen that the front headlock is one of the most dominating clinches. If your opponent is skilled, it can be a difficult position to break out of. One of the best escapes to it. however, is the *short-arm drag*. Using your trapped arm, reach up to grab the opponent's elbow (figure 5.22a; you will be grabbing the elbow of the arm that is encircling your neck). If you cannot reach the elbow, use your other hand to help bring it down within reach. Having grabbed the elbow, drag it hard across and in front of you, then circle behind your opponent. You can punch your other arm over your opponent's back as you attempt the move (figure 5.22b). Should your opponent take the front headlock to the ground, the same move works equally well on the mat.

Figure 5.22 Escaping front-headlock clinch.

CLINCH DRILLS

It is one thing to see and practice a set of moves in the clinch, but to really fight well in the clinch, you need to be able to put moves into effect in a sparring situation with a live, resisting partner. A number of useful drills enable fighters to develop the skills, attributes, and sensitivity needed in a real fight. To keep the drill moving, set a level-appropriate time limit on each drill. Keep in mind that both drills described here are tiring. Initially, you may only be able to work hard for a few minutes. In time, however, you can set rounds of five minutes and work hard with sound technique throughout.

Sumo Drill

The sumo drill is an effective way to develop strength, speed, and reflexes in the clinch. More important, it develops the ability to create movement in your opponent and off-balance him. It is a physical drill that quickly proves exhausting to the beginner. As you develop skills, however, you will substitute technique for strength and therefore will last much longer. More than anything else, the sumo drill develops the skill of hand-fighting, which is the battle for superior hand and arm position that is so important in attaining a solid position and setting up takedowns. You will soon find that the drill is much easier when you can get your hands inside your opponent's hands.

The drill itself consists of you and your partner standing inside a circle. The object is to push the other fellow out of the circle. Each time someone goes out, a point is scored. Another way to score is to snap your opponent down so that he goes down to a knee or a hand. In this case, a point is scored as well. As you attempt to push your opponent out of the circle, he naturally pushes back. This reaction sets up your snapdowns. Soon, you will develop the ability to push and snap your opponent completely out of balance. This ability—with the resultant gains in stamina, strength, and coordination—proves vital in live fighting. Once you can readily off-balance an opponent, you will find it much easier to strike, take down, or submit an opponent in the clinch.

Pummeling Drill

A truly vital skill in the clinch is the ability to work your way into a more dominant position as you grapple. The single best way to develop this skill is the pummeling drill.

Begin in an over-under clinch with your partner. This position is a neutral clinch. The idea is to work from it into a dominant clinch. A point is scored every time you either get behind your opponent to a rear clinch; bring his head down and secure a front headlock or guillotine; or lift both his feet off the ground. You will find it much easier to lift your opponent if you first succeed in getting under both his arms with your arms (a double-underhooks clinch). This move gives great control over your opponent's lower back and hence his whole body, making the lift much easier. Your opponent will therefore not let you secure double underhooks, but he will instead fight hard to secure his own double underhooks. It thus becomes a grueling battle for positional dominance. Should your opponent lock his arms under yours, you need to move your hips back and get square to your opponent, then swim your arms back under his arms to recover your position. Failure to do so results in your opponent's crunching you down to your back.

The pummeling drill is physically exhausting and will get you in great shape for the tough work of upper-body clinch fighting. Nothing else can prepare you so well for the all-important struggle for positional control in the standing position.

You can also play a similar game with the neck clinch. The idea is to lock up a neck clinch on your partner and to keep your hands in position with both arms inside his arms, giving you inside control and, hence, a measure of dominance. Your partner will seek to break your dominant clinch position by swimming his own hands, one at a time, inside yours. This move allows him to lock up his own neck clinch with his arms inside yours, thus reversing the dominant clinch. Each of you must try to prevent the other from maintaining the dominant inside-arm position.

Also try to maintain an upright stance with your hips in tight to your partner. Remember that one of the main uses for the neck clinch is to control an opponent's head so that you can throw knee strikes at him. If your head is low, then the chances of a knockout knee to the jaw are quite high. Therefore, keep your stance upright, your hips in, and your head high for this particular drill. If you are bent over, you are not only vulnerable to knee strikes, but it will also be easy to be off-balanced by snapdowns and pulling on the head.

As you become more confident, you can begin incorporating some knee strikes as you work the neck clinch. Do not perform this exercise too hard. Aim for the ribs, stomach, and thighs with light contact. If you hit too hard, injuries are the obvious result, which will quickly put a stop to your training and, hence, your progress. The emphasis is on controlling the opponent's movement and balance while maintaining your own. Once this is done, the knee strikes are the easy part; therefore, there is no need to hit hard in everyday training.

By working hard on these drills, you quickly develop the most important skills and attributes that allow you to fight successfully in the clinch. Your ability to control the movement and balance of your opponent, while maintaining your own, will dramatically increase. This is really the essence of successful fighting in the clinch. All the offensive techniques in clinch fighting—strikes, takedowns, and submissions—rely on this control of movement and balance. Soon, you will apply the positional strategy of seeking better position and control in a live situation, rather than merely repeating moves with no resistance. This level is as close to the pressure that you will experience in a real fight and is thus excellent preparation. It is really the equivalent of sparring in the clinch, and it plays the same crucial role that live sparring plays in the free-movement phase.

Ground Fighting

Before the reemergence of mixed martial arts (MMA) competition in the early 1990s in North America and Japan, ground fighting was totally overlooked by the mainstream martial arts community. No one really talked about it or paid any real attention to it, and the few arts that did engage in any serious ground work—judo, sambo, wrestling, and shootfighting—were relatively unpopular. Wrestling, in fact, was not even seen as a martial art, but as a school sport almost irrelevant to real fighting.

Unknown to virtually the entire martial arts world was the presence of Brazilian jiu jitsu, a variant of jujitsu perfected over time by the Gracie family of Brazil. They devoted a huge amount of time to the study of ground fighting and put it to practice in many sanctioned and nonsanctioned fights in their native land. This practical experience put them far ahead of every other art in the ground phase of combat. In Brazil, the Gracies forged a great reputation as fighters, and they experienced tremendous success in local MMA competition. This local fame, however, did not cross over into the mainstream martial arts outside of Brazil.

All this changed when the first MMA tournament, the Ultimate Fighting Championship (UFC), was held in 1993 in Denver, Colorado. To most martial artists, this tournament was a revolutionary concept. The idea was to match different styles of fighting against each other with *very* few rules; in fact, only eye gouging was prohibited in the first UFCs. This format was the logical means to settle the age-old dispute about which style of fighting was the most efficient, a question that has run throughout the history of the martial arts. Few people are even aware of the long history of MMA events, which had run throughout the early 20th century in Europe, North America, and Japan. Memories are short, however, and few people in the audience knew of the Fusen-ryu challenges, the work of Maeda and Yukio Tani, or the American catch wrestlers. Even fewer had heard of the Gracies and their 60-year history of MMA prowess.

To the shock of the mainstream martial arts community (and in many cases, to the dismay), the action was totally dominated by a little-known jiu jitsu stylist, Royce Gracie. What was really astounding to most people was the frail appearance of Gracie, a mere 170 pounds, with a thoroughly unimposing physique. Most of the other competitors were rugged looking and had impressive credentials—yet Gracie had little difficulty in making them submit. Not only did Gracie defeat these powerful and dangerous opponents, he did so with little effort and with an absolute minimum of blood and violence. He won through the use of submission holds, a method of victory little used in the mainstream martial arts community, where the emphasis was on striking prowess. People were expecting a bludgeoning match, with heavy hitting as the means to victory. They were stunned to see such strong men submit to innocuous-looking locks and chokes that drew no blood.

Remarkable as this was, it was only a prelude to a long run of MMA tournaments that were totally dominated by grappling styles. In fight after fight, a pattern was seen. Fights would begin with a flurry of punches and kicks; they would quickly go into a clinch; then they would finally go to the ground. Once on the ground, fighters versed in the grappling arts had a massive advantage and won easily. In a short time, it dawned on the martial arts world that the most overlooked elements of fighting—grappling and ground fighting—may well be the most important elements of fighting.

Foremost among the grappling styles in early MMA events was Brazilian jiu jitsu, which concentrated on ground grappling almost to the exclusion of everything else. Specializing in the art of attaining positional dominance and then submission, the Brazilians swept the field and gained a reputation for invincibility in MMA combat. Almost overnight the martial arts world was turned upside down, and ground grappling skill became the measure of fighting skill. More than anything else, these early MMA events demonstrated how vital the ground phase of combat was in real fighting, and it showed just how overlooked it had become in the contemporary martial arts world. In addition, a great many myths of the martial arts were exposed as untenable. Traditional concepts such as "one strike, one kill" were seen as impossible under combat conditions. The oft-heard claim that "I would never be taken down to the ground" rang very hollow indeed. MMA competition was like a blast of wind that blew away all the dust and smoke that had accumulated in the martial arts, leaving a clear view of what was important and workable in real combat.

TWO VIEWS OF THE GROUND PHASE

When MMA competition first revealed the importance of the ground phase of combat, there were two types of reaction. Grapplers received it with delight, a vindication of their style's effectiveness. Traditional strikers, however, were generally horrified, since ground combat largely negated their game. Over the last decade, this dichotomy in viewpoints has persisted, even with the evolution of MMA. In fact, most fighters still have a definite preference for either the ground game or the standing game; only a small percentage are equally comfortable in both. This loyalty to style is due to the fact that most fighters come from a background in one fighting style that puts an emphasis on one phase of combat. Boxers and kickboxers tend to prefer the standing game; grapplers, the ground game. Depending on their background, fighters still have a definite tendency to consider the ground phase of combat as either heaven or hell, which leaves us with two fundamental outlooks.

1. The first outlook is that the ground phase is the best place to take a single-combat, weaponless fight, since this is where the greatest degree of positional control is possible. This is the means by which a fighter can negate an opponent's striking offense and by which he can set up submission holds to allow the fight to be won efficiently. Obviously, this attitude is the trademark of grappling specialists. We saw that the history of modern grappling styles of jujitsu have been the prime examples of this outlook. Mataemon Tanabe, Yukio Tani, Maeda, and more than anyone else, the Gracie family, have all extolled the ground phase as the way to dominate and control a fight.

2. The second outlook is that the ground phase is an inevitable, but undesirable, phase of combat. A fighter needs to know how to get out of the ground phase and back into the standing position as quickly and efficiently as possible. Failing this, he needs to know enough grappling skills to survive on the ground—such as how to avoid submission holds and dangerous pins—until the round ends or the referee intervenes. This outlook tends to be that of fighters who come from a strong background in striking. Their real interest is in keeping the fight in their favored phase of combat, free motion. They recognize, however,

the likelihood of being taken out of that phase and into a ground fight—hence, the need to address the question of ground grappling.

A third outlook that does not merit serious attention is often voiced by many in the traditional martial arts community. This is the claim that the ground is the worst place to be in a real fight and that, consequently, they would simply never go there. This attitude was common in the early days of MMA, but it has since been rejected by virtually all rational martial artists. Experience has proven time and time again the inevitability of ground combat in a real fight. To claim that you simply would not go down is to turn your eyes from the massive store of empirical evidence that demonstrates the contrary. Even those who do not favor ground combat almost always concede the need to address this phase of combat seriously, at least for the purpose of avoiding it as much as possible. As such, we need not consider this third attitude as being relevant.

MODERN JUJITSU AND THE GROUND PHASE

It is quite clear that the modern styles of jujitsu—from the inception of Fusen ryu through the variations of Maeda and the Gracies—have gone in a direction that is radically different from the rest of the martial arts world. No other styles put so much focus on the ground phase of combat, so it is worth asking how they came to choose the ground as the best place to take a fight. To answer this question is to outline the basis of the whole theory of phases of combat and positional dominance, the two cornerstones of modern jujitsu.

The core theory of modern jujitsu is the idea that fighting can be broken into distinct phases, each of which is significantly different from each other. The major differences between each phase require that fighters develop a separate set of skills and attributes to succeed in either phase. As a result, it often happens that a fighter is strong in one or two phases of combat, but alarmingly weak in another. People such as Tanabe, Maeda, and the Gracies all noted that most fighting styles were weak in ground fighting, which made fighters who subscribed to such methods vulnerable to a skilled ground grappler once the fight entered the ground phase.

An additional factor is the idea that the most efficient tactical method to employ in a real fight is to constantly place yourself in a position where you can freely attack your opponent while at the same time he cannot attack you. Applying this method is rather like placing an opponent in a pair of handcuffs before fighting him. A similar result can be achieved by attaining a dominant position on your opponent. The easiest place to attain this kind of positional dominance and control is on the ground because the ground gives a platform on which to pin an opponent and restrict his movement. Add to this the fact that most people do not by nature move efficiently on the ground (since we spend most of our waking lives in an upright position), and you can see that the ground is a wise place to implement this positional strategy.

Finally, there is the simple fact that the ground fight is inevitable in a real fight. A disproportionate number of fights end up on the ground because a fighter's most realistic means of securing victory specifically result from his taking a fight to the ground. For example, if you are hit by a powerful striker, you will be knocked to the ground. If you are thrown by a powerful judo player, you will be thrown to the ground. If a much bigger assailant grabs you in a bearhug, you will trip and fall to the ground. These incidents demonstrate why the ground phase is such an inevitable destination in most fights. It makes tremendous sense, then, for fighters to focus significant attention on this phase of combat and elevate its importance in training.

TRANSITION FROM STANDING POSITION TO THE GROUND PHASE

A standing fight can go to the ground in several ways, and each occurs often in the course of a real fight. More often than not, the transition is a quick one, so be ready! A fight can enter the ground phase as a result of any of the following scenarios:

- *A knockdown as a result of strikes.* This transition to the ground is particularly difficult to deal with since you are usually stunned by the strike. While on the ground, you must recover your wits and defend yourself. Quite often, your opponent does not even follow you down, but instead stands over you and kicks you in the legs.

- *A takedown from a long-range shot.* This means is favored by many wrestlers and jujitsu fighters. It played a seminal role in early MMA events, when observers were stunned with the apparent ease with which grapplers shot in on their surprised opponents from long range and tackled their legs.

- *A takedown or fall from the clinch.* Quite often, two fighters lock up in a clinch while exchanging strikes, or as a result of a high shot. Once in a clinch, a fight has a high chance of going to the ground. Sometimes this is due to the deliberate intent of one of the fighters; that is, he intentionally attempts a takedown. Other times, it is the inevitable result of the extreme pressure that two fighters exert on each other when they battle at full power, with no referee intervention to stop the clinch. More often than not, the two simply trip and fall to the ground. This is the pattern of most MMA fights, and it is even more common among untrained people in street fights, where the two combatants lack balance and athleticism.

You can see then that the likelihood is high that via one of these routes, the fight ultimately goes to the ground—hence the importance of ground training that most contemporary MMA fighters adopt.

CHARACTERISTICS OF THE GROUND PHASE

The early MMA events certainly showed the martial arts world how ground combat was really different from the more familiar phases of combat. Quite often, one fighter would be in trouble until the fight went to the ground. Then, in a total reversal of fortunes, the previously dominant fighter would be quickly defeated on the ground. The reason for this was the sheer difference between the standing and ground positions. This does not mean that there is no overlap between standing and ground skills; however, the differences are significant enough to mean that the nature of the fight does change drastically when it's taken to the ground. This transition is what caused so many fighters who were talented in the standing phases to fail completely in the ground phase of combat. We can enhance our understanding of the ground phase by pointing out the major changes that occur when a fight goes to the ground.

The biggest difference between the ground phase and any other phase of combat is that the degree of positional control and dominance increases dramatically on the ground. There are a number of reasons why this happens.

- *Mobility on the ground is difficult for most people*. The reason for this is simple. We spend the majority of our waking, adult lives in standing or seated positions. Consequently, most of the movement skills we use every day are done while standing. Most people never learn the skills of efficient movement in a supine position (lying on the back). As a result, when they are put on the ground, they move poorly, expending great amounts of energy with few results. Remember: Ground fighters are made, not born. If you are to succeed on the ground, you have to learn the correct movement patterns in the ground phase of combat.

- *When inexperienced ground fighters move, they generally do so in ways that expose them to greater danger*. Without a clear understanding of the possible positions in a ground fight, movement on the ground is usually poorly directed. Often, you will see powerful, explosive fighters who are not well versed in ground fighting use a tremendous amount of energy to get out of one bad position, only to go into another *worse* position. This results from the lack of knowledge and ground training. If they only knew the merits of the various positions, which ones to avoid and which to strive for, they could save themselves.

- *The ground itself plays a critical role*. The ground itself provides an effective platform on which to pin an opponent and prevent him from easy movement. It allows the efficient use of body weight to trap an opponent between your body and the ground itself. In a standing position, fighters can accomplish a similar trick by pushing an opponent against a wall. The wall (like the ground) now plays the role as an inhibitor of movement. But the situation on the ground is even more controlling than the wall because your full body weight (with the aid of gravity) can be pressed on your opponent to crush his movement.

- *Because greater control is possible on the ground, submission holds become crucial*. Locking on a submission hold is difficult as long as your opponent can move about. Since movement can be greatly restricted on the ground, the use of submission holds is far easier. Powerful control over the movement of an opponent is the precursor to most submission holds. This tactic is easiest when fighters perform it on the ground.

- *Striking on the ground is significantly different from striking in the standing position*. In the standing position, successful striking is largely a matter of the explosive application of body weight at the correct time and distance. This is not the case on the ground. In ground fighting, successful striking is the result of superior position and control. Timing, so crucial in standing striking, is almost irrelevant in ground striking, since your opponent cannot move around freely. Distance is a simple factor to maintain on the ground for the same reason. Because hip movement is much more difficult for fighters to attain in the ground-fighting positions, striking tends to be restricted to a battering effect, rather than the possibility of an instantaneous knockout.

VICTORY IN THE GROUND PHASE

We have taken pains to point out that the ground phase of combat is the place where most fights are won and lost. When two unskilled fighters clash, they almost always end up on the ground. The bigger, stronger, more aggressive fighter normally prevails, especially if he lands on top, but this tendency changes when skill and technique are factored into the equation. A skilled grappler can use knowledge of positional pins and escapes to evade and control an opponent. In addition, he can employ submission holds to lock or strangle an opponent and thus swiftly defeat even a larger, stronger fighter. In fact, if a skilled grappler begins the ground fight underneath his opponent, it is still quite possible for him to prevail and attain victory, though he may have to work a little harder to do so. This type of occurrence has been shown numerous times in MMA events, and it is no longer a surprise to most martial artists. The two most common means of victory in a ground fight, then, are the following:

- *Attaining a dominating position, then striking one's opponent with sufficient power and relentlessness to make him submit, to knock him out, to force a referee's stoppage, or to win a judge's decision.* This strategy can be done with varying degrees of sophistication. If you are far larger and stronger than your opponent, it is usually enough to attain any kind of top position and pound away at your opponent. This "ground and pound" methodology is popular among wrestlers in MMA events and has certainly had some success. It has also had many notable failures, however, especially when the size of the two combatants was similar. A much more sensible approach is to employ the positional strategy central to modern jujitsu. The idea is to constantly seek a better, more dominating position, from where a striking attack is not likely to be stopped or countered by a skilled opponent. This position greatly increases the effectiveness of your striking attack and makes it unlikely that your opponent will be able to interrupt your attack with submission attempts.

- *Attaining a dominating position, then looking to finish the fight via a submission hold.* This is one of the most characteristic features of the various grappling styles, especially in modern jujitsu. These submission holds comprise an impressive element—a remarkable demonstration of artistry to win a fight in a bloodless display of pure grappling skill. This is one sense in which modern jujitsu is an *art* form, rather than a bloody, gladiatorial locking of horns in which only strength and endurance prevail.

In actual combat, these two approaches are usually mixed together. It is almost always the case that your opponent will have strong defenses to the basic submission holds. (This is not the case in a street fight, however, since your opponent will almost certainly have no grappling training). Often, this necessitates the use of strikes to open up his defenses. As he reacts to a barrage of strikes, his limbs become exposed, making the application of submission holds much easier.

STRATEGY AND TACTICS IN THE GROUND PHASE

A general strategy lies behind the great success of jujitsu in MMA combat. We have already seen the broad outline of that strategy; now it is time to get into the specifics. Once a fight goes to the ground, whether by accident or design, the two combatants can fall into a large number of possible positions relative to each other. These positions can be ranked according to the degree of control and dominance they allow one fighter to exert on the other. Control and dominance are therefore understood in terms of *the degree to which a position allows you to attack an opponent with strikes and submission holds while restricting his ability to do the same.* Some positions are neutral, offering no real advantage to either fighter. Others are inferior, allowing your opponent to determine when and how he attacks, while making it difficult for you to counterattack. If you reversed positions, then obviously you would find yourself in a superior position. We will soon offer a description of the most important positions in the ground phase of combat.

In addition to the battle for position, there is the battle for ultimate victory—the battle to make your opponent submit. Remember: *Positional control is only a means to an end; that end is to make your opponent quit.* Considered in this light, you can see that finishing skills—the means of ending a fight (striking and submission holds)—are absolutely crucial. Few people submit from merely being held down, but almost everybody will submit when they are pinned and being struck hard, having breaking pressure applied to one of their limbs, or being strangled.

It is tempting to think that finishing skills are *the* most important skill in a ground fight, since they are the direct means to the final goal, to make an opponent submit. There is some truth to this. However, if you lack the ability to first control an opponent (and this is done through the attainment of good position), you will find it difficult to apply any of the submission holds successfully. It is probably fair to say, then, that positional skills and submission skills are roughly equal in importance. Although it is true that positional control is only a means to perform the finishing methods (strikes and submission holds), it is equally true that without positional control, the desired end is unlikely to occur. In other words, positional control and finishing methods are dependent on each other, and thus, fighters must pay equal attention to both skills.

ESSENTIAL GROUND POSITIONS

We have seen that positional control and the passage from one position to more dominating positions form the basis of success on the ground. It is now time to outline the basic positions that occur in the course of a ground fight.

When two people grapple on the ground, they can form any one of a large number of possible positions. In addition, each position has many possible variations. However, we can broadly categorize the essential positions of ground grappling into a simple set, which can be readily understood by a beginner and which form the basis of the ground fighter's positional game. These positions are arranged in order of dominance, starting with the most dominating position (the top-rear mount) and working down to the neutral positions (guard and half-guard). Note that the worst places to be are underneath the dominant positions. Thus, the bottom position in the top-rear mount is the least desirable position to be in.

Rear-Mounted Position

Of all the basic positions that can occur in a ground fight, the rear-mounted position is probably the best. It offers a tremendous combination of control and offensive firepower, in the form of submission holds and strikes. At the same time, it makes it difficult for your opponent to effectively attack you, especially if he is not well versed in grappling technique.

As a fighter, you have two distinct ways to apply the rear mount. First, you can either be on top of your opponent (figure 6.1a) or underneath him (figure 6.1b). Being on top offers a little more control especially if you can stretch your opponent out by thrusting your hips forward into his lower back. Although this move has many alternatives, the most common method of finishing an opponent from this position is the rear naked sleeper choke, also referred to as simply the *sleeper hold (hadaka jime)*.

The bottom-rear mount involves your getting behind your opponent and wrapping your legs around him by placing your feet inside both his hips. In this position, your legs and feet serve a crucial role: They lock you into place,

Figure 6.1 Top-rear mount (*a*) and bottom-rear mount (*b*).

functioning as hooks that enable you to ride your opponent no matter which way he rolls and moves. Be sure not to cross your feet in this position, because this makes it easy for your opponent to apply a simple yet effective footlock on you. Simply place your feet, toes pointed out, inside his hips. Although it is still possible for your opponent to attack your feet in this position, it is not only much more difficult for him to do so, it is also much easier for you to counter any such attack.

From the perspective of your opponent, the man on the receiving end of the rear mount, escape to a better position is the first priority. With certain submission holds, your opponent has possible avenues from which to attack, even from such a disadvantageous position. Nonetheless, these attacks only have a low chance of success. They serve as setups to escape rather than genuine attempts at submission.

Mounted Position *(Tate Shiho Gatame)*

Another dominant position is the basic mounted position, which involves your straddling your opponent's chest and kneeling over him. To execute this move, you can sit up straight to create room to strike, or you can wrap one arm around his neck and get down low to control him, as shown in figure 6.2. From the mount, it is easy for fighters to launch a barrage of powerful punches, and it is difficult for your opponent to respond, since his shoulders and hips are pinned to the mat, thus robbing his punches of any real power. In addition, you can apply a large number of effective submission holds from the mount whereas your opponent has little opportunity to reply.

Often, especially in a street fight against an inexperienced grappler, fighters have opportunities to transition from the mounted position to the rear-mounted position. This move normally occurs when you begin striking from the mount: Your opponent turns away to avoid the punches, giving you his back. By opening your legs a little, simply give him a little room to turn in, then lock in your hooks to secure a rear-mounted position, and thus an easy opportunity to finish the fight with a rear naked choke. This transition is much less common in con-

Figure 6.2 Mounted position.

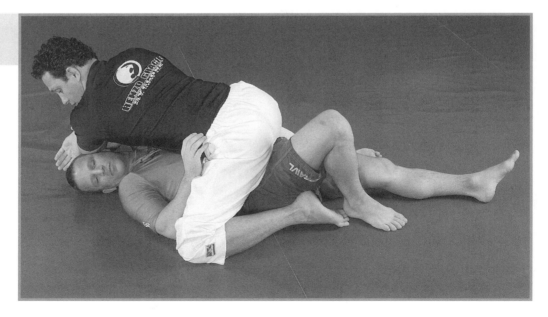

temporary MMA, since most people know that it is foolish to turn under the mount and give up one's back. However, this happens *all the time* in street fights, so you *must* be able to make this transition at a moment's notice. From the persective of the man underneath the mounted position, escape is still the number one priority. The bottom man is generally looking to bridge over and end up on top, just inside his opponent's guard, or he is looking to scoot out and put the top man inside his own guard.

Knee-on-Belly Position *(Uki Gatame)*

As the name implies, the knee-on-belly position has as its central feature the placement of the top fighter's knee on his opponent's abdomen or chest. While his knee is positioned, his hands can be in a number of different places, with the opposite leg placed out wide for balance and the foot secured flat on the ground (figure 6.3).

Opinion is divided on whether the mounted position or the knee-on-belly position is the better one for striking and submitting an opponent. They are both extremely effective platforms for attack. Tradition has it that the mount is the better position, which is why it scores slightly higher in jujitsu competition. The mount is certainly superior in terms of stability and control, and it is also easier for a beginner to use. However, fighters have valid reasons for preferring the knee-on-belly position. It offers tremendous mobility and speedy transitions into submission holds and other positions (especially the mount). The knee-on-belly position is difficult to escape without exposing yourself to locks and chokes. Whatever the respective merits of

Figure 6.3 Knee-on-belly position.

these two positions, it is clear that the knee-on-belly position is an excellent one from which to control and attack an opponent. However, although it is possible for the man on the bottom to enter into a number of submission holds while under the knee-on-belly position, escape is still his most important task.

Side-Control Position

The side-control position is a powerful pinning position that has a great number of variations. The common element in all of them is that you are on top of your opponent, lying across his body, out to one side (figure 6.4). This range of positions goes by many names, such as the *side mount* or *across side (kuzure kami shiho gatame)*. It is a great position to control an opponent and submit him. In addition, it is a great position from which to transition into other positions, such as the mounted position and the knee-on-belly position. The great virtue of the side-control position is its stability. No other position offers the degree of control that is possible from the side position. This advantage makes it a great place to slow the tempo of a fight down, exerting a fatiguing and frustrating positional control on your opponent that makes him tire quickly.

Figure 6.4 Side-control position, underclasp *(a)* and overclasp *(b)*.

Fighters have many ways to hold a side-control position, and each has its advantages and disadvantages. The key elements common to all of them are as follows:

- *Always pin your opponent chest-to-chest.* Make sure that the center of your chest is directly on top of the center of your opponent's chest; ensure that it does not slide down to his stomach or over his side.

- *Keep your hips low and base wide.* If your hips rise up, it becomes easy for your opponent to forcefully bridge and carry you to a bad position. Sink your hips down to use your weight much more efficiently, creating an unpleasant and tiring pressure on your opponent. Also be sure to keep your base of support wide. By this, we mean that you should keep your legs wide apart as you sink your hips down, which makes it difficult for your opponent to roll you over.

- *Keep mobile.* Do not simply hold on grimly to your opponent. No matter how tightly you hold him, he will eventually work his way out. Instead, move in response to his movements, keeping your hips low and staying chest-to-chest as you do so. If he attempts to put you back in guard, do not be afraid to move your hips away from his. You can even walk around his head to the other side of his body (but keeping your hips low all the time). This is a great way to set up submission holds and counter your opponent's movement.

An interesting and important variation of the side-control position occurs when the man on top walks over and around his opponent's head, then stops (figure 6.5). This move puts him in a controlling position, often referred to as the "north and south" position (since you face in opposite directions). This pin has a slightly different feel to it for both the top and bottom fighters.

Figure 6.5 North and south position.

For the man underneath the side-control and north-south pins, the chief concern is escape to a better position. The most common forms of escape involve getting back to the guard position or getting up to one's knees. It is also possible to completely turn the top man over for a reversal or even attempt to submit him. These alternatives are more difficult on an experienced opponent, however.

Turtle Position

The turtle position occurs often in the course of a ground fight. When one fighter is on his hands and knees, head down, balled up tight, he is in the "turtle position." His opponent generally stays on top of him, either in front of him with his arms around the head and one of the arms (front-headlock position), or out to one side with one arm around the opponent's waist for control (figure 6.6). A third alternative is for the top man to position himself directly behind his opponent.

Figure 6.6 Turtle position.

From the bottom man's perspective, the turtle position is a disadvantageous position. By keeping himself in tight, the bottom man can make attack difficult for the top man. Indeed, it is possible for the bottom man to attack with his own submission holds, as well as attempt numerous escapes to better positions. Nonetheless, it is not sensible to spend too much time in the turtle position under an aggressive opponent, since you will often absorb some heavy damage. The bottom man must either escape as soon as possible to a better position or attempt a submission hold. The top man has the choice to either strike his opponent, improve his position, or attempt submission holds.

Guard Position

One of the most talked about positions in ground fighting is the guard position. This position refers to any situation where one fighter is on his back or buttocks with an opponent in front of his legs (figure 6.7). When MMA fighting began in North America in the early 1990s, most people worked under the assumption that if a fighter was on his back, then he was in trouble. After all, in the Western tradition, if a man is on his back, he is pinned and considered helpless. In most people's minds, the very image of helplessness in a fight is that of a man on his back with another man on top, hitting him at will. To the absolute shock of most people, a regular sight in these MMA fights was that of Brazilian jiu jitsu fighters' fighting from their backs and *winning*.

People had simply not realized the enormous difference between pinning a man on his back in a truly dominating position and simply being locked in the guard position. The former involves getting past an opponent's legs and effectively pinning his upper body. The latter means that the man on bottom can use his legs and hips to control the top man's movements to a surprising degree. The quicker you can understand this crucial difference, the quicker your progress in ground fighting will be.

All too often, the difference between winning and losing a fight is this very difference between keeping a man who is on top of you in front of your legs (in

Figure 6.7 Closed-guard position *(a)*, open-guard (butterfly) position *(b)*, and open-guard (opponent standing) position *(c)*.

the guard position) and allowing him past your legs. As long as you hold an opponent in the guard, you have an effective means of defending yourself from strikes and upper-body submission holds while at the same time being able to strike and submit your opponent. The moment your opponent gets past your legs, you lose any semblance of control; thus, you become progressively more vulnerable as your opponent works his way up the hierarchy of positions.

In chapter 7, we shall look at the guard in detail because it is so important to the bottom game in MMA. From the top man's perspective, the guard represents something of a problem. It is possible to win a fight by simply pounding away at your opponent while locked up in his guard; however, it is also possible to lose the fight by following this strategy, as many "ground and pound" fighters have discovered. A much more sensible strategy is to attempt to get past the bottom man's legs and hips into a truly dominant top position that makes it far more difficult for the bottom man to defend himself. This strategy of "passing the guard" (getting past the bottom man's legs) is the one most favored by seasoned grapplers and is a high-percentage approach to the ground game. An alternative strategy is to attack the bottom man's legs with submission holds, which can be an effective shortcut to victory if done well. If done poorly, it can lead to loss of the top position.

Half-Guard Position

Very often in the course of a ground fight and during the application of the guard position, your opponent may attempt to pass your guard (get around your legs). When this happens, you will often be forced to lock your legs around one of your opponent's legs (as opposed to his waist). Since you control only one leg, your opponent is halfway past your guard—hence, the name, *half-guard* (figure 6.8). This is another neutral position. You can submit an opponent from this position, but he can submit you also. The top man has a definite advantage in striking position, but if he overcommits to strikes, he can be swept to a bottom position or attacked with submission holds. Since this position is so common, you must become familiar with it.

Figure 6.8 Half-guard position.

POSITIONAL HIERARCHY

We can now offer a rough guide to the hierarchy of positions. The list begins with the perspective of the top man. Note, however, that if the top man is in a dominant position, then the bottom man is in an inferior position. The more dominating the top man's position, the more inferior the bottom man's position. Thus, the list goes two ways, starting with the perspective of the fighter in the top position, working down to neutral positions (where neither the man on top nor the one on the bottom has a decisive advantage, down to the increasingly bad positions of the fighter on the bottom.

Top-rear mounted position

Bottom-rear mounted position

Mounted position

Knee-on-belly position

Side-control position

Turtle position

Half-guard position

Guard position

Half-guard position

Turtle position

Side-control position

Knee-on-belly position

Mounted position

Bottom-rear mounted position

Top-rear mounted position

Note that there are many variations of each of these positions and other irregular positions that occur in the course of grappling and fighting. In addition, certain other positions (such as headlock variations) are not covered here. Some might disagree with the exact ordering of the positions; after all, each has its own advantages and disadvantages. Nonetheless, this hierarchy can serve as a useful guide to the positional game that is so crucial in a ground fight. Note immediately that the objectives and strategies of the two fighters are different according to whether they occuy top or bottom position—indeed, the objectives of the top and bottom fighters are usually polar opposites. This asymmetry is reflected in the fact that we separate these two different aspects of the ground game and address them in the next two chapters.

Winning From the Bottom Position

In the last decade, ground fighting has become the most talked about aspect of fighting in the martial arts, which is a complete turnaround from the previous decades, when it was almost totally neglected. The reason for this shift in momentum is undoubtedly the influence of mixed martial arts (MMA), where ground fighting has so often proven to be the phase of combat where fights are won and lost. There are, however, deeper reasons that explain why ground fighting currently has the undivided attention of so many martial artists.

First, in a fight without rules, there are no weight categories. You must fight whomever fate places in front of you, which was also the case in the early MMA events. Whenever there is a dramatic difference in size, the likelihood of a smaller opponent being taken down by a far larger opponent is much higher.

Second, regardless of any great disparity in size, there is always the chance of being taken down to your back in a real fight. This could be due to your opponent's great skill in takedowns or a mistake on your part. It is simply a fact that if you fight tough opponents, you have a high chance of being taken down at some point.

Third, fights are usually chaotic affairs, where things never seem to go as planned. Often your opponent turns out to be much more difficult to contend with than anticipated, even when he is untrained. In the swirling chaos of a fight, anything can happen. For example, you can easily trip and end up in the bottom position, despite your intention not to go down.

Perhaps the most important reason for developing your bottom game is the sense of confidence that it will develop in you. For most people, their greatest fear in a real fight is being held down and beaten. This natural fear prohibits them from fighting with confidence. If a fighter is terrified of being taken down, he will be reluctant to apply his techniques. His concern will be that in committing to a strike, he will be taken down and pummeled. However, if he knows that he can survive from the bottom position and even attack from it, then he will have no fear of being taken down. The result is that he will hit with confidence in the standing position. The bottom game is a way of dealing with the worst-case scenario of a real fight—the image of being pinned down and crushed. Jujitsu makes you comfortable specifically in the worst-case scenario. If you can deal comfortably with that aspect of a fight, there is little to fear.

VICTORY FROM THE BOTTOM POSITION

The two most common routes to victory from the bottom position are submission holds, and sweeps and reversals. Submission holds are locks to the joints or neck that threaten your opponent with injury or unconsciousness unless he submits. Many effective submission holds can be applied from underneath your opponent, especially in the guard position. Likewise, there are a large number of sweeps and reversals that allow you to topple an opponent over and take the top position. Once this series of moves occurs, you can begin striking your way to victory, or you can go on to gain a positional advantage and then exploit it with the application of a submission hold from a more dominant position.

Keep in mind, however, that it is difficult to win a fight from underneath your opponent using only strikes. One of the few exceptions to this rule is the use of a thrusting heel kick to the jaw of your opponent as he stands over your open guard. This move is a proven fight-ender in MMA competition. Indeed, one of the most famous instances of this form of striking from the bottom position occurred when Renzo Gracie took on Oleg Taktarov in the Martial Arts Reality Superfight (MARS) MMA event. Taktarov was a skilled grappler with a fine record in MMA competition. After scoring a solid takedown on Renzo, he made the mistake of bending down to control Renzo's feet in the open guard (possibly as a precursor to an ankle-lock attack). Seizing the opportunity provided, Renzo shot a stiff, upward thrusting heel kick to Taktarov's jaw and gained a great knockout.

Most strikes, however, are weaker going *up* to your opponent than ones that he can hit *down* at you. But this disadvantage should not prevent you from attempting strikes from the bottom position. They serve to make your opponent uncomfortable and possibly move him into a submission hold or sweep.

STRATEGY IN THE BOTTOM POSITION

Most of the bottom positions are inferior positions. It is almost always the case that you want to fight on top of your opponent. However, if you fight a bigger, stronger opponent (or one who is skilled in takedowns), you will inevitably end up in the bottom position. Many people claim that they would never fight on their backs in the bottom position—that it is a foolish way to fight. Indeed, jujitsu fighters prefer to fight from on top, but the fact is that what you *want* to do in a fight and what circumstances *force* you to do are usually not the same. If you fight tough opponents, there will be times when you find yourself underneath them, fighting from the bottom position.

Because most bottom positions are inferior, any fighter's emphasis while fighting from underneath is to escape to a better position. Whenever you are forced to fight from underneath, focus on the following strategy:

Get out of controlling, dominating pins in an efficient and safe manner, and either

- escape to the guard position,
- escape to your knees or your feet (and thus get back to a neutral position),
- reverse your opponent, or
- attempt a submission hold.

If you try to reverse your opponent, be aware that some escapes involve turning your opponent over and ending up on top of him in a dominant position. These tend to be difficult and tiring, and there is a risk associated with their use. Should they fail, they tend to leave you in an even worse position than before—and tired to boot. However, done well, they can turn a fight around.

If you attempt a submission hold, remember that this move can be difficult from inferior bottom positions. However, it may force your opponent to back off a little to escape the attempted lock. His reaction may then create the space required to attempt your escape to the guard position or an escape to your knees or feet.

GUARD POSITION

Since many of the escapes from dominating pins and holds involve a retreat to the guard position, we will spend a good deal of time discussing this position. The broadest feature of the guard is that it involves sitting or lying underneath your opponent with him in front of your legs. The advantage of holding an opponent in the guard position is that your legs can be used to control his movements and to work him into submission holds, sweeps, and strikes while at the same time restricting his attacks. Although many forms of guard are available, they all can be divided into three basic categories:

1. Closed guard: This involves locking your legs around your opponent's waist while lying underneath him. This move is what most people associate with the guard position, since this was the variation of the guard that was used more than any other in early MMA matches. The advantage of the closed guard is the ease with which it can be used to nullify an opponent's striking attack. It is rather like a tight restrictive clinch on the ground. You can use it to tie up an opponent's arms and interfere with his punches.

2. Open guard: This is a broad category of positions whose only common factor is that your opponent is in front of your legs. Since you are not really holding your opponent in with your legs, he is at liberty to stand up and walk away from you at any time he chooses, which is an option taken by many strikers who prefer the standing position. The open guard, then, tends to be more effective against an opponent who wants to *keep* the fight in the ground phase and is driving forward into you, trying to "ground and pound" or pass around your legs to get to a better position. In this situation, the open guard offers a great combination of defensive and offensive options, which is due to the great mobility that the position offers to your hips and legs.

3. A third category of guard position—and one of great importance—is the so-called half-guard position. In a full guard, your legs are wrapped around your opponent's waist; thus, *both* his legs are between yours. As you grapple with your training partners, it quite often happens that your opponent attempts to get around your legs. As he pushes past your legs, you have to lock your legs around one of his to prevent him from getting past your legs and into a dominating side position. Since you are controlling only one of his legs, you have him in a "half-guard."

Neutrality of the Guard Position

We have constantly stressed the need of ground fighters to seek better position. It is then worth asking, Is it possible for a fighter to attain a dominant position while he is still underneath his opponent? In the early MMA events, so many jujitsu fighters were able to defeat their unsuspecting opponents from underneath in the guard position that many people came to the conclusion that the guard was a *dominant* position.

In fact, this is not the case. In a fight between two jujitsu fighters of roughly equal ability, the guard is a *neutral* position. Neither the man on top, nor the man on bottom, has a decisive advantage. The top man cannot really pin the bottom man easily, since the bottom man can utilize his legs and hips to move in ways that defy effective control. In addition, the bottom man is still able to move relatively easily into submission holds, and from there, he can also avoid most strikes. It is clear, then, that he is not being pinned in the sense that he is being totally controlled. On the other hand, the top man can attempt his own submission holds reasonably easily (mostly to the legs). His movements are not tightly controlled by the bottom man, so once the guard is opened, he is at liberty to simply stand up and walk away. Clearly, then, he is not being dominated.

In a fight between two equally skilled jujitsu fighters, attacks from the guard tend to rely more on trickery, subterfuge, timing, and deception rather than control and dominance. Seen in this light, one can look at the guard as a neutral position rather than a dominant one, despite its appearance of dominance in early MMA tournaments.

Therefore, we can say the following: *In a ground fight, it is always desirable to be on top, in the most controlling position possible. If, however, you find yourself in the bottom position, the guard is the best place to be.* Although it does not offer the positional control and dominance of the superior top positions, it does prevent your opponent from dominating you, and victory is possible for the man on the bottom. It is absolutely essential that you become familiar with the workings of the guard position, since it is certain that you will need to use it whenever you find yourself on your back. In addition, you will certainly have to work *against* the guard position if you ever put an adept ground fighter on his back.

Case Study in the Use of the Guard Position: Royce Gracie

When MMA competition first came into prominence in North America, one man was associated with MMA fighting skills above all others. That man was Royce Gracie. A large part of Royce's success in the early MMA events was centered on his outstanding use of the guard position. Indeed, it was Royce Gracie who really popularized the use of the guard among MMA fans and spectators. Before Royce's successes, most people thought a fighter on his back was a losing fighter. Royce showed that a smaller, weaker fighter could use the guard to thwart the attacks of a strong, aggressive opponent and then go on the attack and win the fight—all from the bottom position.

At the time, this concept was revolutionary, and Royce's remarkable initial string of victories was largely responsible for starting the grappling craze and for popularizing jujitsu. Royce's success was his mastery of technique in the guard position. With it, he had great patience in waiting for the opponent to commit an error, even when Royce was under extreme pressure. The guard position also allowed Royce to use his superb defensive skills; few people landed blows on him while locked in his guard. These skills, along with the ability to lock on solid submission holds from underneath, proved too much for his opponents.

Defense From the Guard Position

Most people think of the guard as a defensive position in which they can shield themselves from the strikes of an opponent who is on top of them. We shall try hard, however, to dispel the notion that the guard is a purely defensive position in the next section. Nonetheless, it is true that the guard can provide an excellent means of defending yourself from an aggressive, striking opponent when used well.

Fighters have two main options when using the guard as a defensive shield. The first is to hug your opponent as tightly to you as possible in a closed guard, overhooking one of his arms with your arm and holding his head down with the other. This puts you in a tight, supine clinch with your opponent and makes it tough for him to strike you effectively. You can improve your position by scooting your hips out to the same side as the arm that you have overhooked and then getting on your side.

A second option occurs when actually using the open guard. In this case, you generally want to keep your opponent as far away from yourself as possible, since he will be trying hard to punch you. Place your feet on his hips and push him back, making it difficult for him to reach your head. You can also place a foot on his chest, shoulder, or biceps as a means of preventing his coming into range to hit you in the head. Although many other gripping techniques can limit the amount of damage your opponent can inflict on you in the guard position, these two are the simplest and easiest strategies to implement in the chaos of a real fight.

Attacks From the Guard Position

One of the worst mistakes you can make in jujitsu is to consider the guard a passive defensive position where you simply hang on for survival. Although the guard certainly can be used in this way, it is hardly desirable. You want to see the guard as a position from which you can win the fight, not merely hold on for dear life. Remember: *No one ever won a fight by simply holding an opponent.*

It is essential, then, that you develop a proactive attacking game from the guard, taking the fight to your opponent as much as possible. We shall outline a mix of sweeps and submission holds that allow you to attack an opponent in both open- and closed-guard positions, whether he is standing up in your guard or down on his knees. These are high-percentage moves that work well in both MMA and grappling events. We shall also look at moves that have had a high success rate in actual competition.

A good rule of thumb in using the guard is this: *Spend as little time as possible lying flat on your back.* Always look to scoot out to the side of your opponent—sit up, get on your side, get your hips out to one side. These small changes in body position make a *huge* difference; they greatly facilitate your attacks from the guard. If you just lie flat on your back, you really have few offensive options, so move in the ways just mentioned to get your offense under way. The only time you want to lie down is when you want to rest a little, should you feel fatigued.

Attacks From the Closed-Guard Position
When Your Opponent Is on His Knees

Hip-heist sweep. The hip-heist sweep is one of the best moves to employ when your opponent is on his knees inside your closed guard. It is a low-risk move that is seen often in MMA competition at all levels. Done well, it can turn the direction of a fight in a matter of seconds. To initiate the sweep, place both feet on the ground (figure 7.1a). Post one hand behind you on the floor and quickly sit up toward the side you have posted your hand—this will be the side that you will sweep your opponent over. Reach across with your other hand and grasp your opponent's arm (at the elbow) on the side you wish to sweep him over (figure 7.1b). Drive your hips up into your opponent, placing your hips higher than his. Turn your head to look behind you and drop your knee down to the floor on the same side you intend to sweep your opponent. In one motion, roll

Figure 7.1 Hip-heist sweep.

your hips over to the side (figure 7.1c). This will take your opponent over very easily. Drive to the side rather than into your opponent. You will finish in the mounted position.

Guillotine choke. The guillotine choke is the single most common and effective submission hold in MMA. It can be applied from many positions, but the guillotine from the guard is particularly effective as it employs a high percentage of your body's strength against your opponent's vulnerable neck. It combines extremely well with the hip-heist sweep. Whenever one of these fails, switch immediately to the other. It is best applied on an opponent kneeling in your guard. Placing both feet on the floor, sit up and to the side just as you would for the hip-heist sweep (figure 7.2a). Post your hand on the ground behind you and reach around your opponent's neck with your other arm (this is your strangling arm; figure 7.2b). You can scoot your hips away from your opponent a bit to facilitate the encircling of his neck with your arm. With your other arm grab your strangling arm at the wrist (figure 7.2c). Pull your strangling arm up to your sternum. Lie down and scoot your hips out to the opposite side of your opponent's head. Lock your opponent in your closed guard and squeeze the choke (figure 7.2d).

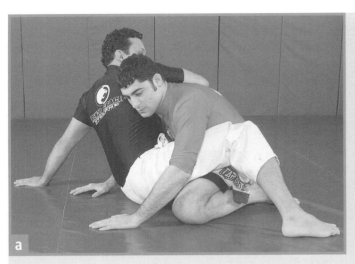

Figure 7.2 Guillotine choke.

Neck-crank turnover. This is an excellent way to either force an opponent to submit or turn him over into the mounted position. With your opponent kneeling down in your closed guard, place both feet on the ground and sit up and to the side, just as in the hip-heist sweep and guillotine choke (these three moves are intended to combine together as they all have the same initial movement). Posting one hand on the ground behind you, loop the other arm around your opponent's neck (figure 7.3a), as in the guillotine. Feed the arm you have looped over your opponent's neck under his armpit, then bring it up to his upper back. The palm of your hand should be facing away from you. Your opponent's head is locked under your armpit. Lock your hands palm to palm and torque your opponent's neck by bringing your hands across his back (figure 7.3 b and c). Quite often this is sufficient to force an opponent to submit. If not, continue applying pressure until he is turned over to his back and you find yourself mounted (figure 7.3d).

Figure 7.3 Neck-crank turnover.

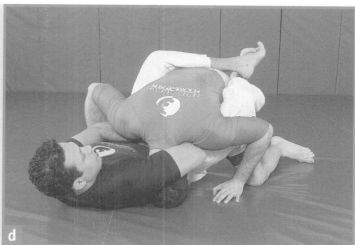

Triangle choke. The triangle choke remains one of the most popular and successful submission holds from the guard position. The variant we look at here is best used from the closed guard when the opponent is on his knees. With your opponent locked in your closed guard, grab both his wrists, forcing one wrist back towards his sternum (figure 7.4a). This allows you to throw your leg over that trapped arm and around your opponent's neck (this will be your strangling leg). This traps your opponent's head and one arm between your legs (figure 7.4b). Try to touch the foot of your strangling leg to the back of your opponent's opposite shoulder to create an optimum angle for the stranglehold (you may have to pull your foot into this position). It is often helpful to scoot your hips out to the side to facilitate the choke. Lock your legs around your opponent's head and arm in the triangular figure-four pattern shown (figure 7.4c). Be sure to pull the foot of the strangling leg all the way under the knee of the other leg (do not merely cross your feet). Squeeze your knees together and pull down on your opponent's head to strangle.

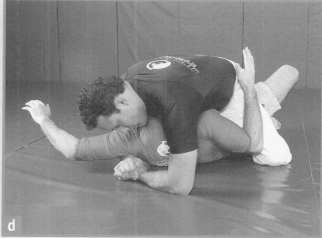

Figure 7.4   Triangle choke.

Attacks From the Closed-Guard Position When Your Opponent Is Standing

Arm bar (juji gatame).   This versatile submission hold can be used in a huge number of positions. Here we see it used against an opponent standing up in the closed guard. Grab the wrist of the arm you wish to lock with your hand and secure it to your chest (figure 7.5a). With your other hand, reach inside his leg close to the ankle and pull your head towards the ankle you have grabbed (figure 7.5b). This sets up the correct angle for the arm lock. Your body should be roughly perpendicular to your opponent. Walk your feet high up on your opponent's back. Do not let your hips drop to the floor as that greatly lessens the chance of a successful arm lock. Swing your leg over your opponent's head to secure the lock (figure 7.5c). Try to touch your hips up into the armpit of the arm you are locking, which tightens the lock considerably. Squeeze your knees together, bring your feet down towards the floor, raise your hips, and pull the wrist of the locked arm down. This quickly puts breaking pressure on your opponent's arm.

Knee bar (hiza gatame).   The knee bar is another submission hold that can be used in a large number of positions. It is particularly effective when an opponent stands up in your closed guard. It combines very well with the arm bar attack just seen, since the initial movement is the same. Should the arm bar fail, the knee bar is an excellent follow-up. As your opponent stands in your closed guard, reach inside his leg with your arm just as you did for the arm lock (figure 7.6a). Pull your head towards the foot of that leg. Open your guard and let your hips drop. Your foot will rest on the hip of the leg you intend to lock, as shown in figure 7.6b. Bring your knee inside the knee of the leg you have grabbed. This is a crucial detail. Swing your other leg around in a wide arc until your foot touches the opponent's buttocks (figure 7.6c). Be sure to bring your hips up and above the knee of the leg you are attacking! If you fail to do so the lock will be ineffective. Squeeze your knees together to control your opponent's leg (figure 7.6d). Lock your arms around your opponent's ankle, arch back, and thrust your hips forward to put breaking pressure on the knee joint (figure 7.6e).

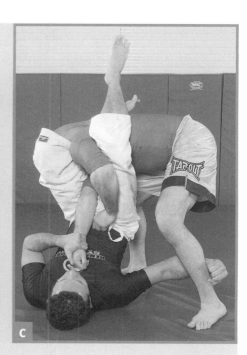

Figure 7.5 Arm bar.

Attacks From the Open-Guard Position
When Your Opponent Is on His Knees

Basic elevator sweep (sumi gaeshi). This great move is best employed when your opponent is on his knees in your open butterfly guard (your two feet are hooked under your opponent's thighs). Sit up and lock your arm around your opponent's upper arm (overhook). With your other hand secure your opponent's elbow or wrist (figure 7.7a). Fall directly to the side of the wrist or elbow you have grasped (figure 7.7b). As you fall, lift with the foot on the opposite side you are sweeping towards. Push off the ground with your other foot (figure 7.7c).

Figure 7.6   Knee bar.

This combined action topples your opponent over to the side and onto his back. Keep driving until you end in the mounted position or across his side (figure 7.7d).

Pressing armlock (ude gatame).   Few submission holds can be applied with the ease and speed of *ude gatame*—one of the very best attacks to use on an opponent inside your open guard on his knees. The moment your opponent extends an arm inside your open guard he becomes vulnerable to *ude gatame*. Slide your hips out to the side (your body should be on its side) and wrap your arm around his elbow as shown (figure 7.8a). Trap the wrist of the arm you wish to lock between your neck and shoulder. Clamp your knees around the shoulder of the arm you are attacking and squeeze. This makes escape difficult. Fold your arms directly over the elbow of your opponent's arm and squeeze in towards your chest, hyper extending the elbow joint (figure 7.8b).

Figure 7.7 Basic elevator sweep.

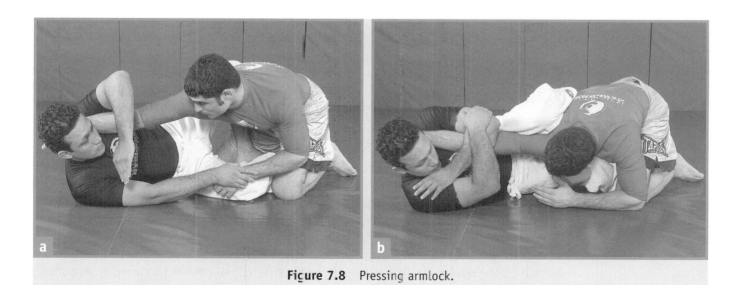

Figure 7.8 Pressing armlock.

Case Study in Offensive Use of the Guard Position:
Antonio Rodrigo "Minotauro" Nogueira

Among contemporary MMA fighters, none has excelled in the use of the guard position to the degree of Brazilian jiu jitsu expert Antonio Rodrigo "Minotauro" Nogueira. In fight after fight, Minotauro locked up the best fighters in the world in his guard and made them quit. Quite often these opponents were far larger than Minotauro, but it made no difference—they found themselves caught up in a barrage of submission attacks inside the guard position. What distinguished Nogueira's game from most fighters was his constant and unremitting attacks from the bottom position. Most fighters use the guard in a largely defensive fashion. Nogueira, on the other hand, constantly looked to lock his opponent in a combination attack using the triangle choke, kimura armlock, and omo platte armlock. As his frustrated opponents battled out of one lock they inevitably found themselves caught in another. In the face of this concerted attack, they could hold out only so long before defeat came by way of another perfectly-executed submission hold.

Part of what made Nogueira such a difficult opponent was his skill in the standing position. He had strong boxing skills and takedowns. Thus, if an opponent attempted to stand up and escape his guard, he faced more punishment on his feet. This threat kept most people down in Nogueira's guard where they were exposed to the submission hold attack. In this way they were put in a dilemma: If they stood up they risked being knocked out or taken down to a bottom position. If they stayed in the guard they would be finished by submission holds. Everybody knew what to expect inside Nogueira's guard. His submission attacks were well known and quite basic. What made the difference was the precision and determination with which they were applied (usually in extended combinations). Faced with the constant pressure from underneath, few opponents were able to mount any effective offense while locked in Minotauro's guard.

Attacks From the Open-Guard Position
When Your Opponent Is Standing

Double-shin sweep. This move is an excellent way to attack an opponent who is standing in your open guard, and it does not expose you to any troublesome ankle and knee locks (unlike many other open guard sweeps). As your opponent stands, place your feet inside his legs at the knees, your lower shins pressing against the inside of his knees (figure 7.9a). Grab both his ankles from the outside (figure 7.9b). Pull with both hands as you punch your hips up off the floor and spread your knees outward (figure 7.9c). This knocks your opponent directly backward to the floor. You can then come up in a top position or attempt an Achilles lock.

Heel hook. The heel hook is a great way to attack an opponent who is standing up in your open guard. With both feet hooked inside your opponent's legs at the knees, reach out and grab the heel of whichever foot is closest to you (figure 7.10a). Pull your hips in close to that foot and kick your foot inside and around that leg (this is the leg that you are attacking) until your foot lands on the hip of the leg you are attacking (figure 7.10 b and c). Your other foot is tucked under the hamstring of the leg you are attacking. Squeeze your knees together for control. Pull the toes of the foot that you are attacking under your armpit. Hook your wrist under the heel of that foot and lock your hands together. Torque the heel across your chest to put breaking pressure on the ankle and knee. Be careful in the application of this technique—injuries are common. Give your partner time to submit while training.

Figure 7.9 Double-shin sweep.

Figure 7.10 Heel hook.

ESCAPES AND COUNTERS IN THE BOTTOM POSITION

It is time for us to look at each of the common positions in a ground fight from the bottom fighter's perspective. We have already mentioned that the bottom fighter's main emphasis is an escape to a better position. An alternative strategy is to attempt a submission hold from underneath. If the submission hold succeeds, consider it a great bonus. If it fails, at least it forces your opponent to defend it, giving you the space needed to escape to a better position. In either case, you have done well. We shall now consider moves that enable you to get out of the more dangerous pins and hold-downs in MMA.

Escaping the Rear-Mounted Position

The rear mount is one of the most dangerous places to be caught in a real fight. Your opponent can rain blows on the back of your head and neck if he is on top, whereas you can do little in return. In addition, he can attack your neck and arms with an array of submission holds. An effective means of escape is thus essential. We shall look at how to escape the two main forms of a rear mount: top and bottom.

Top-Rear Mount

The top-rear mount occurs when your opponent is perched on top of you, riding your lower back and hips with both his legs hooked into your hips. From

Figure 7.11 Elbow escape from the top-rear mount.

this position, he can stretch you out and put you under great pressure. One possible escape is the elbow escape method.

The elbow escape is by far the most useful and important escape method in jujitsu. It enables you to escape the pins and holds of opponents far larger than yourself with relative ease. Generally it results in you placing your opponent back in the guard position. People usually think of the elbow escape as an escape from the regular mounted position, but there are many variants, including this one from the top-rear mount. This can seem like a complicated move, but with a little practice, you will be able to do it quickly and efficiently. Your opponent is on top of you in a full rear mount (figure 7.11a). The most important thing is to remove his "hooks" (his feet in your hips), which give him stability and control over you. To remove the hooks, kick one of your legs back and place it flat on the ground between your opponent's legs (figure 7.11b). This removes one hook immediately. Slide the knee of the leg you have just kicked across and under your opponent's remaining hook (figure 7.11c). Try to touch the knee of that leg to your opposite elbow. This prevents your opponent from

getting his hook back in place. To remove the remaining hook, kick your other leg (the one your opponent is still hooked under) back. Now both hooks have been removed (figure 7.11d). Get up to your knees, keeping your knees and elbows tight together to prevent your opponent from getting his hooks back in place (figure 7.11e). Reach up and grab his arm (figure 7.11f). Roll him over your shoulder (figure 7.11g). The fact that he is not hooked in place makes this easy. As he falls off your back, stay on your knees so that you can take a top pinning position.

Bottom-Rear Mount

The bottom-rear mount occurs when your opponent is not only hooked in behind you, but also underneath you. From here, he can still attack your neck and arms, though his striking power is somewhat less than from the top rear-mounted position. Once again, a sound escape method is needed if you are to avoid his attacks. For example, the slide-out method: It enables you to protect yourself from the usual choke and armlock attempts that you can expect an opponent to do once he attains this great position, while at the same time it takes you out of immediate danger and into a better position.

Your opponent is behind and underneath you in a bottom-rear mount, threatening to choke you (figure 7.12a). He has both feet hooked into your hips. Once again, these "hooks" in your hips are the source of your problem. To escape, bridge up into your opponent as you pull down on his strangling arm at the wrist and elbow. Slide out in the same direction that the fingers of his strangling arm are pointing. Turn your chin down and toward the biceps of the strangling arm. Keep sliding out until your shoulders touch the floor (figure 7.12b). Getting your back and shoulders to the floor is crucial—once this occurs, your opponent is unable to choke you. Try to get on your side and face your opponent (figure 7.12c). In this position, you are safe from the strangle. The danger now is that your opponent will get up on top of you in the mounted position. To prevent this, hook your uppermost foot under your opponent's upper leg at the knee and lift. Hook your arm under the same leg (figure 7.12d). Lift with your arm to prevent your opponent getting up. Kick your leg back and settle into a side pinning position (figure 7.12e).

Escaping the Mounted Position

The mounted position has ended many MMA fights. It allows the top man to strike almost at will. Without a sound means of escape, the bottom man is virtually helpless—thus, the need for the elbow escape.

We have noted already the massive importance of the elbow escape—the king of escapes. In addition to requiring little strength and being effective against much larger opponents, it also exposes the user to little danger as it is being performed. Here we look at a variant that finishes with an offensive move—the Achilles lock. With your opponent mounted on top of you, form a defensive frame by placing both hands on your opponent's hips (figure 7.13a). Bridge to get your hips off the floor. Push with both hands toward your feet (do not push up!) and turn to one side. As you drop your hips, scoot them out to the opposite side that you have turned toward and bring the opposite knee (the knee of your lower leg) between your opponent's legs (figure 7.13b). Your knee should be drawn up to your chest. Wrap your other leg around the leg you intend to attack and place your foot on your opponent's hip (of the leg you are attacking).

Figure 7.12 Slide-out escape from the bottom-rear mount.

Wrap your arm around your opponent's ankle at the Achilles tendon so that the bony part of your wrist is under the Achilles tendon (figure 7.13c). Grab your wrist with your other hand and pull both hands high up to the sternum. Push your hips forward and arch your back to put breaking pressure on the ankle. Perform the lock on your side, not flat on your back.

Figure 7.13 Elbow escape from the mounted position.

Escaping the Knee-on-Belly Position

Only slightly less dangerous than the mount is the knee-on-belly position. Once again, fighters face a real danger of being beaten into submission from this position or being locked in a choke or joint lock.

When you are caught under the knee-on-belly position (figure 7.14a), a good escape method is to off-balance your opponent forward. Do this by bumping your knee into your opponent's buttocks to bring his weight forward (figure 7.14b). Your opponent will need to base out on his hands to prevent toppling over. Turn toward your opponent and shoot your arm (the one furthest from the opponent) around the leg (at the knee) that was placed on your belly (figure 7.14c). Scissor your legs and get quickly up to your knees, tackling your opponent's legs and taking him down (figure 7.14d).

Figure 7.14 Escape from the knee-on-belly position.

Escaping the Side-Control Position

The side-control position is not quite as potentially dangerous as the positions we have seen so far. However, it is the stepping stone to those positions. Even so, considerable damage can be done with strikes from this position. A vast number of submission holds can be done from side control; a solid means of escape is therefore essential. The method of escape from the side-control position is often determined by the way your opponent pins you. We discuss the escape-to-knees method and the escape-to-armlock method.

Escape-to-knees method. When your opponent pins you with an overclasp, a good means of escape is to get to your knees. To do this while pinned down by a determined and skilled opponent requires careful observance of technique. Begin by getting your arms in the good position shown in figure 7.15a—one

Figure 7.15 Escape side-control position (overclasp) to knees.

hand is on your opponent's hip, the elbow on his belt line. Your other arm is tucked under his arm and holds his upper back. Bridge up, turn into your opponent, and throw your hips out and away from your opponent (figure 7.15b). Punch the arm that was on his upper back around your opponent's leg. As you roll onto your stomach, lock your hands around your opponent's leg at the knee (figure 7.15c). Pull yourself into your opponent, getting up to your knees and close to the leg you are holding (figure 7.15d). Drive into your opponent, reaching across for the other leg and taking your opponent down (figure 7.15e).

Escape-to-armlock (juji gatame) method. This method is employed against an underclasp side pin. Your opponent has established a side control pin with underclasp. Form a defensive frame by placing both hands on your upper chest, elbows in tight to your chest (figure 7.16a). Bridge and push your opponent with both your elbows over your head (rather than directly upwards), as shown in figure 7.16b. This creates sufficient space for you to swing both legs up simultaneously. Bring the leg that is nearest your opponent up under his arm

Figure 7.16 Escape side-control position (underclasp) to armlock.

so that your foot touches the back of his shoulder. The other leg goes over his head (figure 7.16c). Bring the foot of that leg down towards the floor as you squeeze your knees together. With both legs push your opponent down and away to off-balance him to his back. Complete the armlock by raising your hips and pulling his wrist down with both hands (figure 7.16d).

Escaping the Turtle Position

The turtle position is difficult to categorize in terms of a hierarchy that is based on degree of danger. In actual MMA competition, the turtle position has been used with great success to defend against attacks in certain cases. In other cases, however, the turtle position has gotten fighters into a lot of trouble, especially from the front-headlock position that we saw earlier in the clinch-fighting chapter. Quite often, the top fighter is able to throw strong knee strikes into the bottom fighter's head as he turtles up, which results in knockouts and severe damage. Indeed, it is no exaggeration to say that in some cases, the bottom of the turtle position is even more hazardous than the bottom of the mounted position.

The trap-and-roll method is an effective means of escape. When you are in the turtle position and your opponent is on top of you in a controlling position, secure the wrist of the arm that your opponent has over your back (figure 7.17a). He has to put his arm over your back in order to hold you down and clamp your elbow to your ribs. It is best to get perpendicular to your opponent before you attempt the roll. Get your hips in close and under your opponent. Look toward him and roll over your shoulder (figure 7.17b). You want to rotate your body under your opponent. This will take him right over your shoulder and onto his back. Roll over with him and turn toward his legs. This is important. If you turn the wrong way he will end in a good position. By turning toward his legs, you come out with a clean side-position pin (figure 7.17c).

DRILLS FOR THE BOTTOM POSITION

A number of useful drills can dramatically improve a fighter's bottom game. We shall look now at some of the best. But before we do, let us quickly review how partners should begin each drill.

Perhaps the best way to gain expertise in escaping from bad positions in a quick and efficient manner is to have your training partner start in each of the dominant positions while you try to escape from them (positional escape drills). Now we can begin with the following positional escape drills.

Rear-Mount Escape Drill

Have your partner start in the rear-mount position (try both top and bottom mounts). He attempts to submit you as you attempt to escape. As soon as either of you succeeds in this goal, swap roles and start again.

Mount Escape Drill

Your partner begins mounted. He attempts to hold the mounted position and apply submission holds while you attempt to escape to the guard position or

Figure 7.17 Trap-and-roll method of escaping the turtle position.

attempt to bridge and roll your partner over. When either of you succeeds, swap positions and start again.

The mount escape drill can be done with the knee-on-belly position and side-control position. Only this time, the top man not only tries to submit his partner, but he also looks to improve his position by getting to the mounted position. The bottom man must resist this move by escaping to the guard position, getting to his knees, or just scrambling out.

Turtle Drill

The top man tries to control and hold down the bottom player, who is in a tight turtle position. The bottom man seeks to escape by getting to the guard position, standing up, or rolling his partner over. The top man then tries to hold the bottom man down, applying submission holds or breaking him down to gain a superior position.

Armless-Guard Drill

The drill that is most useful for developing a strong guard is the armless-guard drill. The idea is to begin with your partner in your open guard. He attempts to pass your guard while you attempt to keep him controlled by your legs and feet. The catch is this: You cannot use your arms to help you. In this drill, you have to rely entirely on your legs to maneuver your hips and body around to keep him in the guard. This drill is extremely frustrating at first. Your guard will be easy to pass. However, if you persist, your leg work will dramatically improve, and your guard become tough to pass. Nothing develops the superior leg work, flexibility, and body position of the guard position better than this drill.

Winning From the Top Position

More than anything else, ground fighting from the top position is characterized by control. This control is not merely over the movements of your opponent's body as you hold him down, but it is also over the direction the fight goes in. The great virtue of working from the top position is that it allows you to determine the nature of the fight. From the top position, it is your choice whether you keep the fight on the ground or whether you decide to stand back up. Thus, the question over which phase of combat the fight goes into is decided by the fighter who is on top.

An added advantage of working from the top position is that you can put your opponent under great and constant pressure, since he is working under your body weight. This is tiring and frustrating for the bottom fighter; it also makes striking and the use of submission holds more difficult than if used from the top position. The top position also greatly facilitates a striking attack on the ground, since striking is so much easier from the top than from underneath. This pressure often creates mistakes on the part of your opponent and sets up the use of submission holds.

TWO APPROACHES TO THE TOP GROUND GAME

When fighting from the various top positions, we have seen that there are two basic approaches, and both have proven highly effective in mixed martial arts (MMA) competition. The first is the so-called "ground and pound" method, which can be performed with greater or lesser degrees of sophistication. Some fighters simply try to hit as fast and hard as they can from any top position that they can get, usually while held in their opponent's guard. This tactic can get results if you are much bigger and stronger than your opponent. All too often, however, it quickly results in defeat when the bottom man locks on a tight submission hold and forces a tap-out.

A much more successful method used by almost all of today's top fighters is to strike with a greater sense of caution, never exposing oneself to the major submission holds and sweeps. By keeping a solid base and by being careful not to overextend one's arms or overcommit to strikes, a fighter can hit successfully inside the guard. This kind of approach rarely gets a submission, though it often gets a decision victory. Better yet is the attempt to get past the guard and into a really dominant position from which a fighter can pound away with confidence. This tactic often leads to submission or referee's stoppage, and it is the highest form of the "ground and pound" game.

A second approach, much favored by the jujitsu fighters, is the use of joint locks and choke holds from the top position. This is the most common means of securing victory by submission. The elegance and artfulness of these holds are what so impressed many viewers of the early MMA events. They seem to represent the martial artist's dream of a clean, efficient, and peaceful victory over a bigger and more aggressive opponent. Remember that you can always combine both approaches to the top game. Indeed, this is probably the most sensible way to approach a real fight in the top ground position.

The biggest impediment to victory in the top position, however, is the guard. The guard position is unusual among bottom positions in that it prevents your opponent from ever really controlling you, even though you are on the bottom, underneath your opponent. Thus, it is absolutely crucial that you learn to deal successfully with the guard position, which means that you must be able to get around your opponent's legs and hips and into side control, without getting swept over or submitted. This battle to get around your opponent's legs and into a truly dominating pin is referred to as "passing the guard." It is the basis of true positional dominance in jujitsu and one of the genuinely essential skills in the top ground game.

STRATEGY IN THE TOP POSITION

From the statements just made, you can easily deduce the guiding strategy for the jujitsu fighter in the top position: Always seek to get past your opponent's legs (passing the guard). Most of the time, this means attempting to get to the side-control position, although one can also pass the guard into knee-on-belly or the mounted position. Once there, prevent your opponent from reestablishing the guard and thus regaining control; seek to move on to still stronger positions. As your positional dominance increases, look to finish your opponent with strikes or the application of submission holds.

Some jujitsu fighters have tremendous leg work and can create great problems when a fighter attempts to pass their guard. In cases where you simply cannot get around your opponent's legs, an alternative strategy is to forego the passing process and attempt to go directly for a submission attempt on their legs. This move can serve as a useful strategy. In general, jujitsu has strongly favored the guard-passing strategy since it leads to control over your opponent's upper body and, consequently, strong and secure positional pins. These upper-body pins allow you to make a choice between striking an opponent from a dominant position or going for a submission hold (often, the former sets up the latter). When you pursue leg submissions, you tend to lose that choice, since you are sacrificing upper-body control. But this does not mean leg submissions are not a good choice; they can work well. Be sure, however, not to make them your only option.

Learning to pass the guard is one of the best ways to learn to really control a resisting opponent. It is done in a way that embodies the proven positional strategy of jujitsu—the constant struggle for better position. It also gives you a great deal of flexibility in the way you fight an opponent. You can simply get into a position where you can hold him down in a truly dominating upper-body pin and either pound him or utilize any one of a large number of submission holds.

TRANSITION FROM STANDING POSITION TO TOP GROUND POSITION

Whenever you take an opponent to the ground, you want to land on top of him. The jujitsu fighter, however, goes to the next level. Instead of being satisfied to secure any top position, always attempt to land in the best possible top position as soon as you hit the ground. Do not settle for landing inside your opponent's full guard; rather, look to land across your opponent's side or in the mounted position. This move allows you to avoid the struggle to get past your opponent's legs while on the ground.

In the transition from standing position to the ground, few people have the presence of mind to land in good position. In fact, most people are totally preoccupied with their fall. As a result, you have an excellent chance of taking advantage of this distraction as you fall to the ground: In the immediate aftermath of the takedown, quickly slip past your opponent's legs and get into good position. By following this approach, you can avoid a lot of needless effort and frustration on the ground.

So then, keep an alert mind in the crucial transition between standing and ground phases. Be aware of the need to land in a dominant position as you are falling down—or even better, land in a submission hold. Take advantage of the confusion and chaos that arise when you take someone down by going straight into a dominant top game.

A NEW THEORY OF PINNING

Most grappling arts are based around the notion of a *pin*, which is the action of holding someone's shoulders and back to the ground. The idea is that by pinning someone to the ground, you exert your control and dominance over him. In fact, of the grappling styles that permit ground grappling, the pin is usually one of the main routes to victory, and it is even often thought of as the ultimate means of victory in the Western wrestling tradition. The idea of the pin as the sign of victory is probably a recognition of the fact that in ancient warfare, being held down was a sure way to be killed by a dagger thrust, either by the person pinning you or his comrades. But this is not a convincing argument, since it is not necessary to pin someone on their back to thrust a blade into them. It is just as easy if they are on their stomach or knees. It is more likely that the notion of pinning arose out of the fact that it demonstrates great control over an adversary. That control is indicative of the fact that in a real fight you could have inflicted great damage, had you chosen to.

The idea of a pin, however, has been radically changed in modern jujitsu. It is no exaggeration to say that this has changed the way contemporary grapplers judge the notions of control and dominance in a ground fight. Taking their lead from Brazilian jiu jitsu, contemporary grappling forms of jujitsu have moved away from classical notions of pinning in three main ways.

1. Modern grappling styles of jujitsu are unusual insofar as they do not recognize the pin as a means of ending a match. Possibly, this is a natural result of modern jujitsu's having evolved away from the battlefield origins of the ancient styles. The truth, however, is that nobody was ever harmed by simply being held down. Pinning itself does not physically harm your opponent; it simply gives one the ability to move on to harmful action, such as striking, submission holds, or dagger thrusts. In modern grappling styles of jujitsu, pins have a distinct interpretation from that of most grappling styles. The pin is only seen as useful insofar as it leads a fighter on to actions that can end a fight.

2. Modern jujitsu recognizes a hierarchy of pins. Not all pins are equal in the degree to which they allow the person on top to strike or finish an opponent. In most ground-grappling styles, a pin is a pin. If you hold a person down on his back for an allotted time, the match is over, regardless of the type of pin

employed. In jujitsu, certain types of pin score higher than others. *The more a pin facilitates striking and submission holds (the two main ways of ending a fight from the top position), the more it is valued.* Holding a pin *never* ends a match in modern jujitsu competition. It simply scores points in proportion to the degree to which that particular type of pin sets up strikes and submission holds. In addition, jujitsu does not recognize the guard position as a pin at all, since it is possible for the bottom man to win the fight from there, despite the fact that his back is on the ground. The same is also true in judo.

3. Jujitsu is unique in that it recognizes pins that do not put the victim on his back. One of the highest scoring pins in jujitsu sport competition is the rear mount, which is equal in points with the mounted position. Here, the victim is often lying on his abdomen. Naturally, the notion of a face-down pin is unusual in grappling styles. Indeed, in most grappling styles, the rear mount scores no points at all and is a position of safety for the player on bottom. In a real fight, however, the rear mount is a potentially devastating position, since you can strike without reply to the back of your opponent's head and neck while simultaneously applying submission holds; hence, it scores high in modern jujitsu.

It is fair to say that the Brazilians brought a sophistication and combative realism into the notion of pinning that was absent in classical grappling styles. This fact is one of the main reasons why they experienced such unprecedented success in MMA competition.

PASSING THE GUARD

We have seen that the basis of positional control in a real fight is the ability to get past an opponent's legs and into a truly dominant pin. When looking at the guard from the bottom fighter's perspective in the previous chapter, we saw that there are two basic varieties of guard position.

1. The closed guard: Here your opponent is on his back with his legs wrapped around your waist and his feet crossed. The first problem that confronts you when you attempt to pass the closed guard is breaking the guard open by uncrossing his feet. Until this occurs, you are not able to pass the guard.

2. The open guard: In this case, your opponent is on either his back or his buttocks with his legs in front of you. Here, you have no need to break the guard open; the issue becomes one of simply getting past the legs.

Passing the Closed Guard

We shall look first at the closed guard. During a fight, fighters first need a reliable means of breaking the guard open so that they can pass around the opponent's legs. The problem is that while a fighter attempts to break open his opponent's guard, he makes himself vulnerable to sweeps, strikes, and submission holds. So always remember that your opponent will not be sitting passively when you come to pass his guard in training or in a fight. On the contrary, he will be doing his best to defeat you. We shall look at one very effective method of breaking the guard open that does not make you vulnerable to your opponent's attacks. First we discuss standing in the closed guard.

There are many advantages to standing up in order to pass the guard. The standing position makes it very difficult for your opponent to punch you or finish you with upper body submissions. It also makes the act of breaking the guard open somewhat easier. Standing up inside a resisting opponent's guard requires precise technique and practice. Start by sitting up fairly straight and placing one hand on your opponent's chest (figure 8.1a). Do not lean forward on this hand. Use it to prevent your opponent sitting up and attacking you. Your other hand pushes down on the hip area. Stand up by stepping forward

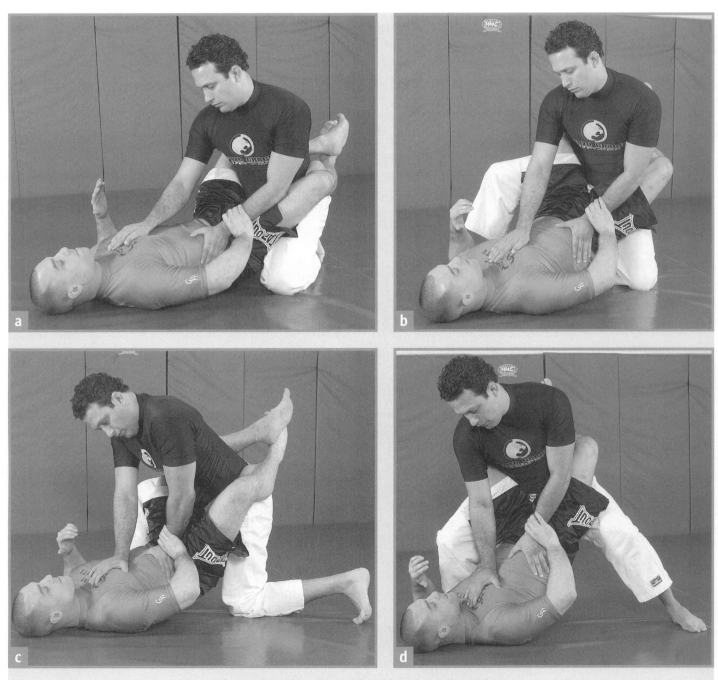

Figure 8.1 Standing up in a closed-guard position.

with the same-side leg as your forward arm (figure 8.1b). Place your foot close to your opponent's ribs to help you keep a strong position as you rise. The next move involves widening your base of support to make it difficult for your opponent to topple you over. You can do this by turning your other foot out wide behind you as shown in figure 8.1c (your knee is still down on the ground). This greatly increases the space between your feet and widens your base. You are now in a strong position to complete the act of standing up. Simultaneously stand and rotate away from your forward leg, corkscrewing into your opponent (figure 8.1d). This strong turning action puts a lot of pressure on his legs (often this opens his guard by itself). You finish with one leg forward and at an angle to your opponent. You are now up on your feet in a relatively safe position, ready to open your opponent's guard and then go into a passing move.

If your opponent has strong legs, he will maintain a closed guard even after you stand up. In order to open the guard, take the hand that was on the hip and move it back until your elbow is wedged into a spot on or just below your opponent's inner knee (figure 8.2a). Push straight down with your elbow to break his legs apart (figure 8.2b). This is not a pressure point attack, though there are pressure point methods of open the guard. You simply use mechanical leverage to open the legs. You are now in a strong standing position with your opponent's guard opened. The next step is to get around your opponent's legs into a strong side-control pin. To do this we shall make use of a powerful means of limiting your opponent's movement that we might call the *control position*.

The Control Position

The great virtue of the control position is that it allows you to instantly switch direction as you pass. Whenever you feel resistance in one direction, simply

Figure 8.2 Opening a closed-guard position.

switch to the other side. This makes it very hard for your opponent to resist the pass. At the same time it nullifies most of your opponent's offensive submissions and sweeps.

To achieve the control position, lift one of your opponent's legs under the knee while at the same time pushing the other knee down (figure 8.3a). Slide your own knee over the knee that you are pushing down, pinning it to the floor. Bring the leg you are lifting all the way up to your shoulder (figure 8.3b). You now have your opponent in a strong control position where movement is difficult for him and from where he cannot attack you with strikes or submissions. The beauty of this control position is that it gives you a tremendously effective and safe platform from which to pass the guard in two different directions.

Figure 8.3 Entering the control position.

Two passes from the control position are the stacking guard pass and the leg-pin guard pass.

The stacking guard pass. Any time you stack your opponent up on his shoulder with his hips and legs off the floor, you place him in a position where it is extremely difficult for him to do anything meaningful from the guard position. Once in a deep stack, your opponent lacks the mobility and position to attack you or to move in ways that allow him to recover the guard. From here, passing into side control is easy. If your opponent makes it difficult to pass by stacking, simply switch to the next method.

From the control position, reach around your opponent's leg at the hip and drive forward, bringing your opponent's knee towards his chin, stacking him up (figure 8.4a). Drive with your hips and stomach and keep a straight back to add to the pressure. Begin to circle around the leg that you are driving forward. Take your other hand and grasp the same leg from the inside close to the knee (figure 8.4b). Pull the leg by you and advance to a strong side-control position. Grasp your opponent under the neck to further control his movements. Take

Figure 8.4 Stacking guard pass.

your time with the pass. Do not feel a need to sprint around your opponent's legs. Often it is more fruitful to work at a slow, grinding pace, using bodyweight and leverage to work around the legs. Make sure you finish in a position where you are chest to chest with your opponent (figure 8.4c). Very often your opponent will resist the stacking guard pass by pushing back with the leg you are attempting to stack. When you feel that forward progress is difficult, switch to the leg-pin guard pass.

The leg-pin guard pass. By pinning one of your opponent's legs to the floor, you create the possibility of passing over that leg into the side-control position. Since his leg is controlled (and thus also his hips), it is difficult for him to attack with submission holds or sweeps. Should your opponent make it difficult for you to pass by this method, simply change direction and pass by stacking.

Push down on the knee that you are pinning to the floor and slide your knee over the inner thigh close to the knee until your foot hooks into the inside of your opponent's knee (figure 8.5a). Lean forward and grasp your opponent around the neck, keeping your foot hooked inside the knee that you are pinning down (figure 8.5b). At this point you still have one leg between your opponent's legs. Step that leg out wide behind you to clear your opponent's legs while maintaining your other foot hooked inside your opponent's pinned knee (figure 8.5c). Now both legs are free of your opponent's legs. Come up onto your knees and establish a firm side-control pin, chest to chest on top of your opponent (figure 8.5d). Use the stacking guard pass in combination with the leg-pinning method. Whenever you cannot make forward progress with one, switch to the other.

Passing the Open Guard

In an open guard, a fighter has no need to first break open his opponent's feet since his legs are already open. The problem you confront in this case is the mobility of your opponent's legs. With skillful leg work, an opponent can make it difficult for you to pass his guard, while at the same time he can attack you with a bewildering array of sweeps and submission holds. What is needed is

Figure 8.5 Leg-pin guard pass.

a quick and effective means of sweeping the legs to the side so that you can move safely into side control. One such means is the side-step method.

Begin by grasping your opponent's legs at the ankles (figure 8.6a). In one smooth motion, push the legs to one side and step across to the other side, landing your stepping foot right next to your opponent's hip (figure 8.6b). If you push the opponent's legs to your right, then your right foot will step across to his right hip and vice versa. From here simply place the knee of the leg you stepped across with on your opponent's stomach and step forward with your other leg, finishing in a perfect knee-on-belly-position (figure 8.6c). Execute the move in a smooth, continuous motion at a fluid pace.

Passing the Half-Guard

In the course of passing the guard, and indeed of grappling in general, it is likely that you will end up in a half-guard position on a regular basis, which can be a frustrating experience. In fact, some jujitsu fighters develop the half-guard position to the point where they even use it offensively, attacking with sweeps and submissions. Therefore, you definitely stand in need of a strong and effective means of getting past the half-guard position if you are to play the positional dominance game.

Fighters have dozens of effective ways to pass the half-guard. One problem is that many of these methods require a precise set of preconditions to work. For instance, the opponent must have his arms and legs in certain positions if the pass is to work as intended. However, the great virtue of the method we shall look at is that it works regardless of the positions of the opponent's arm and leg. It is thus one of the most versatile means of getting past the half-guard, as well as one of the safest, and is known as the sit-out method

Starting inside a half-guard position where your right leg is trapped, place your left elbow on the floor next to your opponent's left ear (figure 8.7a). Sit on your left hip and turn to face your opponent's legs. Shuffle your hips up toward his head as you post your right hand on his left knee (figure 8.7b). In this sit-out

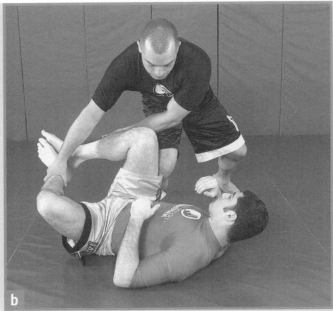

Figure 8.6 Side-step method.

Figure 8.7 Sit-out half-guard pass.

position, slide your left knee on to your opponent's stomach so that your left shin is wedged against his upper legs and hips. Push his legs away with your left shin and use the leverage that this gives you to extract your trapped right leg (figure 8.7c). It often helps to precede this by shuffling your right foot up to your opponent's buttocks. This makes the extraction of your trapped leg much easier. Finish by coming up to your knees in a tight chest-to-chest position in side control (figure 8.7d).

The Achilles Lock

We noted earlier that there are times when a direct attack to your opponent's legs can be a useful alternative to passing the guard. One effective means of doing so is by using the Achilles lock. Done well, it can end the fight quickly and efficiently.

If you feel that a direct attack on your opponent's legs is a viable option, step one leg between your opponent's legs. Let the foot of the leg you wish to attack

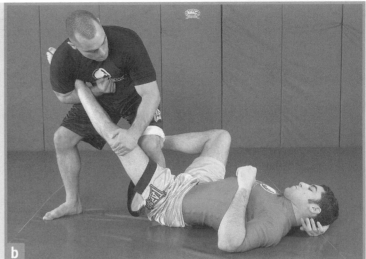

Figure 8.8 Achilles lock.

slide over your hip and place your hand on the knee of that leg to stabilize it (figure 8.8a). Wrap your arm around the leg where the Achilles tendon runs into the lower leg. Step the foot of the leg you have place between your opponent's legs under the buttocks/hamstring of the leg you are attacking (figure 8.8b). At the same time, place your other hand on the knee of the leg you plan to lock for stability. Fall down in a controlled manner and place your outside foot on your opponent's hip, toes turned out (figure 8.8c). To finish the lock, clamp your knees together. Grip the wrist of the hand around your opponent's ankle and pull up to your sternum (figure 8.8d). Lie down on your side until your shoulder touches the ground (do not lie flat on your back). Push your hips forward and arch your back strongly. This puts great pressure on the ankle and results in quick submission.

Turtle Position

Whenever you go to pass the guard on a tough opponent, there is an excellent chance that he will roll up to his knees into the turtle position, rather than allow you to pass into the dominating side-control pin. Another possibility is that as you go to stack him, he will roll over backward and surface in the turtle position. Therefore, you must be prepared to deal with the turtle position as you go to pass the guard.

Attacking the turtle position can be a frustrating experience. We look at two excellent means of doing so. The first is to break the turtle position down by rolling your opponent over into a sleeper hold. The second is to attempt an armlock. We shall look at an effective and reliable example of each.

Rolling method. Position yourself out to your opponent's side. Place one arm under and around your opponent's neck. The other goes over his back and under his far arm. Lock your hands tightly as shown in figure 8.9a. Push your shoulder down on the back of your opponent's head so that his forehead touches the floor. Sprawl your legs out and position yourself perpendicular to your opponent (figure 8.9b). Making sure your chest is tight to your opponent's upper

back, roll over the shoulder that you placed on the back of your opponent's neck (figure 8.9c). You will land in a position stretched out in front of your opponent with your hand-grip still in place (figure 8.9d). Pull strongly with both arms to whip your opponent over on top of you. He will land in your lap. Place your hooks in and attack with the sleeper hold (figure 8.9e).

Wrist-control-to-arm-bar method. From on top of your opponent in the turtle position, reach in behind his armpit and grasp his wrist close to the hand (figure 8.10a). Pulling on the trapped wrist and leaning your weight down on your opponent, begin to circle around his head (figure 8.10b). Stand up and step all the way around your opponent's head, still controlling the wrist and pulling it up and across your opponent's upper back (figure 8.10c). This forces him to his back. Sit down (shuffling backwards as you sit down helps the move), and fall into the arm bar (*juji gatame*) position as shown in figure 8.10d. Be sure to clamp your knees together and control the wrist of the locked arm. Keep the thumb of the captured arm uppermost to make for a more efficient application of force.

SIDE-CONTROL POSITION

The side-control position is the first of the really dominant pinning positions and is almost always the first pin you enter into after having passed your opponent's guard. It is stable, and it is a great platform from which to either submit your opponent, strike him, or move on to still better pins. We shall look at two of these possible strategies from the side control.

Transition from side-control position to mounted position. Many transitional movements exist that take a fighter from one position smoothly and efficiently into another. The idea is to be able to flow from one good position to another, working up the hierarchy of positions. It is not enough to be able to move—you

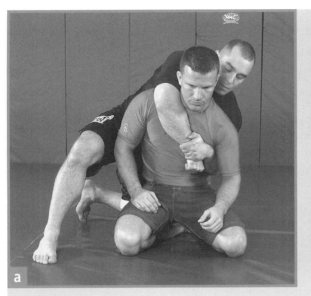

Figure 8.9 Rolling method.

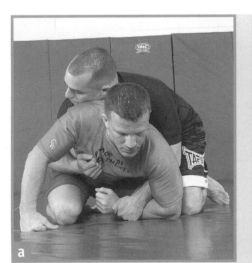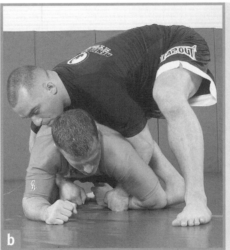

Figure 8.10 Attacking the turtle via arm bar.

must move in a manner that keeps your opponent pinned down and does not allow him to escape as you make the transition. One of the most important positional transitions is that from the side-control position into the mounted position. If this is done well, it takes you into a position where you can put your opponent under tremendous pressure with strikes and submissions. Done poorly it gives your opponent an avenue to escape, thus wasting your good position. Here we look at one of the best means to move into the mounted position, the sit-out method. From the side-control position, sit out toward your opponent's legs (figure 8.11a). Resting on your hip while maintaining chest-to-chest pressure, keep your rear leg well back to prevent your opponent bridging into you and taking you over. In one smooth motion, throw your rear leg over your opponent's legs, landing your foot on the floor on the far side of his body (figure 8.11b). As you pull your body up onto your opponent, push your hips forward to solidify your base and prevent your opponent escaping (figure 8.11c). Promptly put your hands out wide for base.

Arm bar (juji gatame) off the kimura grip. Few submission holds have the versatility of *juji gatame*. It can be used from a vast number of positions. Here we see a particularly useful one from the side-control position. Begin by grabbing your opponent's far arm at the wrist (figure 8.12a). Bring your other hand around and under the elbow of the arm you have just gripped and grasp your own wrist (figure 8.12b). This grip, often referred to as the "kimura" grip, gives you tremendous control over your opponent's trapped arm. One option is to then step around your opponent's head, placing your foot very close to his upper back (figure 8.12c). Then simply turn around and sit down (figure 8.12d). This puts you in a perfect position to execute *juji gatame*. Clamp your knees together to control the arm and straighten the arm out, holding it at the wrist. Push your hips up to break the arm (figure 8.12e).

Figure 8.11 Transition from side control to mounted position.

Figure 8.12 Side control to arm bar.

(continued)

Figure 8.12 *(continued)*

MOUNTED POSITION

Once you are sitting astride your opponent's chest, you are at liberty to pummel him with strikes to the face with little danger of return fire. The pressure of this kind of attack almost always sets up submission holds and makes the mount one of the most sought-after positions in a ground fight.

Transition from mounted position to rear-mounted position. We have already noted the crucial importance of transitional movements that take you from one position to another. This is central to the positional strategy of jujitsu that this book features. One of the really crucial transitions is that of the mounted position to the rear-mounted position. Opportunity for this movement occurs whenever your opponent turns his back on you while you are mounted on him. He may do this when he attempts a wild escape from the mount, or when the pressure of repeated strikes from the mounted position induces panic. The key to successfully getting behind a wildly thrashing opponent underneath you without losing position is to give him sufficient space to roll over unhindered. If you clamp your thighs together you can get flipped over quite easily. As your opponent turns, open your legs in the direction he is turning toward and let

Figure 8.13 Transition from mounted to rear-mounted position.

him roll (figure 8.13a). Keep your feet tucked against his outer thighs just above the knees. If he attempts to get up and escape, slide your feet as "hooks" into his hips to stabilize your position (figure 8.13b). Only after your hooks are in and you have established a sound position should you think about the next logical step—attacking your opponent with the rear naked choke.

Arm bar (juji gatame) from the mounted position. Once again the arm bar figures in our submission attacks, this time from the mounted position. From the mount, grasp the back of your opponent's head or neck to help stabilize your position. With your other hand, reach across and grasp his arm at the elbow (figure 8.14a). Your left hand will grab your opponent's left arm and vice versa. Pull the arm across your body for control. Slide your knee along the floor up to your opponent's ear on the same side as the arm you are attacking (figure 8.14b). Post your other foot up, close to your opponent's opposite ribs until you are in the side sit-out position. At this stage your hand is still cupped under his neck, pulling him in tight. Your other hand pulls his arm in tight to your chest. To enter into the armlock, slide the arm that is under his neck over his face and post it on his far shoulder. Lean forward over your opponent and begin to turn your body in the same direction that his endangered arm is pointing (figure 8.14c). Bring the foot of the leg you placed next to your opponent's ear up and post it on the far side of his head. This is made easier by leaning your upper body down towards your opponent's legs. Sit back and lie down, clamping your knees together to secure his arm (figure 8.14d). Raise your hips to create breaking pressure.

Shoulder choke. One of the safest and most successful submission holds in jujitsu is the shoulder choke. It can be set up in a huge number of ways in many positions. Here we see a very good application from the mount. Any time your opponent pushes up on your chest (a common reaction to the pressure of being struck from the mount), as in figure 8.15a, sit up and knock one of his arms across your body. Slide your face down the back of the arm you have just knocked aside as you snake your other arm around his neck (figure 8.15b). As you come down chest to chest you will have neatly trapped his arm across his own neck

Figure 8.14 Mounted position to arm bar.

(figure 8.15c). This forces his deltoid into one of his carotid arteries; your biceps blocks the other artery. Place the hand of the arm that you have snaked around your opponent's neck on the biceps of your other arm, with your other hand on his forehead (figure 8.15d). Squeeze your elbows together to initiate the stranglehold.

REAR-MOUNTED POSITION

The rear-mounted position is probably the king of positions in a real fight. From here, you can attack your opponent who lacks grappling skill with virtual impunity. Even a skilled opponent finds it tough to work out of this hold unscathed.

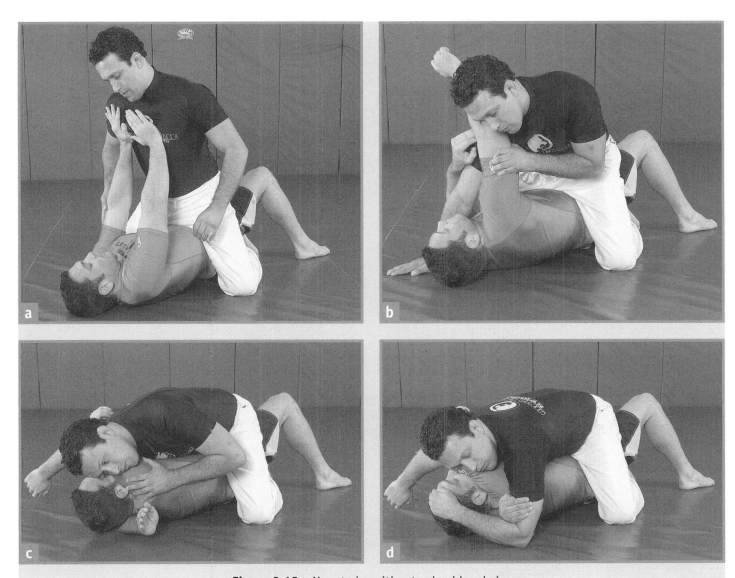

Figure 8.15 Mounted position to shoulder choke.

Rear naked choke (hadaka jime). Of all the submission holds, the rear naked choke (also called the sleeper hold) is one of the most important to learn. It can be used any time you get behind an opponent as a result of good positional play. Once it is clamped on, the fight is over, regardless of size, strength or ferocity. The key to the successful application of the choke is first controlling your opponent by placing your feet as "hooks" in your opponent's hips (figure 8.16). This will keep you locked in place, regardless of your opponent's wild escape attempts. Snake one arm around your opponent's neck, reaching around so that the elbow of the strangling arm rests under your opponent's chin. Place the hand of your strangling arm on the biceps of your other arm. Your other hand is placed on the back of your opponent's neck or head. Bring your head in tight to the back of your opponent's head and squeeze your elbows together. If your opponent does

Figure 8.16 Rear naked choke.

not submit, he will be rendered unconscious. It is thus crucial that you practice with safety in mind. Release the hold the instant your opponent signals submission.

Arm bar (juji gatame). One problem with the rear naked choke is that your opponent can defend it by grasping your strangling arm and lowering his chin, making it hard to complete the strangle. In this case it is often better to switch to the arm bar. With your strangling arm, snatch your opponent's wrist. Feed your other hand under the arm you have just snatched and grasp your own wrist (figure 8.17a). This is a variation of the kimura grip and gives you great control over the trapped arm. Take out the hook on the opposite side of the arm you have trapped and place it on the floor (figure 8.17b). Slide your strangling arm over your opponent's head and push his head away from you. The idea is to get as close to perpendicular as you can. Place the leg you put on the floor over your opponent's head and lie down into the armlock (figure 8.17c). Squeeze your knees together and raise your hips to apply the lock (figure 8.17d).

Figure 8.17 Rear-mounted position to arm bar.

(continued)

Figure 8.17 *(continued)*

DRILLS FOR THE TOP POSITION

Live drills are the best way to develop the skills and attributes that make you a proficient fighter in any aspect of combat.

Positional Drills

In the previous chapter (that dealt with the bottom position), we looked at a series of positional drills where you and your partner begin in the basic ground-grappling positions and work from there. The very same drills can also be used from the top man's perspective. Start in any of the dominant pins we have looked at. From the top position, look to either maintain and further improve your position or submit your opponent as your partner attempts to escape the pin. When any of these goals are accomplished, stop and start the drill again.

Repetitive Guard-Passing Drill

Start in your partner's closed guard. You attempt to pass the guard into either the side-control, knee-on-belly, or mounted position. Your partner attempts either to apply submission holds, to perform sweeps, to stand up, or to get to his knees. If any of these goals are accomplished, stop and start the drill again.

Training and Competition

Most people think of a martial art as a collection of techniques, and they tend to associate a given fighting style with its most distinctive techniques. This response is a natural enough consequence, seeing that most styles put an emphasis on technique as the basis of their art. But it is a rather unfortunate state of affairs. The truth is that technique by itself is of little value. Technique is only as useful as the degree to which it can be used by a practitioner under combat conditions. All the technique in the world is useless if it cannot be applied well. The missing link in most fighting styles (which was quickly revealed in MMA competition) is an adequate training method that allows a student to successfully master a technique under combat conditions.

We saw earlier that Jigoro Kano, the founder of judo, was the man most responsible for the adoption of a superior training method as the basis of his style. What was fascinating about Kano was the fact that he taught a relatively low number of techniques, few of which were original. Despite this fact, his students were able to totally dominate their competition in the grappling matches of the 1880s that quickly took judo to absolute prominence in Japan by the end of the 19th century. The underpinning of his success was the adoption of live training *(randori)* as the basis of judo training. By engaging in live training, the kodokan team was able to utilize their techniques far more efficiently than their competitors could.

Kano realized that there was a tremendous gap between theoretical knowledge of a technique and practical knowledge of a technique. In other words, the knowledge of how to do the technique and apply it on an unresisting training partner is radically different from the ability to apply it under combat conditions on a fully resisting opponent. Repetitive drilling and kata can build great expertise in the former but does not guarantee expertise in the latter. It was this gap between theoretical and practical knowledge that Kano was able to exploit and thus destroy his competition.

THE BASIC PROBLEM OF MARTIAL ARTS TRAINING

One of the impediments to live training in a combat sport is the notion of dangerous technique. Martial arts typically have techniques that are designed to cripple or even kill a potential enemy. Usually, there is no regard for the safety of the opponent, since it is assumed that he or she is a dangerous enemy and that we are engaged with them in a struggle without rules. Many of these techniques are attacks to the groin, hair, or eyes. Biting, scratching, clawing, and a host of other potentially dangerous tactics are commonly employed, as well as joint locks, strangles, and powerful strikes to vulnerable targets. This list of crippling tactics creates an immediate problem that we might well regard as the basic problem of martial arts training. Practice is required to gain expertise in any form of physical activity, but how can you practice the techniques of the martial arts, given that application of these techniques almost always results in serious injury? This is the dilemma that faces all martial arts, and how a martial art attempts to answer this problem is a defining feature of that art. In answer to this problem, there have been two basic types of response.

1. The first response is to include all the techniques of the martial arts, even the most dangerous, but limit their use in training to kata—the restrained, prechoreographed sets of technique practiced with no resistance on a cooperative partner. In other words, the techniques are never performed live on a resisting opponent, but instead they are limited to the abstract movement patterns of a safe kata. This strategy certainly ensures the safety of the students, since the groin grabs, eye gouges, and so on are never actually applied. The problem, however, is that it is only acted out without any real contact. In this sense, the student learns the theory of the move and understands what he or she is supposed to do when a certain attack occurs.

2. Another approach, made famous by Kano, was the removal of the dangerous techniques so that the remaining safe techniques could be used in full-power sporting competition. By removing certain types of techniques that simply cannot be made part of safe, everyday training—such as groin attacks, eye gouging, biting, and the like—one can create a set of techniques that can be used at full strength on a resisting opponent in open competition. Another stipulation of this approach is the adoption of a system of submission, where both participants have an agreement that states the following: When a potentially injurious technique has been successfully applied by one player, the other can give a signal of submission that stops the match. In jujitsu, this signal is made by rapidly tapping the opponent's body or the mat. With a combination of limits on technique and a system of submission, safe sporting competition and training is possible within a martial art. In fact, this system of limiting technique is also common in the Western combative sports. For example, wrestling obviously has a set of limits on technique that make it safe to apply at full power as does boxing, with its limits on what boxers may hit (e.g., nothing below the belt) and how they may hit (e.g., nothing but punches with a gloved fist).

These two fundamentally different approaches to the basic problem of martial arts training have created a deep divide in the martial arts. The issue has created a gap between arts that describe themselves as "pure," insofar as they have no sporting application (since this would be considered too dangerous), and those that do have a sporting application. In fact, martial arts purists have long decried the "degeneration" of martial arts through the adoption of a sporting application. It is argued that this introduces an undesirable set of attributes into martial arts. Obsession with victory, arrogance, and (perhaps most of all) a watering down of technique to only those that are "safe" are the faults most often associated with arts that have taken the second approach to the basic problem of martial arts training. Such purists often dismiss the sporting arts as "mere" sports, as opposed to a truly combative art, with its emphasis on dangerous technique.

Perhaps part of the problem in looking at this divide that has grown in the martial arts as a result of these two approaches is the misunderstanding that surrounds the notion of a "safe technique." When people think of a "safe" technique, they often think of a "harmless" technique. This reference is a clear misunderstanding. Many of the "safe" techniques of modern jujitsu and other combative sports are "safe" only so far as both participants have a prior agreement to stop when the techniques are well applied. Without this agreement, the result would be crippling injuries to the joints, unconsciousness, or possibly death. The potentially brutal joint locks and strangles of the grappling arts should never be thought of as harmless.

Consider also the strikes of the sporting striking arts. Thai boxing and Western boxing both have strict limits on what you may hit and how you may hit. In addition, safety equipment in the form of gloves, cups, and mouthpieces are compulsory. These rules may appear to make them less potentially dangerous than traditional striking arts, which teach strikes to the eyes, groin, and knees in addition to a host of other techniques that could not be made part of a reasonably safe sport. The striking of modern jujitsu as used in MMA competition, however, is much more like Western and Thai boxing than the classical styles of jujitsu, and thus, it would also seem to be open to the same criticism.

Yet there is a definite sense in which it seems obvious which of the two methods is the better approach to martial arts training. To most people, it would seem clear that an art that taught really dangerous technique would be a far more lethal art; it would be one that in a real fight would destroy an art that was limited to a "safe" technique. After all, the pure art would contain all the safe techniques of the sporting arts, plus the really dangerous ones that combat sports lack.

The truth is, however, that the pure arts, so laden with deadly and frightening techniques, suffer from a great disadvantage that has severely detracted from their effectiveness in MMA competition, which is the closest evidence we have for the combat-effectiveness of a fighting style. By making it impossible for students to train with their apparently deadly techniques in live situations, the traditional arts never exposed their students to the pressure and feel of applying technique in a real situation. It is one thing to know the theory of applying a technique on a cooperative partner; it is a completely different thing to apply it on someone who is doing everything they can to resist your technique and apply their own.

TECHNIQUE, CONCEPTS, AND ATTRIBUTES

Few people in the martial arts are cognizant of the fundamental differences among technique, concepts, and attributes, yet these differences are crucial to understanding how combative sports have been able to dominate the pure traditional arts whenever they meet in MMA combat. Let us understand the differences among technique, concepts, and attributes in the following way.

A *technique* is a series of bodily movements that is designed to bring about some desired end. For example, the rear naked choke (if applied correctly) is a technique that has the end result of inducing submission or unconsciousness in the victim. A *concept* is a general rule that guides the application of techniques. For example, the concept "never leave your foot in an exposed position while working from the guard," is clearly not a specific technique, but a general guide to action as you grapple. An *attribute,* on the other hand, is an ability or feature that a given fighter has that enables him to engage in a given task. For example, a fighter can have tremendous physical fitness, which would be a bodily attribute that aids him in applying his technique.

Remember: An effective fighter has an amalgam of techniques, concepts, and attributes. It is important to realize that a technique without concepts and attributes is a technique without value. The attributes that a fighter has are what allow him to apply a technique in a real situation.

It is worth our time to see how this process works. To apply a technique in a live situation, you must have a set of attributes, such as good timing; adequate physical strength, conditioning, and flexibility; recognition of the correct opportunity for a move; and (in some cases) speed and control. Without these attributes, knowledge of the technique does you no good whatsoever.

Think about the basic jab. The technique itself is simple and can be adopted quite well in a short time, even by a novice. However, the actual application of the technique is quite a different matter. At this point, you need to do much more than perform the technique itself; you must also engage all the attributes that allow you to apply the technique under combat conditions. For example, you must *time* the blow correctly and throw it with *accuracy*. Failure to do so results in a failure to hit the target. In addition, the blow must be thrown with adequate *speed*, or an opponent will easily evade it. Should you lack *conditioning*, fatigue soon sets in, destroying your ability to perform the technique correctly. You can clearly see, then, that the actual application of a technique involves much more than the physical movement associated with it. Rather, proficient execution involves the technique itself combined with an array of attributes that make for successful application.

Herein lies the great weakness of martial arts that train only with kata. Because the techniques they teach cannot be performed safely in a sparring match or sporting competition, they can only be taught by repetitive drilling on a cooperative partner. Such kata training never develops the attributes that are required to accompany the technique if the fighter is to successfully apply it under combat conditions. In other words, kata simply builds technique, not attributes. This imbalance is the great failing of the traditional martial arts and one that has been readily exposed in MMA combat. Combat sports, on the other hand, allow the students to apply their "safe" techniques at full power, and thus they strongly develop the essential attributes that make the successful application of technique possible. This rationale explains the irony of how an art limited to "safe" techniques can regularly defeat arts packed with deadly or dangerous techniques. Once the distinctions among technique, concepts, and attributes are clearly spelled out, the wisdom of Kano's training method becomes clear.

Modern forms of jujitsu, most notably the Brazilian style, have taken the same approach. Limiting the techniques to those that can be made part of a safe sport (though placing far fewer limits than Kano did), the modern forms of jujitsu have broken away from the classical schools in the all-important area of training method. This trend also applies to the striking aspect of contemporary jujitsu, which is based around Western and Thai boxing, which have both utilized the idea of limiting technique to that which can be made part of a safe sport. Just like modern practitioners of jujitsu, boxers develop the necessary attributes far more proficiently than do classical martial artists because boxers and modern jujitsu fighters can both train the same way they fight.

In fact, there is an axiom of martial arts training that everyone ought to know: *The way you train is the way you will fight.* Martial arts that allow you to apply your technique at close to full power in daily training and sport allow you to constantly use those very techniques in almost exactly the same way during a real fight. This consistency creates a tremendous familiarity with the technique and with its real-world application.

TRAINING OUTSIDE THE DOJO

Most of your training in jujitsu will consist of the strategy, skills, concepts, and attributes that you learn and rehearse inside the dojo. It would be a mistake, however, to limit your training to these elements of jujitsu, as many beneficial training methods can be done outside the dojo that can lead to great improvements in your overall game. The two most obvious are conditioning and cross-training.

Conditioning

In a street fight, conditioning does not always play a crucial role, though it certainly can. Quite often, street fights are over in a short time, usually as a result of the use of cheap shots, sucker punches, or bystander intervention; thus, great conditioning is not always a prerequisite of success. However, in an MMA fight between two athletes over a specified time, conditioning plays a huge part in the final outcome. No matter how refined and developed your technical skills are, if you are exhausted, your ability to apply these skills will be totally negated. It is important, therefore, that if you wish to perform to the best of your technical ability, you develop yourself physically so that your levels of conditioning, flexibility, and strength are adequate for the tasks you set for yourself.

Obviously, if you are preparing for a professional fight, then the level of conditioning that you require is far higher than someone who is preparing for a local grappling tournament in the novice division. Do not delude yourself: Strength and conditioning play a definite and often decisive role in a fight. Too often, one hears claims that strength is unnecessary to win a fight and that technique is far more important. There is a lot of truth to this. You should do everything you can to develop your technical skills. When you train, you should do so in ways that encourage the use of technique over strength. However, this does not mean that strength and conditioning are irrelevant or unimportant. You should spend a good deal of time working on these attributes as well. Usually, development of strength and conditioning occurs as part of a separate program outside the dojo, but there is disagreement as to which exercise program is best for the MMA fighter (there always appears to be as many theories as there are fighters). A rational analysis of the needs of an MMA fighter quickly reveals a few key points.

Endurance

Endurance is the most important physical attribute, more important than size, strength, and flexibility (though these are undeniably important as well). The reason is simple to grasp: When two well-trained fighters clash, it is unlikely that one quickly overwhelms the other. Most of the time, the match is drawn out, since each can defend the other's attacks. Each fighter needs stamina to last the duration of the fight; thus, endurance is the most vital characteristic required by the combat athlete.

Two types of endurance are required. The first is cardiovascular endurance, which pertains to the strength of your heart and lungs. It is best developed by aerobic activity such as running, cycling, using aerobic exercise machines (such as a stair stepper), and live sparring. The second is muscular endurance, which is your ability to exert your muscles for long periods of time in a clinch or ground-grappling situation. It is best developed by calisthenics that focus on body weight, such as push-ups, sit-ups, pull-ups, and dips, in addition to live wrestling, yoga, and certain kinds of weightlifting regimens (such as circuit training).

Physical Requirements

Each phase of combat has a specific set of physical requirements, and you must be able to cope with all of them. For instance, while standing, you may be moving about freely, in which case you need the attributes of speed, explosiveness, and aerobic conditioning. When you lock up in a clinch, you need balance, gripping strength, and driving power. On the ground, you require anaerobic conditioning, strength, flexibility, and grappling endurance.

Very often, a fighter who can train comfortably for long periods of time in one phase of combat can quickly become exhausted when taken into another phase of combat that he is not familiar with. This is partially from a lack of the technical knowledge needed to move efficiently in this unfamiliar situation; hence, he compensates by using (and thus wasting) a lot of strength. However, it is also due to the different physical demands that each phase places on fighters.

Movement of Body Weight

The greatest feature of an MMA fight is that of moving your body weight (and often that of your opponent as well) through a range of distinct physical scenarios. During a fight, you are constantly engaging your whole body to perform a range of athletic movements. The mastery of moving and controlling your own body weight and that of your opponent's is thus the defining physical feature of an MMA fight, which should tell you something about the types of exercises that are most relevant to developing the conditioning level of an MMA fighter. It is the movement of your own body and your opponent's body in both the standing and supine positions that most characterizes a fight.

It makes perfect sense, then, to think of exercise that involves the movement of your own body weight (and to a lesser degree, that of your opponent's) as the most important form of conditioning for the MMA fighter. Thus, it is calisthenics (exercises that involve the movement of your own body weight) that has consistently proven to be the most important form of conditioning for the jujitsu fighter. Always remember: If you gain weight, you have to carry that extra weight as you move about during the course of the fight, with the result that you will fatigue more quickly.

Cross-Training

Another element of training that has become popular among MMA fighters is that of cross-training. By this, we mean the idea of training in several different fighting styles, each of which is specialized in one phase of combat. Cross-training is designed to create a truly complete fighter, versed in all three phases of combat. So, for example, a fighter might train in Thai boxing to gain expertise in the free-movement phase, Greco-Roman wrestling for the clinch phase, and Brazilian jiu jitsu for the ground phase. In this way, he hopes to cover all the possible elements of a real fight. There is much to commend this approach. It results in a fighter who is comfortable with almost any possible situation in the course of a fight.

There are, however, some problems with the notion of cross-training. These different arts were originally intended as complete and autonomous arts. As such, they have their own set of rules and viewpoints, some of which clash with those of the other arts under study. For example, the rules in boxing prohibit any kind of offensive technique other than with the hands. As a result, it makes use of some techniques and concepts that can be a cause of trouble in an MMA fight.

Consider the common movement of bobbing and weaving, which is the use of body motion as a defensive mechanism in boxing. By bobbing under a punch, you can avoid damage while staying in range to launch your own offense. In a boxing match, this tactic is an excellent strategy. In an MMA fight, however, there is no restriction on the use of knees and, in some cases, elbows. By grabbing the head in a neck clinch, one fighter can launch into a devastating knee and elbow attack against a fighter who bobs and weaves. This is only one instance out of many where a technique that is good for one type of combat style can be potentially disastrous in MMA competition. Thus, fighters must be sure to master from the various arts only those techniques that are appropriate for MMA events.

Perhaps the most useful lesson that can be taken from cross-training is that it teaches you the strengths and weaknesses of the various fighting styles that you can expect to face, either in competition or on the street. By becoming familiar with the strategy and techniques of a given style, you become much more comfortable in dealing with that style under combat conditions. In addition, most fighters come from a background in one or two fighting styles. As such, they tend to fight according to the prescriptions of that particular style. If you are familiar with the strengths and weaknesses of that style, you stand an excellent chance of negating your opponent's attack and successfully taking him out of his comfort zone. Thus, the sincere study of other fighting styles is a crucial part of the path to victory in combat.

In addition to learning the strengths and weaknesses of a style, you must also be able to judge the strengths and weaknesses of an individual fighter. As you spar with him, you must make mental notes on the reactions he makes to your attacks. This is the process of "feeling out your opponent." As you observe your opponent's reactions, you can quickly get a sense of where his skills lie. Having deduced his weak area (or areas), you often know where to keep the fight—although if his weaknesses coincide with your own, you may not want to do this.

INJURIES

Modern jujitsu is a combat sport, and as such, there is always going to be the risk of injury. The locks can be applied too quickly, takedowns can turn into slams, and strikes can hit too hard. Even with a responsible training partner, there is always the chance of things going wrong with injury as the inevitable result. Obviously, there are different grades of injury. With experience, however, you will be able to tell which injuries are serious enough to prevent you from training and which are merely inconveniences that you can train around.

TRAINING FOR DIFFERENT TYPES OF COMPETITION

Very often, people who are engaged in the study of jujitsu seek a competitive sporting environment in which to test their skills. This attitude is normal and healthy. Three types of competition are popular among modern jujitsu fighters, and all three stem from the influence of Brazilian jiu jitsu. These are Brazilian jiu jitsu sport competition, submission grappling, and MMA events.

Brazilian Jiu Jitsu Sport Competition

This is the standard competition of Brazilian jiu jitsu. It is based on the rule and point system designed by the Gracies to reflect the nature of a real fight. Positions are awarded points based on the degree to which they would enable you to strike and control an opponent. Takedowns, the means of getting an opponent to the ground where he can be much more easily controlled, are given two points. Getting past your opponent's legs to a position of genuine control is given three points. Should the man on the bottom sweep his opponent over before he can get past his legs, he is rewarded with two points. Getting to the best striking positions—the knee-on-belly position and the mounted position—are awarded three and four points, respectively. Getting the coveted rear-mounted position is also worth four points. No matter what the score, though, a match is automatically ended if either man can get the other to submit, just as it would end in a real fight.

Using this point system, fighters are rewarded according to the degree of position, control, and submission that they would want to achieve in actual combat. Thus, Brazilian jiu jitsu ingrains in students the same habits in sport competition as would be used in an actual fight. The wearing of a *judogi* (kimono) is compulsory. As a result, the knowledge of how to use the *gi* (Japanese jacket) for throws, control, and submission is absolutely crucial. It is no exaggeration to say that jujitsu competition with the gi is quite different in feel from grappling without the gi. Fighters will often perform much better in one than in the other.

Submission Grappling

Many different rule systems exist for submission grappling. It is fair to say, however, that in recent years the form of submission grappling that has taken precedence around the world is that used in the unofficial world championships of submission grappling in Abu Dhabi. In a sense, it is simply the standard Brazilian jiu jitsu without the gi. After all, the positional point system is nearly identical, so there is a lot of truth to this claim.

However, there are some important differences between the two sports as well. Fewer restrictions are put on submission holds in submission grappling. Unlike Brazilian jiu jitsu competition, all manner of twisting-leg locks are legal. A simplistic but fairly accurate statement would be that the takedowns of

Brazilian jiu jitsu are more similar to those of a judo match (hardly surprising, given that both use a similar gi) whereas those of submission grappling closely resemble Olympic wrestling. Thus, the games have a different look, feel, and dynamic from each other.

The takedowns of submission grappling are different because competitors do not wear a judogi. The judogi has a dramatic slowing effect on the competitors in a Brazilian jiu jitsu match, which is a result of the fact that it provides the competitors with a multitude of grips and handles that can be used to stall an opponent's progress. Because of this element, there are often long periods of comparative inactivity, where both players appear deadlocked. In submission grappling, on the other hand, the matches appear faster because of the reduced friction (sweat quickly accumulates on the bodies of the athletes) and the comparative lack of handles and grips to hold an opponent and slow his motion.

MMA Events—Vale Tudo, No-Holds-Barred (NHB)

Without a doubt, MMA events have proven to be the most popular with television audiences and martial arts enthusiasts. We have seen that the basic idea is to test the relative combat-effectiveness of the various styles by pitting them against each other in a fight with few rules. This is as close to a real fight as civil society will allow. As such, it represents the best empirical evidence we have for the effectiveness of a given fighting style.

A strong argument can be made that MMA combat is the ultimate sporting test of a martial artist's combat prowess. It involves the full spectrum of martial skills, strikes, takedowns, clinching, and ground grappling. Such MMA competition obviously requires a good deal of preparation if you wish to avoid serious injury. In addition to the great skill level required for success, you must also be in great physical condition. The constant impact, grappling, and motion are utterly exhausting to those who are not well prepared.

Note immediately that MMA competition is not currently standardized. Each organization has its own set of rules and regulations. Make sure you check into these before signing up. Local tournaments are often run according to rules intended to ensure the safety of participants. For example, they may limit the type of striking that is allowed by banning elbow strikes and closed-fist strikes.

It is probably fair to say that you should enter these three types of competition in the order they are presented here. Begin with Brazilian jiu jitsu competition, move on to submission grappling, then, if you desire, take the step up to mixed martial arts. You must learn to take the impact of strikes before moving onto MMA competition, so do not attempt it without engaging in regular, live sparring (obviously with protective equipment). It is also important for you to face someone of your own skill level and size when you start out. To ensure that this happens, you must participate in a responsible organization with promoters who hold the fighter's safety in high regard.

Jujitsu For Self-Defense

People give all kinds of reasons why they study martial arts. Physical fitness, discipline, spiritual growth, and social liaisons are all common reasons that students give for joining a school. Ultimately, however, the prime motivation for studying a fighting style is the idea of defending oneself from an attack. All other motivations are merely attractive additions. Any of the other commonly stated benefits can be readily obtained from any other type of physical activity. The ability to defend oneself only comes from the serious study of combat. The strongest appeal of martial arts training is therefore the personal sense of confidence that comes from knowing that you are prepared to overcome physical threats to your well-being.

MARTIAL ARTS AS EFFECTIVE SELF-DEFENSE

We have stated that people undertake the study of martial arts to gain confidence and to be able to defend themselves from physical attack, but an apt question from the outset is whether this actually occurs. In other words, does the study of martial arts actually allow you to defend yourself from attack? One often hears stories about people who have studied a martial art in-depth, only to be soundly trounced when they actually got into a real fight. Thus, there is a legitimate concern among many that martial artists walk around with a dangerously false sense of confidence that is not based on any real fighting skill. In addition, asking martial artists whether their style is really effective is never itself a reliable means of answering our question because most martial artists are convinced that their style is more effective than any other. Indeed, few human activities have more claims that are as grandiose and that are made on such weak evidence than those of the world of martial arts.

The only adequate means of answering our question is to seek some form of unbiased empirical evidence as to the effectiveness of a martial art, as used in real combat with real participants. This inquiry was in fact the original motivation of MMA combat. By getting the various fighting styles to compete against each other with few rules, organizers and participants felt they could gain an accurate picture of the relative effectiveness of each fighting style.

As witnessed in the heat of open competition, observers could easily conclude that the most traditional of the martial arts failed the test of combat-effectiveness. By this, we mean that the practitioners of traditional fighting styles consistently failed to fight according to the major precepts and doctrines of their style. Once the fighting began, they were quickly forced into situations that they had specifically professed they would avoid. For example, most traditional martial arts eschew going to the ground in a real fight, yet on virtually every occasion, these traditionalists quickly found themselves in a ground fight for which they were totally unprepared.

In fact, none of the major traditional arts could impose their style's game plan on the fight. Boxers and kickboxers alike proved unable to keep the fight in the free-movement phase that their style prefers. Karate fighters proved totally unable to act out the "one strike, one kill" theory, and Wing Chun kung-fu fighters proved unable to keep the fight in a trapping range. The list of stylistic failures is long, and it could well have created a sense of total failure in the martial arts community, especially since practitioners of the well-known arts appeared to lose to fighters who had only a small amount of formal training. Not only did they lose, but many did so in a truly pathetic way. In many cases, supposedly highly-skilled practitioners were reduced to futile and frantic flailing about on the ground, looking no better than an untrained fighter.

The only saving grace for the martial arts world was the great performance given by the various grappling styles. The grapplers were the only fighters who consistently demonstrated a real ability to act out the claim made by all martial arts—to enable a smaller, weaker fighter to overcome and defeat a larger, stronger fighter with a minimum of violence and bloodshed.

Obtained from an objective public source, this evidence allows jujitsu fighters to make a legitimate claim to fighting proficiency. Their claim is not an empty one made without real evidence. Their style really does work. It is a claim that has been *proven* in actual MMA combat, before millions of skeptical viewers, on a significant number of occasions. This is why many students of modern jujitsu feel a special confidence in the effectiveness of their art. Their confidence is based on a wealth of real evidence that it works exceptionally well, even against larger, stronger attackers.

Even though a great deal of evidence suggests that modern grappling forms of jujitsu are highly effective in a real fight, practitioners certainly do not consider themselves untouchable. Every fighting style, including jujitsu, has its limits, and quite often these limits are simply human limits. As a human being, you have definite boundaries as to what you can and cannot do, regardless of what kind of training you participate in.

Yet, strangely, these obvious human limits are sometimes ignored in the martial arts. One constantly hears wondrous stories of fighting prowess and superhuman endeavor that are totally divorced from reality. Even more strangely, many martial artists (who are otherwise sensible people) are willing to accept these fables as factual. The reason for this strange state of affairs is that all too often, people engaged in martial arts training are catering to their martial *fantasies*, rather than the reality of combat. People are simply entranced by the idea of superhuman fighting prowess.

It is wise, then, for people to always keep in mind their own human limits in the world of self-defense. You will never be bulletproof or knifeproof, nor will you be able to crush 10 powerful opponents without effort. Rather, fix your attention on developing your skills to the best of your ability while keeping a healthy humility in your personal assessment of your ability to defend your life and limb. If you fight, things can and often do go wrong. Chances are that you will not win without shedding some of your own blood. Your skills do not make you immune to weapons and groups of determined attackers.

What you *can* realistically hope for is to greatly increase your chances of evading serious punishment while dominating and controlling a single weaponless attacker. Any more than this and the chances of getting through the altercation without serious harm begin to rapidly diminish. Your jujitsu training (when taken seriously) definitely gives you a major advantage in weaponless combat over a single untrained attacker, even if he is far larger and stronger than you are. But do not let this fact create an arrogance or haughtiness in you. In a real fight, anything can happen, and overconfidence may well be your undoing.

SIX CATEGORIES OF MOTIVATION FOR ATTACK AND DEFENSE

In civil settings, six types of situations usually result in a need to defend yourself. In no particular order, they are the ego fight, a robbery, an assassination, a rape, a sociopathic attack, and a professional intervention in a violent confrontation.

1. *The ego fight:* Without doubt, the ego fight is the main cause of physical altercations between people. We all carry around a sense of self—our ego—which often feels challenged by the actions and words of another person or group. In a large number of cases, people fight to preserve their sense of who they are, even if this action is totally irrational (indeed, most ego fights are characterized by the irrationality of both parties). Our sense of pride, self-image, public image, vanity, and a host of other factors are all part of our ego, any one of which can drag us into a fight at any given time.

Whenever the ego is challenged, we typically have an emotional response that drives us toward some kind of retaliation. This reaction is matched by the other person, and a process of escalation occurs. In a short time, both parties feel so offended that neither is willing to back down. The severity of the fight is then dependent on the mental and physical toughness of the combatants and the degree to which they are prepared to go. In most cases, they begin with a fairly low level of intensity, but the process of escalation quickly takes the intensity of the two parties to higher levels, high enough to start fights and even go all the way to aggravated assault or murder.

The actual process of escalation, however, is a fascinating phenomenon to observe. In the majority of cases, people who become embroiled in ego fights begin the confrontation with no intention of physically fighting another person. What happens is that each side of the dispute feels a need to match and surpass the perceived wrong that has been done to them. We feel that by allowing someone else to have the last word in a dispute, we somehow demean ourselves, which is a situation our ego cannot tolerate. An upward spiral of insults and threats ensues. If the cycle of increasingly strong taunts, gestures, and posturing is not broken by one side's withdrawing, backing down, or by some outside intervention, the confrontation almost invariably turns physical.

The physical element of the confrontation itself comes in degrees as well. It typically begins with both sides' getting physically close to each other in an attempt at intimidation, then it progresses to pushing and shoving, then to open fighting. Each time the level of the conflict is raised by a new insult or gesture, it becomes more difficult for each participant to pull out of the cycle of violence. Ironically, the majority of ego fights begin over matters so small and insignificant that neither side would be willing to fight for them. What happens is that the dispute gains its own momentum, and the initial cause of the dispute is completely forgotten. A sense of entrapment occurs where the two protagonists feel themselves locked into the escalating dispute and unable to pull out. To do so would leave them with a sense of damage to their self-image that they would find unacceptable. As you understand how this cycle works, you can see how easy it is to avoid this type of fight. By simply withdrawing from the game of one-upmanship, you can leave your antagonist with a smug feeling of superiority that almost always allows him to walk away with a satisfied ego.

2. *Robbery:* An age-old form of aggression is simple robbery. Here the threat or use of violence has a definite goal: to take your money or goods from you. Often, the attacker bears you no personal malice but launches his attack on a purely professional basis. You can take advantage of this fact to avoid physical harm easily—simply surrender the goods. If this sounds undesirable, ask yourself whether the goods you wish to defend are really worth the possible price that you may pay by defending them. You may have some kinds of property that you are simply not willing to surrender. In this case, a strong defense is in order.

A robber is usually only interested in financial gain. Fierce resistance may well be more than he is prepared to risk to gain your property. Just like ego fights, robberies come in different levels of intensity. Sometimes the robbers are amateurish and inept, and the robberies themselves offer little chance of serious harm. Other times, the robberies are carefully planned and potentially dangerous undertakings that involve weapons and a real chance of death or serious injury. Obviously, your reaction should be based on your perception of what form of robbery is taking place. It is wise, however, for you to always err on the side of caution when deciding to respond physically in a robbery. The level of violence can quickly escalate with dramatic and unwanted results.

3. *Assassination:* Of all the forms of attack, the assassination is the most difficult to deal with; though, thankfully, it is the rarest. The assassin is interested in ending your life. This circumstance can happen for many reasons, political or social. Sometimes, it is simply the act of revenge from someone who bears a grudge against you. Other times, it involves the work of a professional assassin hired by some person or group who prefers the idea of a world in which you do not exist. This is a particularly tough form of attack to deal with, since your attacker is a paid professional with (presumably) expertise and a plan of action in bringing about your demise.

Defense against assassination is more a case of preparation and anticipation. You must make yourself a difficult target, which can be done by keeping an erratic schedule, a low profile, and by staying away from areas and times where a hit is likely. The idea is simply not to be there when someone comes to take your life. This strategy has little to do with the physical skills of jujitsu and much more to do with intelligent planning and forethought. Given that your life is at stake, you are clearly licensed to use all techniques at your disposal in defending yourself, including those that are potentially life-threatening (along with improvised weapons). For example, the chokes so commonly used in MMA events can obviously be used in a lethal way simply by holding on to the victim until he dies. Normally, the chokes can be released when an opponent submits or passes out, but in the case of a genuine attempt at assassination, the usual standards of behavior are typically waived.

4. *Rape:* Sexual attacks form another category. Such attacks are disturbingly common. Rape, like most forms of physical attack, comes in degrees of physical severity. Sometimes, the attack is made by a total stranger and involves a vicious assault. Other times, the people involved know each other, and the physical coercion may be quite mild. In almost all cases, however, the rapist is looking to control the body of the victim in a way that allows a sexual act to be performed. Almost always, this coercion involves taking the victim to the ground in some form of pin. This fact makes modern grappling forms of jujitsu (which strongly

emphasize ground-fighting skills) one of the best ways for women to defend themselves against sexual attack.

Stated again: *Grappling jujitsu is most effective in the very area where sexual attacks almost always occur, on the ground.* This fact should not be overlooked by people interested in defending themselves from the various forms of rape. There are few (if any) martial arts better suited to the needs of women who seek a means of defending themselves from sexual predators. The severity of technique used to defend oneself from sexual attack can be chosen according to the severity of the attack. The public generally favors the rape victim when self-defense technique is used, so one can err on the side of overkill without too much concern.

5. *Sociopathic attack:* Like assassination, this form of attack is relatively rare. The distinguishing characteristic of such attacks is the lack of a normal motivation. In robbery, the perpetrator seeks money; in a rape, sexual power; in an assassination, revenge or some sociological or political motivation. A sociopathic attack, however, seems to occur for the sheer sake of violence itself. Through the eyes of the attacker, the attack is a joy. Some people simply appear to enjoy the pain and suffering of others—or at least, they are just unable to feel remorse for their victims. Sociopaths engage in both planned and unplanned attacks on other people for no apparent reason other than excitement or fun.

Sociopathic violence manifests itself in many ways. Sometimes, it is the behavior of gang members or disaffected youths who simply enjoy violent activity. Other times, it is the work of a loner looking to act out violent urges or fantasies (i.e., serial killers). Obviously, in a case such as this one (just like assassinations), you are permitted to defend yourself with all the powers at your disposal. Jujitsu offers the full range of possibilities in defense, including many techniques that can maim or kill.

6. *Professional intervention in violent confrontation:* Another scenario involves intervening in a physical fight as a *neutral third party.* This situation most often occurs in professions that deal specifically with this kind of altercation. For example, police officers, nightclub bouncers, professional security guards, and the like all must defuse violence where they have no personal involvement, but only a professional interest.

It can, however, happen to nonprofessionals as well. Quite often, people intervene to stop a street fight, especially if one person is being badly hurt. This form of combat is not really self-defense at all, since you are not defending yourself but another person. You are not personally involved, so you must fight "cold," insofar as you are emotionally detached from the fight. If you allow yourself to be emotionally drawn into the conflict, you will quickly find yourself locked up in an ego fight.

A distinguishing characteristic of this kind of confrontation is the need for nonviolent restraint techniques. As a professional third party who is interested in ending the dispute in a way satisfactory to both sides, you cannot be punching and kicking the protagonists and turning them into a bloody mess. Jujitsu is well suited to this kind of situation because it focuses so heavily on control and restraint. It allows you to control someone to a high degree without causing them grievous bodily harm. This is not an exhaustive list of the possible scenarios of self-defense, but it does cover the main possibilities. But enough about the broad categories of the motivations for street attacks. How should one *react* to these various possibilities?

We have seen that each category (with the exception of assassination) comes in degrees of severity. How you react is obviously going to be determined by the degree of severity used in the attack. However, we must now look at a general point that one must bear in mind when attempting to defend oneself. This is the issue over what constitutes a victory in a street fight. We saw earlier that the notion of *victory* is often defined differently in a street fight than it is in an MMA event. We need to describe this difference and explore its ramifications for self-defense.

VICTORY IN A STREET FIGHT

In a sporting fight, both fighters seek positive victory over the other within the rules of the event. A sporting fight is a zero-sum game in which one man wins and the other man loses. In a street fight, however, the goal is often not to defeat your opponent, but to simply survive. Thus, a person who surrenders his wallet to a mugger with a gun and emerges unscathed with only a small financial loss has, in an important sense, emerged victorious, since he has obviously survived in an acceptable state.

In another case, say you are attacked by a man twice your size, and he pushes you over, then lands on top you. You quickly lock him up in a tight, defensive guard position, and you hold on to him until help arrives and you are pulled apart. As a result, you emerge unhurt from the encounter. This, too, would constitute a victory in a street fight.

In a less dramatic case, say you are verbally abused by a group of thugs on the corner. Much as your temper flares, you walk away, knowing that the chance of defeating a group of thugs in an actual fight is remote. By walking away, you emerge totally unscathed and with nothing more than an annoying memory. You have attained victory, even without a physical encounter. Thus, it is not necessary to defeat your opponent in a self-defense situation. Victory does not necessarily equate to your opponent's defeat. This concept means that there are many other possible ways for someone to act than via the ways demonstrated in an MMA fight. The simple avoidance of fighting and the consequent saving of your body from physical harm is a victory. Do not think, then, that you have to commit to a victory *plus* the crushing of your opponent every time you get into a self-defense situation in the street This is usually not the case. Consider the notion of victory in a street fight in terms of survival, rather than a positive victory to your opponent's defeat. More often than not, you will see that there is much more to self-defense than physical fighting. If you survive a street confrontation, then you have succeeded.

DIFFERENCES IN THE WAY FIGHTS BEGIN

An important, often overlooked point in formal martial arts training is that street fights begin quite differently than do sporting fights, and this distinction plays a crucial role in the outcome of real fights. Because most street fights tend to be relatively short affairs, the beginnings of a fight are therefore *very* important. Whoever gets off to a strong start in a street fight tends to go on to victory, especially among those who are untrained. In an MMA fight, the fight begins with two combatants who advance across the ring (or cage) and square off. There is no prelude to the confrontation. Once the referee officially begins the fight, it is immediately understood by both sides that the fight is on and that both men must look to defeat the other within the rules of the event.

In a street fight, on the other hand, the beginning of a fight is quite different. Consider the case of an ego fight. These almost always begin with a verbal prelude and with attempts at intimidation. Ego fights are as much an attempt at enforcing a sense of social dominance as an attempt to hurt somebody. In other words, they are part of a social phenomenon, rather than a merely physical one. Ego fights almost always begin with some kind of social interaction between the two protagonists—insults, cursing, challenges, and threats. The standard pattern is one of a bitter verbal exchange that increases in intensity over time. One of the main problems that confronts a person engaged in the preliminary stages of an ego fight is the ambiguity of the situation. It is not clear whether either person really wants to fight. Actually, people often engage in confrontational behavior with no intention of getting into a physical fight. This question of motive marks a clear difference from the start of an MMA fight, where clearly both fighters have come with the specific intention to fight.

In the street fight, a period exists where both protagonists must determine whether the other is serious about fighting. As this process occurs, the two combatants typically get close to each other and engage in taunting and behavior suggestive of social dominance. The complex interplay between ambiguity, social domination, body language, verbal posturing, and close proximity make this a time when the participants can use all kinds of trickery and deception—sucker punches, groin shots, head butts. All are easy to use at this close range as the posturing process goes on. In fact, the distance between the two protagonists is so short that the fight almost always begins with them face-to-face. In a situation like this, the fight is really beginning in the clinch, which is a crucial point and marks a major point of departure from an MMA fight, and there is little need for the ritual of closing the distance that is so crucial to the beginning of most combat sports.

An appropriate question to ask at this point is this: Does the fact that most street fights begin differently from MMA fights require a change in our tactics at all? The answer is clear. Once the fight begins, you fight in a manner similar to an MMA fight. However, the preliminary posturing that occurs shortly before the fight breaks out definitely requires us to change our tactics to suit the occasion. You need to accommodate the major differences that exist between these two situations. The most important differences are as follows:

1. Close proximity to each other
2. Ambiguity over intentions
3. Social factors; attempts at social domination
4. Witnesses who will report your behavior to the law

These factors make your decisions about what to do all the more difficult. For instance, you have to ask yourself, Does the other person really intend to fight, or is he bluffing? You also have to bear in mind that there is a danger that the fight will escalate if you appear too aggressive. On the other hand, you face the danger of being attacked if you appear too defenseless. Additionally, if you seem to be the aggressor in the dispute, this may count against you in the eyes of the law if witnesses watched the confrontation.

However, these conflicting factors can be rendered much more manageable by a fighter's use of a special stance in these posturing bouts, which almost always seem to occur as a prelude to ego fights. This is the *prayer stance*.

THE PRAYER STANCE

The adoption of the prayer stance is an effective way of simultaneously handling the many factors involved in the tricky prelude to physical violence. This stance would be of no use in an MMA fight, but it is useful during the verbal precursor to real fighting that so often erupts in bars, clubs, the street, the highway, and so on. The chief advantage of this stance is that it is nonthreatening and safe. In other words, it does not lead to escalation, and it protects you if your antagonist judges you a weakling and decides to physically bully you. It also gives potential witnesses the impression that you were on the passive side of the dispute while giving you the time and confidence to determine if this person is serious about fighting or merely bluffing. To help you get the best out of a potentially hazardous situation, the prayer stance uses a combination of body language and sound positioning: The former helps defuse the situation and give the impression of passivity; the latter keeps you protected and able to move into the attack at a moment's notice.

The prayer stance involves your standing in front of your opponent with one leg slightly forward between your opponent's legs. This position helps protect your groin from any cheap shots. Keep your legs flexed, rear heel off the ground—this is an important detail. If you are flat footed, you are vulnerable to be being shoved backward. When your rear heel is raised and your weight is carried on the balls of your feet, it acts as a shock absorber and thus allows you to absorb a hard shove much more easily. In addition, it helps if you need to move quickly in any direction, should the situation get physical. Your two hands are pressed together as a person does in prayer. The tips of your fingers are around chin height. See figure 10.1.

Figure 10.1 Prayer stance.

The advantage of this stance is that it appears submissive. Your antagonist does not feel threatened by someone with his palms pressed together as though in prayer. This impression of peace is a real advantage. It prevents him from feeling the need to match and exceed your physical movements with his own. Most people make the mistake of either aggressively pointing their fingers, placing their hands on the other person, adopting a belligerent pose, or acting out some other physical action that escalates the dispute to another level.

Not only is the prayer stance a good way to calm the situation, it is also an excellent way to give yourself a real

Figure 10.2 Inside control.

physical advantage should the dispute turn into a fight. When your hands are held together as though in prayer, you have the crucial advantage of inside control. Whenever your hands are inside your opponent's hands, it is easier for you to control his upper body and quickly work your way into a dominant clinch or takedown (figure 10.2). In addition, it allows you to block his punches at the shoulders or shove him backward. Thus, the prayer stance is much more than a way to defuse the process of escalation, it is also a great way to stack the odds in your favor should a fight break out between you and your antagonist.

Another detail of the stance is your head position. Tuck your chin, and fix your gaze on your opponent's upper chest. Do not make the common error of lifting your chin and looking down your nose at your opponent. This makes it easy for your opponent to sucker punch you or step into a devastating headbutt. By fixing your gaze on his chest, you are not engaging in direct eye contact, which often leads to an escalation of violence. It gives the impression of somebody who does not start trouble, but who is prepared to act decisively if trouble arises.

Let us briefly run through the chief advantages of the prayer stance as a way of holding yourself in the preliminary period of a real fight.

1. It gives you a safe defensive posture: All the main targets (chin, groin, solar plexus) are protected.
2. It permits a rapid transition to offensive movement.
3. The hand/eye position conveys dismissive body language that does not escalate the cycle of violence.
4. It starts you out with the crucial advantage of inside control.

The prayer stance is so useful in that it permits the user to avoid demonstrating a desire to be aggressive. The danger of these situations is that by appearing too aggressive, you escalate the situation into a fight that you may well not even want. One of the most common actions on the part of an aggressive ego fighter is to walk up close to the person with whom they are in dispute—thus, the phrase "in your face." From this close range, the aggressor demonstrates his intimidating dialogue, body language, and posturing. At such close range, your potential adversary is dangerous. Many fights are lost because one fighter allows another fighter to get too close, which leaves the former undefended once the latter blasts into the attack. As the nonaggressor, you have two choices at this point.

1. *Start fighting:* If you decide that a fight is inevitable, simply skip the whole escalation process and start fighting. There is much to commend this approach. It ensures that you will definitely not be the victim of a sucker punch. By attacking first, you almost always take the initial momentum of the fight in your favor, which is an important advantage in street fighting. Certain problems,

however, surface with this method. Sometimes you simply do not want to fight, and in these cases, a kind of de-escalation to the conflict is necessary. In addition, if the fight occurs in a public setting in front of witnesses, you can put yourself in legal strife by hitting first. If you are working in a security-related vocation, such as a police officer or bouncer, then hitting first may not be an option. Your primary task would be defusing violence, not starting it.

2. *Attempt to avoid a fight:* You can enter into a dialogue with the other participant and try to control the situation. The big problem with this approach is that your antagonist is so close that if he quickly goes into a physical attack, it will be difficult for you to counter. This is where the prayer stance comes in. It protects you, and it avoids presenting yourself as a threat to the other person.

To review: Stand in front of your opponent, chin tucked, hands in front of your upper chest, eyes fixed on his upper chest. Move your eyes only to investigate the movements of other people, especially if he has comrades with him. If he attempts to place a hand on you or if he brings his hands up in a threatening manner, bring your hands inside his. This move is made easy by the fact that your hands are initially pressed together at your center, which automatically gives you inside control. Doing so quickly grants you inside control of his arms, which gives you an important advantage should he attempt to shove you or punch you. In fact, by controlling his arms from the inside, you can not only dominate his arm movement but you can set up your own entries into a series of strikes (especially elbows and headbutts), dominating clinches, or takedowns.

When standing in the prayer stance, you can decide to engage in dialogue with your antagonist, verbally calming him while not leaving yourself exposed to his attacks. If you sense the dispute is about to get physical, you can then decide to use your inside control in one of two ways. First, you can use it to clear his arms and move straight into elbow strikes, headbutts, clinches, or takedowns. Second, you can choose to avoid a grappling fight by using your inside control to shove him back thus creating the space necessary to strike him with punches and kicks.

Offensive Moves From the Prayer Stance

Once a confrontation turns physical you must be able to move quickly and efficiently from the prayer stance into offensive moves that will end the confrontation as quickly as possible and with a degree of force appropriate to the situation. If you have decided to engage in the fight, you need to be able to step into your opponent and apply an appropriate technique. There are two main methods of stepping into your opponent. The first is the inside step, where (as the name implies) you step your lead foot deep inside your opponent's feet. The other is the outside step, where your lead foot lands outside your opponent's feet. Both are very useful.

Inside step to double-underhooks clinch. Very often confrontations get physical in ways that are not very serious. Arguments and disagreements can turn into pushing and shoving matches that are not likely to escalate much further. What is needed here is not brutal technique that results in serious injury, but simple control. The double-underhooks clinch is a great way to control an opponent and resolve a situation without doing any real harm. Lower your level and step deep inside your opponent's feet. Pass your hands under his arms and lock your hands palm to palm around his lower back (figure 10.3). Your head is on his chest, pushing into him. Keep your hips in under his for control. Pull his hips and lower back in tight as you drive your head forward. In this manner you can totally control his movement and walk him where you want. If the situation demands, you can easily take him down with the outside trip demonstrated earlier in the book.

Outside step to elbow strike. If the situation is more dangerous, you may need to begin with a quick fight-ending strike. Few are better for this task than the horizontal elbow. Step toward your opponent with outside step penetration and whip your rear elbow into the jaw, nose, or eyebrow while keeping your other hand high in the manner of a covering block (see page 78) for protection (figure 10.4). Be prepared to follow up if necessary.

Inside step to knee strike. Another great striking method that is generally less bloody than the elbow strike is the knee strike. Step forward with inside step penetration and throw your rear knee to the groin, stomach, liver, sternum, or jaw (figure 10.5). It is best to grasp your opponent with both hands at the biceps or shoulder or in a neck clinch, snapping him forward into the knee. Again, be prepared to follow up. One of the best follow-ups to the knee is the guillotine choke (see page 151), since the knee tends to bring the opponent's head down where it is easily locked in a guillotine.

Figure 10.3 Inside step to double underhooks.

Figure 10.4 Outside step to elbow strike.

Figure 10.5 Inside step to knee strike.

Seatbelt clinch transition to rear clinch—the throw-by. In a real fight one of the very best things you can do is get behind your opponent with control. Once locked in behind him, it is exceedingly difficult for him to attack you with the usual methods used by (unarmed) street thugs. You can attack him with some of the best fight-enders in jujitsu (such as the rear naked choke) or simply control him as you please. What is needed is a fast and reliable means of getting behind a determined opponent. One such method is the throw-by. Begin by stepping in with outside step penetration to a seatbelt clinch. The idea is to wrap one arm under your opponent's arm and around his waist (like a seatbelt). Your other arm controls his far arm at the elbow (figure 10.6a). Keep your head tight to his chest. Your base must be wide, your hips below and tight to his hips. Make sure you are not in front of him but at his side. This seatbelt clinch is a very safe and controlling clinch for street fighting. You can execute many positional transitions, throws, takedowns, and elbow and knee strikes while controlling your opponent. To transition to the rear clinch, reach around with the arm around your opponent's waist and grasp his forearm (figure 10.6b). Now you are controlling that forearm with the strength of two hands. Keeping your hips in tight, shuffle a little behind your opponent. In one explosive movement, duck your head and throw the shoulder of the arm around your opponent's waist forward. This will put you right behind your opponent with total control of his waist and one arm (figure 10.6c). From here it is very difficult for him to harm you, while you can attack him at will.

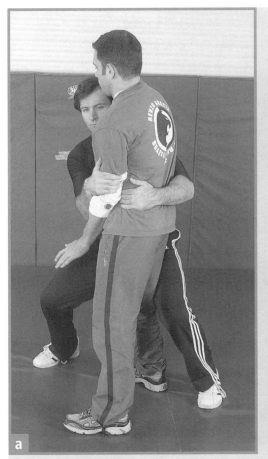

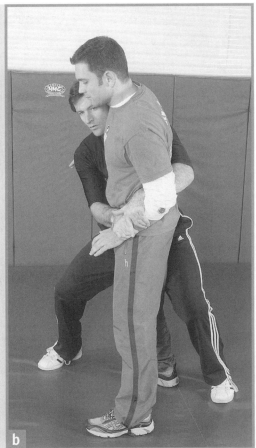

Figure 10.6 Transition from seatbelt clinch to rear clinch.

MOST COMMON FORMS OF WEAPONLESS, PHYSICAL ATTACKS IN THE STREET

Street fights are wild, chaotic affairs. Interestingly, however, they do have repeating patterns of behavior that usually reflect a definite lack of experience and training on the part of the attacker. Remember, most adults fight only a few times in their lives. When they do, they are unlikely to do so efficiently. The fact that many of them are in a blind rage when they fight does not add to their technical proficiency. Other times, the method of attack actually reflects a streak of cowardice or ruthlessness in the attacker. These cowards often use "sucker" punches, where the idea is to hit someone from behind or without warning. They achieve victory by surprise and deceit, rather than skill.

In other cases, a group will attack an individual or a much smaller group and seek to win by virtue of outnumbering their opponents. This scenario is often the modus operandi of the criminal classes and those of a violent temperament who "fight" (read: ambush) on a regular basis. Their idea is not so much to win a fight but to hurt another person. To achieve this end, the ambush is an effective (yet cowardly and ruthless) tactic. Thus, technically inexperienced rage and ruthless deceit are the two major mind-sets that lie behind most street fights. Occasionally, one will see fights of honor, where two people square off and fight one-on-one, as if they were in an MMA fight. Their fight will even resemble something more like a boxing match. Setting aside these fights of honor, however, let us analyze the more common forms of weaponless attack.

Simple Shove

Probably the most common form of physical aggression in street fights is the simple open-handed shove to the chest or face. This act usually occurs in the gray zone of an ego fight. just as the dispute is switching from a verbal dispute to a physical one. As the dispute heats up, one of the combatants decides to take it to the next level and shoves the other, looking for a reaction and hoping to either set up a more devastating technique, manhandle his opponent into a wall, or shove him all the way to the ground. The shove itself is not dangerous. What is dangerous is the follow-up.

If the shove takes you either off-balance, to the ground, or it causes you to freeze with fear (a common reaction in many people), then it will make you vulnerable to a powerful second attack that may well be at a new level of intensity. The shove is best countered with inside control of the opponent's arms, which greatly lessens your opponent's ability to shove you with any power. You can follow up with a powerful snapdown by taking advantage of your opponent's forward pressure to set him off-balance and thus make him vulnerable to attack. The sumo drill in chapter 5 is an excellent way to prepare yourself for a strong shove and how to counter it.

Sucker Punch

One of the most commonly used techniques among street fighters is the sucker punch. This move involves any form of attack (not just punches) that takes the victim by total surprise—for example, by hitting an opponent from behind or from the side, or by initially distracting him by some form of ruse. A sucker punch is simply any method of getting a powerful first strike in without giving your opponent any opportunity to defend himself or launch his own attacks. This approach has many advantages. First, the attacker has little risk of a counter, since the opponent does not see the attack coming. Second, the strike almost always has a catastrophic effect on the victim, since he is not braced to take the blow. As a result, sucker punches often result in knockouts or at least severe stunning effects.

Such attacks take little skill to perform; hence, they can be used by anybody and can produce great results. The only skill needed for a sucker punch rests in the setup. Experienced street fighters are experts in getting surreptitiously behind a victim or out to the side. Others feign weakness, friendliness, or fear, then they smash their victim with total surprise. There is no counter to a sucker punch for the simple reason that you do not see it coming. Obviously, you cannot counter a technique that you do not see.

The key to avoiding sucker punches is not a technique at all. Rather, it is keeping yourself in a state of awareness that prevents people from taking you by surprise. You can employ a number of tricks to make it tougher for someone to catch you unaware. To prevent rear attacks, place your back against a wall (if possible). Tell your antagonist to keep his distance from you. Inform him that if he gets within a certain distance, the fight is on. *Do not bluff with this threat.* If you do not act on your threat, you will be seen as a weakling. If you are reluctant to initiate the fight, avoid the verbal threat and simply adopt the prayer stance. This position makes you much less vulnerable to a sucker punch than standing in front of your antagonist and arguing.

Wide, Swinging Punch

Most people lack training in the combat arts. They fight only a few times in their adult lives. It is no surprise, then, that when they do fight, they do so in a way that is bereft of skill. In fact, the majority of people in a street fight throw punches rather than any other technique since a punch is the most commonly known method of hurting another person. These punches are almost always wild swings from out wide, thrown with great enthusiasm but with little skill.

Fortunately, these wild swings are easy to avoid. If you practice the correct method of striking and defense in the free-movement phase along with sparring as outlined in chapter 4, you will find it an easy matter to avoid these sloppy punches and thus counter strongly. To block the punches, you can simply employ any of the standard defenses to strikes (as shown previously in this chapter). An even better reaction is to forego defense altogether. Instead, take advantage of the wide, slow, swinging motion by quickly blasting straight punches into your opponent's chin, knowing that your straight punches will arrive on target sooner than his wide, looping punches. Another alternative is to close distance under the punches and either clinch or take him down. From there, you can go to work while in the clinch or on the ground.

Tackle

Another common form of attack in a street fight is the tackle. Superficially, this appears similar to a double-leg takedown or bear hug. Because it is performed by untrained people, it actually tends to be done rather poorly, more like a football tackle than a true takedown. Typically, street fighters charge in with poor balance, head down, bent over at the waist, neck extended, and arms out wide—a really dreadful attempt at a takedown. This ineptness makes the tackle easy to counter, especially if you practice your takedown defenses as shown in chapter 4. You can simply block the tackle by posting your hands on your opponent's head or forearms. From there, you can counter with a knee strike to the head. Another solid option is to sprawl out on your opponent and lock a front headlock (chapter 5). Perhaps the best counter is to lock on a tight guillotine choke (chapter 5) and finish the fight right there.

Groin Kick

Many people view the groin kick (or knee kick) as the magic formula of street fighting. They believe that a solid kick to the groin immediately ends any fight and that such a kick is easy to perform. In fact, it is not so simple. Many times, a determined fighter keeps going even after a strong kick to the testicles. Also, the target must be hit precisely if it is to work as desired. Nonetheless, the belief persists that the groin kick is the king of techniques. Accordingly, you must be prepared to defend it, given the likelihood that someone will attempt to use it if you get into a fight. To block the kick, simply raise your lead leg up with your foot drawn back toward your buttocks, then draw it across in front of you, effectively blocking the groin (figure 10.7). This move is similar to the defense of the roundhouse kick to the leg shown earlier in the book.

Figure 10.7 Block a kick to the groin or legs.

Headbutt

The headbutt is a highly effective technique that can have devastating results on your opponent if done correctly. The idea is that an attacker steps into his opponent and slams his forehead into the nose or mouth without "winding up" by drawing his head back. Sometimes fighters grip the opponent's head and immobilize it, thus creating a truly devastating headbutt.

The key to defending the headbutt, however, is distance. By keeping away from your opponent, you make it impossible for him to hit you with such a strike. It is in the clinch and on the ground where the headbutt becomes a real problem. You can negate a headbutt attack in the clinch by working into dominant clinches yourself to gain inside control. On the ground, the headbutt is most commonly used when your opponent is in your guard. To prevent this situation, place your open hand on his forehead or hug his head tight to your chest. These positions control his head movement and effectively negate the headbutt.

Common Headlock

One of the all-time favorite techniques among people engaging in a street fight is the common headlock. We say the "common headlock" to differentiate the poorly applied headlocks used in street fights by untrained people from the powerful headlocks used by trained grapplers. The basic idea of all headlocks is the same. When you control the head of an opponent, you control his whole body, since the spinal column runs down from the head to the middle of the body. When a trained grappler uses any form of a proper headlock, it is a powerful form of control that can effectively immobilize, control, or throw an opponent. Untrained fighters try to mimic this kind of control by grabbing the head as best they can and attempting to control it. Unfortunately, they usually do a poor job.

Their intention is to hold the head with one arm and pound away with strikes with the other arm, hitting the face and side of the head. Other times, they attempt to pull the head down and drag the opponent down to the ground. The problem with these common headlock attacks is that they usually gain insufficient control of the head and upper body. As a result, a person with adequate technical skills can slip out of the headlock relatively easily and get quickly into a position behind his opponent so that he can go on the attack.

Massed Attack

A sad fact of life is that many people lack the courage to fight alone against another person. Often, they attack as part of a group, using their superiority in numbers to win an easy (and cowardly) victory. Of all the weaponless self-defense situations, this one is the most difficult to defend. People give all kinds of advice on how to defend this situation. Many claim that mobility is the key, that if you just keep moving and striking, you can create angles between you and your attackers and pick them off one by one. Others say that you should severely bloody one attacker to scare the others off (though it never seems to occur to them that this might inspire a powerful revenge). All of this certainly sounds good, and it all appears exciting in Hollywood movies. Unfortunately, reality has a way of ruining such delightful fantasies. Serious attackers do not attack one at a time. They rush in together, one high, one low, and within seconds you find yourself under a barrage of strikes, grabs, and tackles. Invariably, the next stage involves your falling to the ground, where the ultimate step is usually a fearful stomping at the hands of your attackers.

The best counter to such an attack is almost always a good burst of speed. There is no guarantee that this will work, however, since they may well be faster than you, in which case you will then merely take your beating in a state of exhaustion. Other times, running is simply not an option; you may be with a loved one or in a confined space. Another counter that is effective is the use of a weapon.

Weapons are great equalizers. If you are carrying a dangerous weapon, you can intimidate even a group of attackers. Should they pull out weapons in response, then you are truly in trouble. Remember that you do not have to carry a weapon to have one at hand. Improvised weapons are all around us: Broomsticks, bottles, pool balls, chairs, belts, and a host of other everyday objects all make excellent improvised weapons that can even things up when a group threatens you. An excellent idea, then, is to take a quick look around you before the attack occurs to procure an improvised weapon. The danger of this approach is that it usually inspires your attackers to pick up their own improvised weapons and take your beating to a whole new level. Failing this, there is not a lot you can do when a determined group attacks you.

With certain kinds of groups, you can verbally challenge them into fighting one on one, berating them for their cowardice and appealing to their sense of pride or decency. Other times, you can plead for mercy; however, this does not work in every case. People who are ruthless enough to attack in groups are usually not impressed by such arguments. Sometimes, you just have to be fatalistic and accept that you are about to take a beating and therefore do as much damage as possible before going down.

Talking about massed attacks in these realistic terms is disappointing to many people. Often, they have been told that resounding victory is a definite possibility when attacked by even a large group. It comes as a letdown to be told that victory is unlikely, the same way that children feel disappointment when they learn that Santa Claus does not exist. Still, it is much better to learn the unpleasant truth. At least the hard truth dissuades people from foolishly attempting to fight with a group, except when it is utterly unavoidable. As for the martial artists who claim the ability to defeat groups of people, let them publicly demonstrate this ability on a group of people who are trying seriously to attack and defeat them. Only then will their arguments have any credence.

SPECIAL CHARACTERISTICS OF JUJITSU FOR SELF-DEFENSE

Modern styles of jujitsu offer an approach to self-defense that is quite different from most other accepted methods. The defining features of modern jujitsu as an art of self-defense are as follows.

1. A commitment to the idea that most fights do not go as planned. People always talk about how they want a fight to unfold, forgetting that the opponent is generally unwilling to go along with the program. Fights generally have a wild, unpredictable element to them. As a result, you must be able to fight well

in any of the three main phases of combat because you are not always able to determine which of the three phases a fight moves into. Thus, competence in all three is essential if you wish to be capable of defending yourself against a serious unarmed attack.

2. The majority of fights do not end with a single blow, but instead they quickly go into a grappling situation. In other words, the fight is first on the feet, then on the ground. Knowledge of grappling skill in both the standing position and on the ground is therefore critical to your ability to defend yourself. The reason almost all fights go into a grappling phase is simple. When a fight begins, the two protagonists invariably attack each other with blows. At any given time in the fight, one of the two gets the better of the exchange. The other fellow invariably tries to recover by grabbing his opponent and nullifying the strikes. This natural chain of events is repeated in almost every unarmed street fight.

3. Jujitsu gives you a vast range of possible responses to aggression that can be tailored to every given scenario. People often think that all fights are struggles for survival where only one man walks away alive. This is certainly true in some cases, but by no means all. Quite often, aggression comes in much lower levels than this. To respond to all acts of aggression as though they were pitched battles for your very existence is to overreact in ways that are likely to send you to prison. The techniques of jujitsu are based around control. This control allows you to determine the severity of response to the opponent in a way appropriate to the scenario. In a low-level conflict, it involves simply immobilizing an antagonist. In a much more dangerous situation, it may involve either severely damaging his joints, performing strangleholds to render an assailant unconscious, or utilizing vicious strikes from a controlling position. The important difference is that you place yourself in a control position where you can adjust the severity of your response to a level appropriate to the situation.

CONCLUSIONS

We saw in the chapters concerned with the history of jujitsu that the art had its beginnings as a supplemental battlefield art of the Japanese warrior caste. Over time, it settled into an art concerned with self-defense in a civilian setting, and contemporary forms of grappling jujitsu are in this category. They offer the student a powerful array of techniques that can range from peaceful restraints to crippling locks and potentially lethal strangles. In the wide range of possible self-defense scenarios that can confront us, some of these techniques will be appropriate. If used well, they make the difference between a humiliating or traumatizing beating and a confidence-boosting victory. In more serious cases, they determine the difference between life and death. Always bear in mind, however, our human frailty. Do not let your training become a source of unhealthy arrogance. Defeat is always a possibility in a real fight. Keep this in mind when deciding to engage in a fight. In the case of fighting, it is better to err on the side of caution. Do not enter fights frivolously, as the consequences can sometimes be far heavier than you anticipated. Let your jujitsu training be a source of pride and confidence. If you are required to defend yourself, your training will qualify you well for the task.

INDEX

ABOUT THE AUTHORS

One of the most successful and active members of the world-famous Gracie clan, **Renzo Gracie** has spent almost 30 years training in Brazilian jiu jitsu. Competing at the highest levels of mixed martial arts (MMA), grappling, and no-holds-barred (NHB) events, he has won the Brazilian jiu jitsu national title twice, the World Combat Championships (MMA event), and the martial arts reality series superfight. He is also a two-time winner of the world submission grappling championship (held annually in Abu Dhabi) and a multiple winner in Japan's premier MMA venue, PRIDE.

Gracie has instructed many current UFC competitors and students who have gone on to become world Brazilian jiu jitsu champions, PRIDE champions, and Pan American Games champions. His New York City academy is one of the largest and most popular in the United States. Gracie continues to teach, train, and compete throughout the world. He resides in New York City.

John Danaher (left) and **Renzo Gracie**

An instructor at the Gracie School of Jujitsu in New York, **John Danaher** has been Renzo's training partner for several years. He holds a PhD from Columbia University and has written another book, *Brazilian Jujitsu: Theory and Technique*, with Renzo and his brother Royler Gracie. Danaher has the distinction of being involved with the highest authorities in the sport and the formal writing skills to convey it. He resides in New York City.